Japanese Education in an Era of Globalization

Japanese Education in an Era of Globalization

Culture, Politics, and Equity

EDITED BY
Gary DeCoker
Christopher Bjork

FOREWORD BY
James J. Shields

Teachers College,
Columbia University
New York and London

Published by Teachers College Press, 1234 Amsterdam Avenue, New York, NY 10027

Library of Congress Cataloging-in-Publication Data

Japanese education in an era of globalization : culture, politics, and equity / edited by Gary DeCoker, Christopher Bjork ; foreword by James J. Shields.
     pages   cm
  Includes bibliographical references and index.
  ISBN 978-0-8077-5423-8 (pbk. : alk. paper)
  I. DeCoker, Gary, editor of compilation. II. Bjork, Christopher, editor of compilation.
  LA1312.J323 2013
  370.952—dc23

                                     2012050574

ISBN 978-0-8077-5423-8 (paperback)

Printed on acid-free paper
Manufactured in the United States of America

20 19 18 17 16 15 14 13   8 7 6 5 4 3 2 1

For Tom Rohlen,
an inspiration to so many of us

Contents

Part III:
Minority Groups and Educational Reform:
The Intersection of Domestic Reform, Policy, and Global Forces

Part IV:
The Outcome of Educational Reform: Evaluating Policies
Introduced to Mitigate Inequality and Expand Opportunity

Foreword
Genesis and Goals

Japanese Education in an Era of Globalization is deeply rooted in the history of the Comparative and International Educational Society (CIES) and its relationship to research in Japanese education. Each critical stage in the development of the book took place in conjunction with a CIES annual conference. The Japan Foundation, New York, provided support for a planning session held at the 2008 annual conference, followed by a similar event in Charleston in 2009. At these sessions, scholars and graduate students from a range of academic disciplines discussed major issues and reforms in Japanese education from a comparative and international perspective.

At a 3-day meeting held before the May 2011 annual CIES conference in Montreal, supported by the Japan Foundation, Canada, the book editors assembled scholars from Japan, the United States, Canada, Australia, Great Britain, and Korea to present drafts of possible chapters focused on such broad themes as cultural and social diversity and equality and academic achievement within the context of recent, multidisciplinary, cross-national qualitative and quantitative research. Most of the chapters in *Japanese Education in an Era of Globalization* grew out of the critical discussion of these chapters in Montreal.

The genesis of this book goes back even earlier to the 2007 annual CIES conference in Baltimore where Christopher Bjork and I organized two sessions on Japanese education. These panels led to an announcement posted on the conference bulletin board for a follow-up session to continue the dialogue. As it has turned out, 10 of the 17 contributors to *Japanese Education in an Era of Globalization* had participated in this impromptu gathering.

Christopher Bjork, Victor Kobayashi, and I made a proposal at the 2007 conference for the creation of a CIES-Japan Special Interest Group (SIG) that was accepted and later approved by the CIES board of directors. Its purpose was to create a group that would encourage ongoing collaboration among young and established scholars on projects, publications, and grant proposals related to Japanese educational studies, research, and reform.

The first official Japan SIG meeting was scheduled the following year at the 2008 CIES conference. The conference, held at Teachers College Columbia University, attracted more than 1,200 university faculty, graduate students, and staff affiliated with international organizations from all over the world. Among them was Gary DeCoker, who joined the ongoing project. Subsequently, at the 2009 CIES meeting, two Japan SIG sessions were held to solicit ideas and identify appropriate contributors for the book. Among the more compelling themes that surfaced in our discussions were: Japan as an important "Other" for the West and model for East Asia; changing educational goals and priorities; the classroom as a microcosm of the larger political and economic world and a starting point for educational reform; historic and new immigrant populations; teaching and learning practices; the interplay of public and private interests; and pupil relationships and control issues, among other topics. To varying degrees, each of these themes was eventually incorporated into the book.

Although a major impetus for the creation of this volume was to document the significant changes that have occurred in Japanese schools and society since the collapse of the nation's economic bubble, the issues explored in the chapters have deep historical roots. The value of looking back to understand the present reminded me of my own experiences studying Japanese education and editing *Japanese Schooling: Patterns of Socialization, Equality and Political Control*, originally published in 1989.

One of the scholars who inspired me to study Japanese education was Herbert Passin, with whom I become acquainted when I was a student at Columbia University in the late 1950s and early 1960s. In that period it was still possible to meet many of the early icons of Japanese comparative and international educational studies, including two Teachers College Columbia University professors, Isaac Kandel and Goodwin Watson, who both served as members of the U.S. Education Mission, created by General Douglas MacArthur to reshape Japanese schooling after World War II.

Two even more world-renowned Columbia University professors, John Dewey and Edward L. Thorndike, had been considered for the U.S. Educational Mission, but in fact did not serve, probably because of their advanced age. Nonetheless, historically, both played prominent roles in the cross-cultural rhetoric and practice of educational reform in Japan. The impact of Dewey, who actually visited Japan and China before World War II, is evident in the areas of cooperative and experiential, community-focused learning. For Thorndike, the connection is centered on issues related to the quantification of knowledge and testing that originally were considered radically progressive.

In the early 1980s, to my surprise, I found John Dewey's ideas on cooperative and experiential learning and social justice widely featured in the publications of the Japan Teachers Union (*Nikkyôso*) and in teacher education, especially at the early schooling levels. Today, it is Edward L. Thorndike's ideas related to the quantification of knowledge and testing that dominate Japan's educational reform agendas, often to the detriment of educational equity and social justice. This is true, not only in Japan, but also in the United States and worldwide, as we move toward a more universal model of schooling based upon Programme for International Student Assessment (PISA), Trends in International Mathematics and Science Study (TIMSS), and other testing instruments.

In conclusion, it should be noted that in the face of the challenging paradoxes and contradictions of education in Japan and around the world, it is more important than ever that we seek better ways to understand each other and our educational systems and societies as a foundation to improve our respective lives and the world we live in. In Shinto ritual, the mirror has always played an important role in Japan's sacred traditions and in defining its identity. The mirror also can be borrowed for use as a metaphor to describe the contribution made by *Japanese Education in an Era of Globalization.* As Robert Rosenstone (1988) mentions in *Mirror in the Shrine: American Encounters with Meiji Japan,* the study of Japan in international and comparative perspective presents us with a powerful opportunity to hold up a mirror to Japan and learn more about our own culture, and each of our individual identities. In other words, in pursuing an understanding of the "Other," we expand the growth of self-understanding.

James J. Shields

REFERENCES

Rosenstone, R. A. (1988). *Mirror in the shrine: American encounters with Meiji Japan.* Cambridge, MA: Harvard University Press.

Shields, J. J., Jr. (Ed.) (1989). *Japanese schooling: Patterns of socialization, equality and political control.* University Park: The Pennsylvania State University Press.

Preface

Gary DeCoker & Christopher Bjork

Japanese Education in an Era of Globalization presents a rigorous yet readable set of essays that place contemporary Japanese education in global context. Sustained attention to the links between education and wider social trends in Japan makes the book a useful resource to readers focused particularly on school reform and also to those with a broader interest in Japanese society and culture. The book would be a valuable addition to undergraduate courses offered by Asian studies, anthropology, sociology, and education departments as well as seminars for policymakers and practitioners. It also provides insight into contemporary youth culture, links between families and schools, and broader questions about societal change as a society grapples with issues such as growing social inequity and a recent influx of immigrants.

Contributors to the volume received invitations from the editors to write essays for the book. Then we held two meetings of authors and additional researchers to discuss ways to improve each essay and bring them together into an integrated volume. Participants told fascinating stories of how schools they were studying had adapted to fit shifting social, economic, demographic, and political conditions. We also came to a strong consensus that the literature on Japanese education has not kept pace with those changes.

Through the process of developing this volume, we encouraged contributors to focus on concrete repercussions of changes in and beyond Japanese society. Rather than offer a strictly theoretical treatment of education, we sought to provide readers with information and analyses that will deepen their understanding of conditions in actual schools. Particular attention is paid to the impact of reform on the learning opportunities for students with diverse ethnic and economic backgrounds. We believe that *Japanese Education in an Era of Globalization* provides unique perspectives on the ways that education is shaped by social and material contexts in Japan as well as abroad.

In addition to the authors represented in the book, the following scholars attended a meeting: Christopher Bondy, Julian Dierkes, Mark Langager, Lary MacDonald, and Tomoko Tokunaga. We are grateful for their contributions. We discussed Ryoko Tsuneyoshi's chapter, although she was unable to attend our meeting due to circumstances related to the Tohoku earthquake and tsunami disaster. Akiko Hayashi and Joe Tobin attended the initial planning meeting and later agreed to provide their chapter. Kazuhiko Shimizu and Yeon-Jin Lee contributed by communicating directly with their chapter coauthors. Nina Selligson, Chris Bjork's student at Vassar College, assisted with the manuscript preparation. We also would like to thank everyone at Teachers College Press for their guidance, especially our editors, Brian Ellerbeck and Aureliano Vazquez. Finally, we are grateful to the Japan Foundation for its support throughout the project.

Please note that we made certain accommodations for readers unfamiliar with the Japanese language. When referring to the Monbukagakushô (often abbreviated as MEXT) in the text, we used the translation "Ministry of Education" (MOE) rather than the official "Ministry of Education, Culture, Sports, Science and Technology." For Japanese scholarly references, we only provide the English translations. Japanese names are written in the Anglo-Western style with given name first followed by family name. Our authors also use the term *middle school* interchangeably with *junior high school*, in both cases referring to grades 7 to 9.

PART I

Framing the Discussion

CHAPTER 1

Enduring Issues, New Contexts

Gary DeCoker

When I started graduate school at the University of Michigan in January 1980, there was a small meeting room next to the Center for Japanese Studies offices. About eight people could squeeze around the table. The shelves that lined three walls of the room contained books on Japan organized by discipline. This little library, according to my fellow graduate students, contained all of the books about Japan written in English. As graduate students, our task was to master this knowledge, set off across the Pacific to conduct research, and later add a few books to the collective knowledge of Japan.

My field, education in Japan, didn't even take up one shelf, with books by Passin, Dore, and Anderson, next to a few World War II/Occupation-era books and some others published by Japanese government institutes and universities. In retrospect, I'm sure that the meeting room didn't contain all of the books on Japan, but from our perspective, as future scholars, we owed it to ourselves to try to master whatever anyone wrote about the country we had chosen to study. Now, some 30 years later, you could probably fill a room that size with books written in each of the academic disciplines that make up the field of Japanese studies. Indeed, books and articles on Japan, not to mention blogs and other Internet sources, now number in the thousands, making it difficult to keep track of, let alone master, all the scholarly work on Japan. At this point, for me, it is difficult to read all of the English-language publications in the single field of Japanese education, while also trying to stay familiar with Japanese-language publications on education, which also have flourished over the last few decades. Putting all of this work into the context of comparative education in general seems sometimes overwhelming.

Another thing that I remember from the beginning of my graduate study was a lecture by Ezra Vogel based on his new book, *Japan as Number One: Lessons for America* (1979). Some of my professors grumbled about Vogel cashing in on his name with a nonacademic book that patronized the Japanese and garnered sizable royalties from its Japanese-language edition. But despite Vogel's generalist approach and the criticism he received, his book had a serious premise, i.e., that modernization could lead to the development of a non-Western country into a liberal democratic capitalist state that surpassed Western nations.

Japan as Number One set the tone for much of the research on Japanese institutions during the economic "bubble" years of the 1980s and early 1990s. As Vogel put it, "Convinced that Japan had lessons for other countries, I was no longer content to look at Japan only as a fascinating intellectual mystery. I wanted to understand the success of the Japanese in dealing with practical questions" (p. viii). "One of the best vantage points for looking at our institutions, for reexamining our assumptions and considering alternatives, is from another place that faces similar problems but finds different solutions" (p. 4).

Vogel's Chapter 7, "Basic Education: Quality and Equality," seemed to define the challenge for Americans hoping to improve the U.S. educational system by using Japan as a model. Nearly a decade later, in "Implications for American Education," the epilogue to the 1987 U.S. Department of Education publication *Japanese Education Today*, U.S. Secretary of Education William Bennett echoed Vogel by stating:

> It is the American belief in the value of universal education that the Japanese have so successfully put into practice, and the American quandary over "equality" and "excellence" that the Japanese seem rather satisfactorily to have resolved. *Our* educational ideals are better realized in a large scale in Japan than observers have tended to realize (p. 69; emphasis in the original).

For many Americans in the 1980s, learning about education from another country, especially a non-Western country, was something new. The United States was challenged by pre–World War II German education and Cold War Soviet education, but in responding to these challenges for technological superiority, the educational systems of these totalitarian states offered little to emulate. Japan in the 1980s and 1990s, despite its "foreignness" as a non-Western country, was viewed as a challenge *and* a potential model.

Japanese education took on many meanings as Americans confronted the idea that Japan's economic boom might result in its surpassing the United States in education, wealth, and ultimately influence. Politicians, pundits, and educators all seemed to start with the simplistic notion that the strength of Japan's economic growth came from its superior education system, and, conversely, the cause of America's economic malaise was its school system. This argument, convenient for the business community and politicians looking for a scapegoat, rarely was questioned in media discussions.

The lessons that Reagan-era politicians seemed to want Americans to learn from Japan followed from those outlined in *A Nation at Risk: The Imperative For Educational Reform*, the 1983 presidential commission report, i.e., a rejection of U.S. progressive policies of the 1960s and 1970s and a move to a more teacher-centered, time-on-task, back-to-basics vision of education. Infatuation with Japanese schooling, motivated in large part by the desire to turn around all that ailed the United States, was so great that Japanese commentators began joking that flights arriving at Narita from the United States carried mostly educators looking for ideas. In the mid-1970s, a university press editor rejected Tom Rohlen's seminal book, *Japan's High Schools*, adding, "How much of an audience would there be for a book about that?" By the time the book eventually appeared in 1983, however, interest in the topic led to record sales for the book and countless print and television interviews for Rohlen.

Much of the best work on Japanese education during this time period came from anthropologists and other social scientists using ethnographic methods. Their scholarship was picked up piecemeal by the media and used by those hoping to promote a certain educational reform agenda. One of the first persons to use extensive quantitative data in comparisons of Japan, the United States, and later China was Harold Stevenson, who once told me that he sought to examine some of the generalizations made by ethnographers in order to find out definitively why Asian students were outperforming their American counterparts. Stevenson delighted in pointing out in specific terms the strength of the Japanese model. His overarching idea was that hard work, both by students and teachers, resulted in academic achievement, an idea that was embraced by the conservative establishment of the Reagan era.

From the late 1970s to the early 1990s, interest in Japanese education resulted in the creation of what is arguably the most sophisticated English-language body of comparative scholarship on the educational system of any country in the world. Regardless of method (quantitative, qualitative, or a mixture of both), however, much of the research published during the closing decades of the 20th century portrayed the Japanese society as monolithic. In retrospect, these generalizations about Japanese culture and society seem a bit too sweeping, and tended to essentialize Japan. As Hoffman (this volume) points out, the themes that emerged out of this voluminous research continue to resonate decades later in current descriptions of Japanese education.[1]

There are various ways to categorize postwar research on Japan and its educational system. Sociologist Yoshio Sugimoto (2010) describes seven phases in the development of such scholarship, beginning with Ruth Benedict's (1946) *Chrysanthemum and the Sword*. It is only in the sixth phase, which includes the 1990s, that research begins to move away from broad generalizations and includes a focus on the internal variation of Japanese society. Jennifer Robertson, in examining anthropological research on Japan, uses the term *bricolage* to describe the need "figuratively speaking, to refabricate the received and homogeneous (and homogenizing) portrait of 'the Japanese' in the multifaceted mode of a 100-headed Kannon (Bodhisattva of Compassion)" (Robertson, 2005, p. 8). Robertson also challenges anthropologists to make use of information from a diverse set of individuals and groups, to read from a range of Japanese-language materials, and to pay attention to historical context.

The fundamental and foundational research issues noted by Hoffman, Sugimoto, Robertson, and others raise the question of what to do with the extensive volume of research on Japanese education. Willis and Rappleye (2011), in their edited volume, make a strong and compelling case for "reconceptualizing what Japan means" and "rising above older images and paradigms" (p. 18). They end their introductory chapter by stating:

> But let us be clear: our attempt, manifest across all of the chapters, is just the beginning of a movement to help restore the voices of suppressed forms of knowledge, to rethink the confining assumptions of the past, to stimulate mutual dialogue and debate, and to unite around common questions *of our own making.* (p. 40; emphasis in the original)

Given the ideological and rhetorical excess that overlaid much of the research in the heyday of Anglo-Western interest in Japanese education, and the theoretical and methodological blinders that seemed to move much of the research on Japan toward "normative templates" (Robertson, p. 8), the desire to sweep away the past and start again with a fresh reexamining of Japanese education is understandable, even laudable. Ironically, our book, begun about the same time as the Willis and Rappleye volume and including some of the same scholars, took a different, but not contradictory, approach. While paying attention to the changes that have taken place in Japanese society and education over the last few years and recognizing the theoretical complexities of studying another culture, we have chosen to start with the assumption that certain fundamental issues have endured through the years of Japan's economic boom and economic malaise and into the current era of globalization. Careful examination of these "enduring issues," we believe, can deepen our understanding of an education system that is often mischaracterized, sensationalized, and misunderstood.

We seek to provide concrete, accessible information about conditions in Japanese schools, especially as they affect the educational opportunities and experiences of students. We hope that the chapters in this book will provide a nuanced framework for evaluating the outcomes of educational reform efforts and that the studies included in the volume will generate empirical evidence to help educators and policymakers better understand the context and ramifications of their decisions as they attempt to modify school policy and practice toward producing educational and societal change.

FIVE THEMES THAT EMERGED FROM OUR WORK

The chapters of this book in many ways can stand alone, but when the authors met to share drafts of their work, five themes emerged that cut across many of the chapters, thereby providing a useful overview for the reader.

Global Interactions

Since the 1990s, educational researchers have been using globalization as a lens to understand changing educational contexts. Following this approach, a number of excellent books and journal articles have situated recent reforms of Japanese education in the context of international achievement tests and global policy recommendations. This research has pointed out how Japanese politicians and the media, using Programme for International Student Assessment (PISA) test results and other data, have placed the educational system into a crisis framework that requires drastic and immediate changes. Most of these Japanese domestic policy narratives are backward-looking in orientation, making the claim that Japan somehow abandoned successful practices for a more progressive, but less successful, present.

In proposing solutions to the "crisis" in Japanese education, neoconservatives focus on patriotism and the importance of preserving a sense of Japaneseness in the face of internationalization. Neoliberals, more willing to follow global educational policy that advocates bringing market forces into the educational landscape, advocate policies that loosen the regulations of the Ministry of Education (MOE). For either group of conservative-leaning politicians and reformers, however, the outside world of global forces cannot be limited to terms and conditions set by domestic political actors and their agendas.

The chapters in this book remind us that global interactions and grassroots responses have been part of Japanese education for decades. One longstanding global influence on education is immigration. Schools for immigrant children have operated in various MOE categories since old-timer Koreans, who remained in Japan at the end of World War II, created more than 500 ethnic schools with the initial goal of repatriation. Since then, the lack of a comprehensive central government policy has left local governments to develop their own policies and make adjustments to national ad hoc notices regarding the education of foreign nationals. Many of these ethnic schools retain a connection with the educational system of the home country, which could involve loosely following a foreign curriculum, gaining outside accreditation, or receiving funding from abroad. These schools operate under varying MOE school recognition from no legal status, to miscellaneous, to mainstream (Okano, this volume).

The influx of newcomer immigrants during the 1980s and 1990s economic boom created many challenges for the Japanese educational system. Brazilian schools, guided by the home-country curriculum, focused on Portuguese language maintenance in order to ensure smooth transition home, and parents found schooling a convenient form of child care. As Brazilians increased in numbers and in the duration of their stay in Japan, learning the Japanese language and assimilating into the host country became more important. But their ambiguous status as "foreign Japanese" and shifting definitions of Japanese identity have required an adjustment of government categories for the educational support of marginalized students (Gordon, this volume; Tsuneyoshi, Okano, & Boocock, 2011).

Foreign observers of Japanese education by their very nature bring an international perspective. Although most policymakers in the developed countries who admired Japan's high scores on international examinations in the 1980s and 1990s have turned their attention to other countries that now dominate these rankings (Tucker, 2011), many educators still look to Japan as an example of renewal and rebirth, especially in a world of shrinking resources (Kobayashi, this volume). And among East Asian countries looking for a model of an industrialized, free-market economy, the collapse of the "economic bubble" has not diminished interest in Japan. In other ways, too, Japan's educational organizations have a global reach. Private, for-profit Kumon and other supplementary, *juku*-style schools thrive in countries around the world, as do Suzuki music, martial arts, and other practices.

The discussion of globalization that animates the research included in this book seems to make obsolete a domestically focused approach to educational reform. As Baker and LeTendre point out, long-term comparative studies, global migration, and the availability of information about other countries have created a "global environment of national school systems" in which "the grammar of schooling is global" (2005, p. 9). Japan is clearly at the center of this phenomenon, and a study of its educational system is, therefore, an inquiry of domestic and global dimensions.

Changing Societal Context

For many outside observers of Japan, its educational system still has the reputation of intense competition for all students. This stereotype emerged in the 1980s and seems to have lingered despite many educational, economic, and demographic changes that have made it somewhat outmoded. Competition still shapes the experiences of Japanese students who aspire to attend one of Japan's leading universities, but, given the dramatic decline in the population of school-age children, educational competition now is largely between universities as they strive for full enrollment.

The competition that came to characterize Japanese education resulted from a post–World War II combination of rapid population and economic growth and an education system that initially lagged behind. When the postwar baby boomers began to enter school, the reconstituted prewar elementary and junior high schools absorbed the increasing enrollment for the compulsory education years. Available spaces in high schools, on the other hand, could not meet the needs of the growing population of students who were pursuing enrollment, resulting in increased competition to enter high school. In addition, high schools had varying reputations, often based on the success of their graduates in enrolling at elite universities.

By the mid-1970s, high school enrollment had become nearly universal, but competition continued as students and their parents came to associate specific high schools with success later in life. This competition went both ways as companies also competed to ensure that they would be able to hire enough competent employees. Many companies established linkages with high schools and universities, offering a predetermined number of jobs each year to graduates of specific schools.

The dual nature of this competition—students working to be accepted and employers working to hire the best graduates—provided schools with a built-in motivation system. Students knew that they needed to work hard in order to succeed in school, but they also knew that at the end of the educational process, they would be rewarded with a job. And many of these jobs, under the system of that time, were accompanied by an assumption of permanent employment until retirement.

The intense competition that defined Japan's education system came under increasing criticism by the public and media. As early as the 1970s, the MOE began exploring ways to "relax" pressure on students, ultimately leading to a major curricular revision that was implemented in 2002. At the same time, however, the population of Japan's 18-year-olds began a precipitous decline from about 2 million in 1992 to 1.5 million in 2002 (and an estimated 1 million in 2020). The 1990s also brought dramatic changes in the Japanese economy, which resulted in a decline in employment opportunities for young people.

For the authors represented in this book, these societal changes raise many interesting questions. The lack of incentives for Japanese young people, for instance, seems to have affected the teacher–student dynamic, resulting in increasing numbers of junior and senior high students who overtly reject school culture and teacher guidance (Bjork & Fukuzawa, this volume). As teachers attempt to respond with varying strategies, some abandon common approaches, thereby fragmenting schools that used to be characterized by consistency in educational approach. At the classroom level, the tradition of children monitoring each other is no longer as effective, exacerbating various social problems such as bullying (Akiba & Shimizu, this volume). In contrast, preschools exhibit more continuity in the longstanding, implicit approaches that are passed on from experienced to younger teachers (Hayashi & Tobin, this volume).

Parents, in turn, have begun placing different expectations on *juku* (private, supplementary schools). Rather than focusing entirely on examination preparation for already motivated students, *juku* first must find ways to induce students to see education as a worthwhile pursuit. Many *juku* teachers emphasize their responsibility to provide reassurance to parents and aspiration to students. As a result, *juku* has become an "insecurity industry" responding to "hyper *kyôiku mama*" (education mothers) who express growing concern but themselves have few strategies for success. Schools, too, must adjust, especially in rural areas characterized by a lack of jobs and declining population. Some districts, for instance, have combined or eliminated schools (Tsuneyoshi, this volume).

For their part, Japanese young people (the "lost generation") face an uncertain future. As Mary Brinton (2011) notes: "Lost in the transition from school to work, the lost generation is a reflection of a deeper transition in Japanese society—a transition away from social institutions that helped guide individuals from one life stage to another" (p. 2). The authors of the chapters in this book point out that the vocabulary used to describe Japanese education (jobs, *juku*, bullying, and so on) has remained, but the changing context has given those words different meanings.

Diminishing Role of the Ministry of Education: Grassroots Change

For Americans, who often incorrectly assume that their decentralized system is the international norm, any form of centralized educational system would seem to illustrate unbridled power concentrated at the national level. In Japan itself, the image of a powerful Ministry of Education remains and is often cast in negative terms—power gone awry, somehow leading to all that is wrong within the education system and even the younger generation itself.

The prewar Ministry of Education might best illustrate the ultimate control that the MOE once had over the country's schools. At any particular time of the day, a Ministry official, often with military connections, could have turned to the nation's curriculum guidelines and stated with certainty the exact page of a particular textbook that all, say, 3rd-grade children would be reading. This was the MOE that U.S. Occupation forces quickly worked to disempower. After rewriting textbooks, eliminating moral education classes, and giving local boards of education an increased level of control, the Occupation forces left Japan in 1952.

Within a couple of years after the Occupation, the MOE had made many moves to reestablish itself, setting off a long series of confrontations with the Japan Teachers Union. These battles, and the media attention that they engendered, reified the domestic public perception of the all-powerful MOE. Internationally, the textbook revision process did the most to create a similar impression. From the 1960s through the 1980s, historian Saburo Ienaga's legal challenges to the MOE's control of textbook content seemed endlessly in the news, and these reports were punctuated by occasional international outbursts that arose whenever a political leader from one of Japan's Asian neighbors complained that a new MOE promulgation was "revisionist" in its denial of Japan's World War II military aggression.

In the midst of these postwar disputes, the MOE hardened its positions, trying to maintain the control it felt necessary for education to do its part in Japan's rapid economic development. During the boom years, despite the perceived relationship of Japan's education system to its economic success, criticism of the MOE and the education system was a constant feature of Japanese media reporting and parental griping. The high-growth economy seemed to require unacceptable sacrifices of citizens, and the education system somehow came to represent much of what was wrong with Japan's domestic policy.

Along with the end of the Ienaga litigation came the weakening of the Japan Teachers Union, and the growing sense that the country needed to reassess its longstanding goal of economic development and turn instead to creating a more "livable" society. During the 1990s, the MOE's planning arm, the Central Council for Education, began exploring ways to respond to some of the criticisms directed at the educational system, and these ideas were represented in the 2002 reforms under the rubric *yutori kyôiku* or "relaxed education."

The 2002 reforms also reflected the move toward neoliberalism in the Koizumi administration, resulting in a further shifting or relaxing of MOE policies and more flexibility at the local level. Funds were provided to support initiatives that focused on strengthening unique aspects of each school. And new MOE policies offered local boards of education more latitude in implementation, which made variation among local schools even more visible.

Explanations for this broader MOE flexibility are varied. Perhaps it stems from a desire to reduce local budgets or maybe to minimize local and prefectural resistance to more controversial, top-down reforms. Recently, public support for the 2002 reforms has weakened in the face of mounting media and political criticism of the effects on academic achievement. It remains to be seen whether the MOE's backpedaling on the 2002 reforms is an initial concession to conservative pressure that will be followed by more aggressive national policy initiatives, or a continued weakening of the MOE and a shift of power to local communities.

To illustrate the changing MOE role, many of the chapters in this book describe examples of the grassroots education initiatives. Whether this shift in power means that the MOE is losing effectiveness or merely changing its strategies vis-à-vis the political establishment and local/prefectural boards of education is a question that comes up repeatedly in the analyses of our authors. Suffice to say that the outdated image of an all-powerful MOE, regardless of whether it was ever accurate, must be replaced by a more nuanced view that our authors are attempting to bring forth.

Equity

American academics and policymakers who praised Japanese education in the 1980s and early 1990s most often focused on the high scores of Japanese students on international achievement tests. Typically, however, they noted that Japan's international standing was not bolstered by the high scores of Japan's best students: The top 10% of U.S. and Japanese students had similar achievement levels. The key to Japan's overall high achievement was the bottom 50%, where the greatest difference between the two countries existed. To make matters worse for U.S. education, the high school graduation rate in Japan at that time was a bit over 90%, compared with a bit less than 80% for the United States. Japan, so U.S. pundits kept repeating, combined high achievement with equity. And the data seemed to support this interpretation. Looking at achievement test scores of the two countries side by side revealed that Japan's scores were clustered tighter around the mean, higher overall, and comparable with the United States at the highest range.

One important conclusion that seemed to point to differences between the educational systems in the two countries came from their definitions of "equal opportunity." In Japan, the term meant that everyone received the same treatment (Okano, this volume). In the United States, at least since the 1960s Great Society programs, the educational system was to "compensate" for societal inequalities though compensatory education programs geared toward bringing everyone to at least a basic level of math and language literacy. This difference in approach, some American reformers concluded, resulted in Japanese teachers teaching to the top level of students, while U.S. teachers and policymakers focused their attention on struggling students.

The Japanese public became accustomed to seeing its students as top performers on international achievement tests. When the Organization for Economic Co-operation and Development (OECD) released the international results of the initial PISA tests, Japanese politicians, media, and the educational community expected success. The initial examination, taken in 2000, measured math and science levels of 15-year-olds, and Japan's scores were in fact first and second respectively of the 31 participating countries. On the second test, administered in 2003, however, Japan's math scores appeared to decline. Coincidently, this took place 1 year after the implementation of the new curriculum guidelines that included many changes aimed at "relaxing" Japan's educational curriculum.

The conservative backlash and media frenzy regarding Japan's supposed decline has been well documented, as has the MOE response that curtailed reforms in order to appease critics and limit the "damage" done by the efforts to ease curricular standards and encourage local initiatives. The *yutori* reforms also are suspect with regard to equity because educationally savvy parents seem better able to work the more flexible system to their advantage, leaving less sophisticated parents at a disadvantage. As a result, the current major revision of the MOE national curriculum guidelines, implemented from 2011 to 2013, contains responses to the "excesses" of the 2002 reforms.

The irony of the current debate in Japan is that most of the discussion fails to take advantage of the sophisticated analytical possibilities that PISA allows. Evidence from these data seems to be pointing to growing inequality in Japan's student achievement, although the source of this trend remains an open question (Park & Lee, this volume). Despite what is said about the effect of educational reform, the cultural capital of a student's family still seems to have great influence on achievement, as it did during the economic heyday (Nomi, this volume). But in the 1980s this inequality was overlooked, perhaps because the economy was booming, high school enrollments had rapidly increased, and postsecondary enrollment surpassed 50%. Given this situation, even if the pie was not being shared equally, everyone was getting a pretty large piece. This economic and educational growth allowed the rhetoric of equality to continue, even when disparities were becoming more evident.

Parents have had to adjust to the shifting terrain caused by recent reforms. A majority of parents, especially those in urban areas, continue to purchase supplementary education in the form of *juku*. But *juku* have never been a place where exceptionalities (learning disabilities and so forth) have been addressed. A few *juku* exist for remedial education, but most provide preparation for entrance examinations. Attempts to limit the influence of *juku*, such as the movement to create a 6-6 system by combining junior and senior high schools, have made *juku* more important for even younger students. Junior high school entrance in some metropolitan regions, for instance, has become a critical point, heightening examination pressure for some families (Nomi, this volume; Tsuneyoshi, this volume).

Over the last 15 or so years, the term *unequal society* has increasingly been used to describe Japan. Although inequality is not a new issue for Japan's schools, recent reforms and the long-held belief that equal opportunity defines equality make it hard to overcome inequities through top-down public policy. The chapters in this book illustrate various local school responses to an issue that had been set aside, but now attracts a growing amount of media attention. Ironically, the issue of inequality had been limited primarily to the disparities in achievement between "mainstream" students and those from various minority populations (Frey, this volume). Just as groups such as *Burakumin* and Ainu have begun to reach the norm in terms of high school completion rates, the Japanese media now seem to have realized that there may be other ways to parse a society when searching for inequities, most notably the growing economic disparities of the post-"bubble" years.

Minorities

For an outside observer, Japan often becomes a country of misconceptions. Pithy phrases that seem to capture its essence turn out to be wrong: "Japan is a small, island country" is a description that still gets repeated, even though Japan's land-mass exceeds that of most European countries and is similar to unified Germany. And the statement "Most Japanese are middle-class" belies the great differences in wealth that exist in modern Japan along with a growing underclass.

One of the most common bromides about Japan is that it is a homogeneous country: Everyone is "Japanese." Here, too, a statement that seems to make sense distorts reality. Although at first Japanese society may appear ethnically homogeneous, the "minority" population of Japan is estimated to be about 5%, a number that is well above the minority population of many European countries and similar to Germany and the Netherlands (Sugimoto, 2010). The Anglo-Western scholarship on Japan's minority population typically begins with theories and categories developed outside Japan (Hoffman, this volume). A Japanese definition of "minority," however, focuses on a different set of characteristics. One rather distinct Japanese category is the "returnee" (*kikoku shijo*), a child who experiences an extended stay overseas, typically when the father has been posted abroad for work. In Japan, returnees become a minority because their foreign experience has resulted in an identity that sets them apart from the rest of the country's young people. The category has evolved, as has the treatment of these students, but their differences from the mainstream still result in the perception that society, especially the education system, must make adjustments for them.

The most common way for domestic and international scholars to approach the study of Japan's minorities has been through descriptions of individual minority groups. Some of the early postwar research on *Burakumin* was produced primarily by Anglo-Western scholars at a time when taboos and social exclusion limited Japanese scholarship on this group. Koreans in Japan, the largest among Japan's minority groups, would seem to be an easier group to research, along with the smaller population of residents with Chinese origin, but here differences regarding origin and time of entry to Japan create subcategories of a group of people that would on the surface seem to require a less nuanced description. The earlier Korean population that existed at the end of World War II, for instance, became defined by the partition of the Korean Peninsula, some showing allegiance to the North and others to the South. This division resulted in different approaches to the education of their children within Japan.

In the 1980s, during the arrival of newcomer minorities, the original population of Koreans became "old-timers," who were distinguished by a fluency in Japanese language and culture that allowed most of them to "pass" as Japanese merely by taking a Japanese name. Newcomer Chinese, too, made that population hybrid, especially if you add the repatriated Japanese nationals and their families who remained in China after the end of World War II. This group might also be called "returnees," although their extensive residency in China, during which their prospects of return diminished, gave them a foreign identity that other returning expatriates did not necessarily possess.

In addition to blurring categories, the recent influx of non-Japanese also has resulted in changes in the way scholars and policymakers approach the study of Japan's minorities. As several of the chapters in this book illustrate, interactions between minorities have become more prevalent. Although non-*Burakumin* groups have long benefited indirectly from the efforts of the *Buraku* Liberation League and other groups to overcome the legacy of discrimination, the number of hybrid organizations that lobby the government for more services has increased. A notable example of this is the cooperation of minority organizations after the Kobe earthquake in 1995. And the MOE itself showed a propensity to support such efforts when, in 1991, it extended programs aimed at Koreans to all minorities (Okano, this volume).

In some ways, the Japanese government's homogenizing approach to minorities mirrors the school environment, where distinctions often are blurred. Identities, however, can get stamped out in the process (Gordon, this volume). As a result, the more the government moves toward broadly defined minority policies, the more each minority group becomes forced to define itself in terms of its distinctiveness, even while joining forces with and drawing upon international and domestic organizations and movements. For instance, Ainu organizations look to other Indigenous peoples, even though the Japanese government does not treat them as an Indigenous minority, nor report their number to the United Nations as such (Frey, this volume). The government's rationale, a conflation of ethnicity and nationality, comes from the belief in the primacy of Japanese citizenship over all other differences. Minority groups and their communities also negotiate policy changes in different ways, some making use of newly opened spaces in the curriculum, such as integrated studies, to bring in domestic and international agendas related to their particular group. Finally, the groups themselves are not always distinct, as the Brazilians of Japanese origin illustrate by bringing with them their former minority status as *Burakumin* or Okinawan (Gordon, this volume).

SUMMARY

The goal of this edited volume is to present 12 integrated chapters that place enduring issues in Japanese education in a global context, with particular attention given to how the Japanese education system is responding to changing expectations and pressures that emerge from rapid social change. More than a decade has passed since the collapse of the "economic bubble." In the ensuing years, Japanese society has gone through a long and extensive period of self-examination. Social, political, and economic institutions all came under fire from domestic critics searching for antidotes to Japan's economic maladies and accompanying fissures in the nation's social fabric.

Recent societal and global changes have challenged Japanese citizens to reexamine the goals and structure of their education system. In an era of global interaction and uncertainty, Japan's experiences offer opportunities for understanding Japan itself and for insight into other countries as they, too, confront issues related to equality, academic achievement, privatization, population diversity, societal expectations, and the influence of the media, parents, and political movements.

By placing Japanese education in this emerging global context, *Japanese Education in an Era of Globalization* provides a nuanced framework for evaluating the outcomes of educational reform efforts. The studies included in this volume generate empirical evidence that will help educators and policymakers better understand the context and ramifications of their decisions as they attempt to modify school policy and practice toward producing educational and societal change.

NOTES

1. A recent example of the repetition of themes found in earlier research on Japanese education is the edited volume *Surpassing Shanghai* (Tucker, 2011), which in Part I presents individual chapters on the educational systems of 5 countries, including Japan, followed by Part II titled, "How the United States Can Match the Best Performers."

REFERENCES

Baker, D., & LeTendre, G. (2005). *National differences, global similarities: World culture and the future of schooling*. Palo Alto, CA: Stanford University Press.

Benedict, R. (1946). *Chrysanthemum and the sword: Patterns of Japanese culture.* Boston: Houghton Mifflin Company.

Bennett, W. J. (1987). Epilogue: Implications for American education. In R. Leestma, R. L. August, B. George, & L. Peak, *Japanese education today* (pp. 69–71). Washington, DC: U.S. Department of Education.

Brinton, M. (2011). *Lost in transition: Youth, work, and instability in postindustrial Japan*. Cambridge, U.K.: Cambridge University Press.

National Commission on Excellence in Education. (1983). *A nation at risk: The imperative for educational reform*. Washington, DC: U.S. Department of Education.

Robertson, J. (2005). Introduction: Putting and keeping Japan in anthropology. In J. Robertson (Ed.), *A companion to the anthropology of Japan* (pp. 3–16). Malden, MA: Blackwell Publishing.

Rohlen, T. P. (1983). *Japan's high schools*. Berkeley: University of California Press.

Sugimoto, Y. (2010). *An introduction to Japanese society*. New York: Cambridge University Press.

Tsuneyoshi, R., Okano, K. H., & Boocock, S. (Eds.). (2011). *Minorities and education in multicultural Japan: An interactive perspective*. New York: Routledge.

Tucker, M. C. (Ed.). (2011). *Surpassing Shanghai: An agenda for American education built on the world's leading systems*. Cambridge, MA: Harvard Education Press.

Vogel, E. (1979). *Japan as number one: Lessons for America*. Cambridge, MA: Harvard University Press.

Willis, D., & Rappleye, J. (Eds.). (2011). *Reimaging Japanese education: Borders, transfers, circulations, and the comparative*. Oxford, U.K.: Symposium Books.

CHAPTER 2

Reading Japanese Education
Enduring Tensions, Emerging Challenges

Diane M. Hoffman

What is Japanese education? Or, rather, what do we *say* Japanese education is? This essay considers some of the broad ideas that have shaped and continue to shape academic scholarship on Japanese education at the beginning of the 21st century. In particular, it argues that writing on Japanese education constitutes a genre that has been shaped very powerfully in relationship to conceptualizations of Japanese culture. Culture is thus itself worthy of being read as an ideological frame that constrains the interpretation of Japan and Japanese education in particular ways. As in any genre, texts on Japanese education do not stand alone, but in relation to each other, and they work together to create something called Japanese education. Just as partners in conversation depend on knowing something about "where the other is coming from" to make sense of a given statement, reading and writing Japanese education requires familiarity with some of the themes that characterize the ideological environment of the genre. These themes influence both the texts as well as the kinds of messages that audiences ultimately take away from them.

Clearly, given the enormous attention Japanese education has received from social scientists, a project such as this requires some limits. The goal is not to provide a comprehensive overview of the literature on education in Japan, nor is it to engage in analysis of specific texts (though both, in the long run, would be helpful); rather, it is to delineate the contours of the discourse in ways that will highlight the role and place of culture in analyses of Japanese education. Obviously, culture is an explicit reference point in the large corpus of ethnographically informed texts on Japanese education, but it is also a reference point in much of the nonethnographic work. While it is often helpful to look at Japanese education as a lens on Japanese culture, I consider how Japanese culture frames writing on Japanese education. I am thus offering a *reading* of Japanese education, one whose aim is to raise our consciousness of the constructed nature of education in relationship to culture and to a national entity called Japan.

JAPANESE EDUCATION AND THE ANTHROPOLOGY OF JAPAN: THE VICISSITUDES OF "HOLISM"

Since my focus is on culture, it is helpful to begin with a look at the larger anthropological context in which studies of education in Japan may be situated. For much of the 20th century, a strong tendency toward a "grand models" approach to Japanese culture and society (e.g., Nakane, Benedict, Doi) was evident. In articulating themes central to the organization of Japanese cultural life, these scholars proposed theories that were grounded in holistic accounts of Japanese culture. As Kelly (1991) observes, in part this work has fueled "a broad range of competing national characterizations that reify Japan in contrast to equally totalizing images of the West" (p. 396). Though in recent years, the grand models approach to Japanese culture and society has been superseded by descriptions that emphasize locality, situationality, and heterogeneity, a persistent tendency to explain Japan and its relationships with others in terms of national characterizations has proven very difficult to break away from.

According to Sonia Ryang (2004), one reason for this is that the anthropology of Japan has not yet sufficiently divested itself of a focus on uncovering the "cultural logic" of Japanese practices. This has led to the twin problems of over-exoticizing and over-romanticizing Japan. While the persistence of national characterizations can be seen as a partial response to a broad tendency on the part of Western social science to over-assume the salience of Western models such as modernization in the Japanese context, Ryang sees the problem more in terms of the ways culture and nation have been conflated in scholarship on Japan. The nationalization of Japanese culture in effect naturalizes the role played by the Japanese state, making it invisible in its actions and effects, and leading to one-sided interpretations that bias an overgeneralized and essential "culture" (and in which the *Nihonjinron* [theories of Japanese uniqueness] discourse, too, is itself complicit).

What, then, of education in Japan? How has the well-critiqued tendency of monolithic representations of Japanese national culture affected the way culture comes to be constituted in scholarship on Japanese education? Many writers on Japanese education have critiqued what they see as the mythologizing tendencies in representations of Japanese education (Kubota, 1999; LeTendre, 1999a, 1999b; Lewis, 1995; Peak, 1991), often directing attention to the ways in which ethnographic evidence contradicts commonly held ideas about Japanese education as group-oriented, conformist, teacher-centered, lacking creativity, and almost inhumanly competitive. At the same time, though, as some visions are being contested, the question is, are others being put in their place? As Cave (2007) points out, in reference to the Japanese self, some observers see Japan as a group-oriented society where individualism is frowned upon, while others see it as a society of "strong-minded individuals who endlessly challenge or subvert an official ideology of collective harmony" (p. 2). For some (e.g., Holloway, 2000), the holistic lens in scholarship on Japanese schooling has encouraged a pervasive misreading that paints overly positive and uniform images that fail to capture the reality of a diverse and contested educational landscape. This dichotomizing tendency, built upon a certain retained attraction to grand cultural narratives, seems readily available as a structure upon which to build interpretations of Japanese education.[1]

Yet, the persistence of holism in cultural accounts of Japanese education raises other, perhaps even more interesting questions. First, is this holism simply the result of the lens we have brought to it, influenced as it has been by what Ryang identifies as the failure to separate "culture" from "nation" in our accounts of Japan? Perhaps holism is simply a by-product of the pervasiveness of the nation as a unit of analysis—a nation, moreover, often characterized implicitly if not explicitly as homogeneous. Or is holism in accounts of Japanese education more the result of the way the anthropology of education has evolved in a well-defined national context? Or—most importantly, perhaps—might it even be a reflection of the ways in which education is indeed an overarching and central force in Japanese society, organizing it in ways that demand our attention to the larger and deeper ideas that shape Japanese life?

In this regard, it is useful to distinguish between holism in an anthropological sense and what might be termed its less welcome cousin, mythologizing, which casts a more evaluative or moralistic eye on patterns, tending to represent them more monolithically. It is certainly clear that in the literature on education in Japan, there is no dearth of efforts to "understand the ways patterns of learning are organized in whole societies" (Rohlen & LeTendre, 1996, p. 2), or, alternatively, as elements in a "Japanese cultural theory of teaching" (DeCoker, 1998, p. 69). Much of this work, conducted both in and outside of schools, has provided us with a vision of a society in which education does appear as a central organizing theme, one that derives its significance from its integration across the lifespan, and one where distinctive approaches to learning and teaching are organizing principles across diverse domains of everyday life. One thinks of the many rich studies of education in nonschool-based settings, for example, that have greatly contributed to our understanding of important themes characterizing education, such as the value of hardship, or the centrality of ideas related to mastery of self. While holistic in orientation, this scholarship is not mythologizing, and does not seek to erase diversity or to represent Japan as a model. In this sense, it is perhaps possible to argue that the emphasis on underlying themes in Japanese education is both a function of the ethnographic genre itself, in combination, perhaps, with what may indeed be a distinctive culturally patterned approach to education in the context of Japanese views on human life.

Another important factor to consider is the utility of Japan and accounts of Japanese education in comparative contexts. While there are dangers (probably of the mythologizing type) associated with any kind of national level cultural comparison, there is also value in such an exercise because it allows us to uncover the deep nature of the concepts with which we are dealing. For example, a cultural analysis of patterns in Japanese education can illuminate the extent to which cultural discourse on U.S. education is shaped by powerful conceptual dichotomies that are simply accepted as natural. These include characterizations of classrooms as teacher-centered versus child-centered; or oppositions between rote learning and critical thinking; ideas about national curriculum as being antithetical to teacher autonomy; or notions of academic/cognitive learning as being separate from social and emotional learning.[2]

By contrast, a cultural analysis of Japanese education shows that these conceptual dichotomies are far from inevitable or natural. In fact, there is ample evidence, for example, that rote learning can be seen as the best route to deep, critical thinking (Sogen Hori, 1996); that whole-class, teacher-directed activity can be at the same time child-centered, eminently engaging, and appropriate to individual children's needs (Lewis, 1995); that teacher autonomy can coexist with a national curriculum (Baker & LeTendre, 2005; DeCoker, 2002; Lewis, 1995); and that cognitive academic learning is not a tradeoff for a focus on social and emotional development but something that is integral to it (Cave, 2007; Lewis, 1995; Sato, 2004; Tsuneyoshi, 2001). In this sense, then, holistic, cultural accounts of Japanese education, when placed in a comparative context, accomplish what other kinds of accounts fail to do: They open up for consideration the deep conceptual structure that in effect constructs education as an object of inquiry and research. In this way, they represent a hermeneutic frame for discovery, inquiry, and interpretation that is not so much about what is, but about what and how we *think* about what is.

SOME GUIDING THEMES AND TENSIONS IN JAPANESE EDUCATION

The representation of culture in writing on Japanese education encompasses a broad territory, so my account is necessarily partial. Though one could identify specific substantive themes that have been dealt with in the literature, instead

I present more of a meta-view that emphasizes the ways in which certain core or key overarching themes have shaped our thinking about culture in Japanese education. In my view, these themes present themselves as tensions in the ways phenomena associated with Japanese education are explained and represented, both within the academy as well as to a larger audience beyond. While they can be identified in the chapters in this volume, they also resonate across the broader corpus of texts on contemporary Japanese education. Ultimately, their significance lies in the ways in which they constitute an ideological field that informs the perception and conceptualization of contemporary educational issues in Japan.

Cultural Versus Structural Effects

One of the primary tensions in discussions about Japanese education concerns the extent to which observed phenomena are attributed to the influence of Japanese culture, or to structural features of Japanese society, e.g., educational and social policy, resource availability, features of institutional organization, local and national politics, and so on. This concern is certainly not unique to discussions of Japanese education, but it acquires a particular significance given the previously discussed issues concerning "national culture" in Japan.

A reading of the literature on Japanese education through the 1980s to the present reveals that writers are not shy about discussing Japanese culture as a primary influence, particularly in the everyday practices of classrooms and in nonformal learning settings. In fact, in some cases, authors are concerned with showing how culture exerts a more powerful influence than structural factors. A nice example is Shimahara and Sakai's *Learning to Teach in Two Cultures* (1995), where the authors compare Japanese and American teacher training, observing how structural similarities in teacher preparation are in fact secondary to the kinds of deep-seated cultural values and perspectives that ultimately exert far greater influence on teacher learning and activity in the classroom.

At the same time, in other works, there appears to be an explicit concern with highlighting the impact of structural influences, perhaps as an antidote to cultural reductionism. Contributors to LeTendre's (1999a) *Competitor or Ally?: Japan's Role in American Educational Debates,* for example, are in some cases explicitly concerned with showing how differences in American and Japanese educational systems are not just due to culture, but to differences in institutional organization and educational policies. Dissatisfaction with overly culturalist interpretations of Japanese education among some authors is linked to the ways that such interpretations feed into the mythologizing tendencies critiqued earlier.

The tension between cultural and structural forms of explanation remains, however, and has perhaps gained an even greater salience in the context of discussions about globalization in the Japanese educational system. As discussed by Hayashi and Tobin (this volume), Japanese teaching and learning in preschool is strongly shaped by a "cultural logic" that is more resistant to change than one would expect in the face of economic and structural changes associated with globalization. Indeed, it is this cultural logic itself that Japanese are trying to preserve by recognizing the essentially conservative role the preschool can play as an instrument of cultural maintenance and continuity (Tobin, Hsueh, & Karasawa, 2009). Cave (2007) also found that despite policy changes associated with waves of reform in Japanese education, core cultural values associated with personhood and with the role of the school in contributing toward learning selfhood remained recognizable, indicating that at some level Japanese educational practices are perhaps more self-consciously "cultural" in ways that accommodate but do not reduce to structural forces.

Individual Versus Collective Selves

As an enduring focal point for analysis of Japanese education, concepts of person, self, and self–other relationships undergird many contemporary discussions of education, from bullying (Akiba & Shimizu, this volume) to globalization (Hayashi & Tobin, this volume). The anthropological literature on Japanese education, in particular, has had an enduring preoccupation with both school- and nonschool-based learning as sites and processes intimately connected to the formation of selves. Whether this is because a discourse about "self" is more explicit and/or prominent in the culture of teaching and learning in Japan than elsewhere, or whether this reflects the kinds of research interests or perspectives brought to the study of Japanese education, it is clear that the formation of personhood is a major theme in the literature, and that it is inevitably associated with moral if not political agendas (see Kondo, 1990).

But what is most significant about this theme is that at the level of official discourse (such as that driving Japanese education policy reform) one finds ample reference to a perceived need for the supposed collective or group-oriented Japanese self to change, to become more independent, individualist, creative, and so forth. However, at the level of actual practice, the characterization of the group-oriented self as somehow being in contradiction with attentiveness to children's autonomy and individuality seems not to hold true, as Cave (2007), Sato (2004), and Hoffman (2000a, 2000b) point out. In fact, in the classrooms that are explored by these authors, cultivation of a community of interdependent learners exists alongside cultivation of self-direction and autonomy, rendering the official discourse somewhat redundant (as some of Cave's teachers pointed out). What may well be a tension between individualist and interdependent models of self at the official level of discourse dissolves at the informal level of practice, raising questions as to how certain constructions of Japanese culture gain legitimacy (and perhaps political utility) while others remain unrecognized but perhaps more powerful at the level of ordinary practice of teaching and learning.

Education for Belonging Versus Education for Transformation

A related theme that emerges perhaps most visibly when reading the ethnographic literature on Japanese education concerns the goals for education in Japan in the context of forces for cultural continuity and change. This theme is certainly present in this volume (e.g., Hayashi & Tobin on preschools; Bjork & Fukuzawa on guidance; Tsuneyoshi on market-driven reform), but is perhaps most illuminating when explored in the context of ethnographic literature on situated learning in Japan.

This body of work presents us with a rich portrait of teaching and learning outside schools, from bathhouses to baseball fields, bars, and banks. The diversity of settings in which teaching and learning have been studied is remarkable: One thinks of shellfish divers (Hill & Plath, 1998), taiko drummers (Powell, 2006), Zen monks (Sogen Hori, 1996), urban factory workers (Kondo, 1990), bankers (Rohlen, 1984), Noh actors (Hare, 1996), baseball players (Kelly, 1998), and violin teachers (Hersh & Peak, 1998), among many others. As Singleton points out in his edited volume on the topic (1998), what is common across all these diverse settings is a view of learning that focuses in part on the acquisition of a personal identity as a member of a "community of practice" (Lave & Wenger, 1991).

What is particularly interesting about these accounts is that so many of them are first-person narratives. Among other things, the first-person approach makes vivid the level of personal transformation that is involved in this learning seen from the inside. Inevitably, they also illustrate that becoming a member of a community of practice in Japan appears to require a significant coming to terms with one's own self, in which themes of struggle, sacrifice, and development of a sense of obligation toward others play key roles. The learning process itself is also culturally distinctive in that it is mediated by strict standards of cognitive/skill performance, often ritualistic in nature, yet predicated on a simultaneous experience of deep emotionality. The end point of such learning is integration of the self within the community: While individuals necessarily experience learning as a personally transformative process, the ultimate goal is the continuity of the collective, its survival predicated on the creation of selves committed to the goals and worldviews of the collective.

This is an old theme, in fact, in the anthropology of education, but it takes on new salience in the context of discussions concerning forces for globalization and change in Japan. As Kondo (1990) suggests in her first-person narrative about learning in an ethics institute, there is a tension between an education for appropriate modalities of selfhood and an education for social transformation; the former is inherently conservative and does little to change the status quo. In Japan at present, however, cleavages in the social system, in particular the rise of new forms of social inequality, the decline in levels of public trust in social institutions, changing demographics, and economic pressures, have raised new questions about how education should respond to these developments. While there are at present strong elements of continuity—and indeed a consciousness of the need to preserve what is positive in the educational experience of children—concerns about the future of society and how best to prepare for it are increasingly a part of discourse on education in Japan. Are models of belonging as traditionally understood and enacted sufficient? Or is there a need for a new paradigm of belonging, oriented to perhaps different goals and as-yet-untested methods for its realization?

Homogeneity Versus Diversity

The theme of diversity has been preeminent among the "new" trends in writing about Japanese education. Scholarship on the experiences of minority groups in and against the Japanese mainstream, the changing nature of families and their relationships to schools, new youth cultures, social class stratification, and inequalities of opportunity represents a clear shift away from earlier portraits of Japan as a defiantly egalitarian society built on the bulwark of its "educational success."

Yet for some anthropologists of Japan (e.g., Ryang, 2004) it is wrong to see diversity in Japan as new; what is new is its visibility. And this newfound visibility is a correlate, if not a result, of the insertion of Japan into the discourse of critical cultural scholarship, where the "new" lenses of social reproduction, stratification, multiculturalism, class, and disability can work their demythologizing magic.

While it's clear that Japanese homogeneity (whether real or imagined) has had a long run, this leads one to consider what the representation of Japan as a diverse society may actually accomplish. Rather than liberating Japan from the straitjacket of one kind of homogeneity, does it reimpose another—this time, a conceptual—kind, where what may be distinctive about diversity in Japan is erased in the application of concepts of diversity, stratification, and so on, drawn from the globally circulating discourse? It may be the case that "new" discourse about diversity merely represents other ways to reinscribe Japan within an analytical frame whose terms are still set by others, and in which diversity is constructed as a problem to be solved. The deep lesson in all this, of course, is that Japan still needs outsiders in order to develop an adequate consciousness of itself.[3]

JAPAN AND ITS OTHERS: CULTURE, POWER, AND
DIFFERENCE IN READING JAPANESE EDUCATION

If there is one overarching idea that repeatedly surfaces in accounts of Japanese education, it is the shifting status of Japanese education itself in the global arena. Japan has served at various times as a mirror for self-examination, a source or model for envisioning alternatives to given practices, as well as a case to be avoided at all costs. Numerous writers have identified the ways the American and Japanese views of each other's education systems have changed, depending on the domestic political and economic climate, and the relative international standing of the two nations (e.g., Kelly, 1991; LeTendre, 1999a, 1999b). In fact, book titles themselves rather tellingly reflect this shifting status, as we have moved from *The Japanese Educational Challenge* (White, 1988) to *Challenges to Japanese Education* (Gordon, Fujita, Kariya, & LeTendre, 2009).[4]

Whereas Japanese educational success was once a model that challenged America to rethink its own practices, now Japan faces its own internal challenges as it struggles to deal with growing social disparities, declines in international standing, and an uncertain political economy. As Cummings (1989) and Willis, Yamamura, and Rappleye (2008) also point out, scholarship on Japanese education remains trapped, as it were, between scripts that represent Japan as a "model" to learn from, versus portraits that see Japan as "at risk."

Representing Japanese education as newly beset with challenges that did not exist in the past (regardless of whether or not the claim is true) serves another function. By pointing out that the system faces many of the same kinds of problems that are faced by other nations, not only is Japan less of a model, it is also less of a threat: The proverbial "Other" is tamed, made to appear no more or no less different—in a word, domesticated.[5] When Japan's problems are just like those found anywhere in the world, everyone is more comfortable: What may be the perverse distinctiveness of a Japanese culture of education is subverted by the dynamics of global systems and global problems. Culture is no longer tied to foundational differences in worldview but to localized methods of dealing with universal problems. In this way, as its challenges are internalized instead of directed outward, Japan is made ordinary, its difference tamed.

The "taming" of Japanese education also reveals the extent to which power has long been undertheorized in the field. As a central theme in poststructuralist scholarship, the connection between culture and power raises important questions about Japan's relationship with the rest of the world and the role of national (cultural) identity in those relationships. Power both frames the Japan–Other relationship as well as the internal dynamics of teaching and learning, the social organization of schools, teachers' lives, students' lives, bullying, violence, educational reform, ethnicity, and diversity. But what power means in Japan, and the way it relates to other culturally valued domains of experience and action,[6] is not a given, and it may not conform to expectations or assumptions that shape understandings of power in other cultural contexts. Thus, lest Japan again be subsumed to a globalizing discourse about power that homogenizes, so too must it be carefully contextualized and seen through lenses that prioritize the particular forms it takes in Japanese contexts.

Greater consciousness of how culture and power intersect in Japanese education in fact offers an unparalleled arena for exploring and testing assumptions about what are and what ought to be the goals of education more generally in a changing world. As dialogues and debates on topics of global salience are addressed within the context of Japan, both Japanese and their interlocutors can work out their own visions for education. This means taking a hard look at what makes some systems successful in some ways but inadequate in others.

On the positive side, this effort permits and perhaps even requires expanding both one's capacity for self-critique as well as imagination, as encounters with difference construct spaces of potentiality that are opened up by honest self-confrontation. It is in this sense that the culture of Japanese education is not fixed or isolated in some space of incommensurable alterity, where it remains an alternative *to* us, but can be rather seen as offering alternatives *for* us (as inimitably phrased by Clifford Geertz, 1994). On the negative side, the mirror can distort, as well as encourage complacency, when it fails to promote adequate self-reflection and simply confirms readers' own views about what is good and valuable when it comes to education.

A transformative role for the genre is dependent on its capacity to generate culturally adequate understandings of education that maintain the weight of differences and yet avoid the reductionist and essentialist tendencies of globalizing lenses. As Japanese education itself is increasingly defined by the tensions and challenges that affect education more broadly around the world, reflecting perhaps an inevitable global convergence at some levels of educational discourse and practice, there is a danger that a Japan that is so *unlike* the rest of the world will now become a Japan *just like* the rest of the world. If culture continues to be a significant part of what scholars think about when it comes to Japanese education (as it should), then what is needed is a way of talking, writing, and representing education that gives culture its due without engaging in the excesses of holism or the negations of structural over-determinism.

NOTES

1. At the same time, it probably fails to do justice to the complex ways in which both collectivity and individualism flourish side by side within local spaces and cultural activities.

2. See Hoffman, 2009, for a discussion of the latter.

3. One might argue that *Nihonjinron* was a failed attempt at such, predicated as it was—ironically—on the borrowing of Western concepts to capture and represent Japanese "uniqueness."

4. It is interesting to note that while the direction or nature of the challenge has changed, we still cannot get away from identifying Japan with challenge. Ryang (2004) and Roesgaard (2006) both have the word *challenge* in the titles of their books; while writing this essay, I suddenly recognized that even I used the word *challenge* in my title for this chapter!

5. See LeTendre (1999b) for further analysis of Japan as "Other" in American educational debates.

6. Such as intimacy; see Hoffman, 1999.

REFERENCES

Baker, D. P., & LeTendre, G. K. (2005). *National differences, global similarities: World culture and the future of schooling*. Palo Alto CA: Stanford University Press.

Cave, P. (2007). *Primary school in Japan: Self, individuality, and learning in elementary education*. New York: Routledge.

Cummings, W. K. (1989). The American perception of Japanese education. Comparative *Education, 25*(3), 293–302.

DeCoker, G. (1998). Seven characteristics of a traditional Japanese approach to learning. In J. Singleton (Ed.), *Learning in likely places: Varieties of apprenticeship in Japan*. (pp. 68–84). New York: Cambridge University Press.

DeCoker, G. (Ed.). (2002). *National standards and school reform in Japan and the United States*. New York: Teachers College Press.

Geertz, C. (1994). The uses of diversity. In R. Borofsky (Ed.), *Assessing cultural anthropology* (pp. 454–465). New York: McGraw-Hill.

Gordon, J. A., Fujita, H., Kariya, T., & LeTendre, G. (2009). *Challenges to Japanese education: Economics, reform, and human rights*. New York: Teachers College Press.

Hare, T. (1996). Try, try again: training in Noh drama. In T. P. Rohlen & G. K. LeTendre (Eds.), *Teaching and learning in Japan* (pp. 323–344). New York: Cambridge University Press.

Hersh, S., & Peak, L. (1998). Developing character in music teachers: A Suzuki approach. In J. Singleton (Ed.), *Learning in likely places: Varieties of apprenticeship in Japan* (pp. 153–171). New York: Cambridge University Press.

Hill, J., & Plath, D. (1998). Moneyed knowledge: How women become commercial shellfish divers. In J. Singleton (Ed.), *Learning in likely places: Varieties of apprenticeship in Japan* (pp. 211–225). New York: Cambridge University Press.

Hoffman, D. M. (1999). Turning power inside out: Reflections on resistance from the anthropological field. *International Journal of Qualitative Studies in Education, 12*(6), 671–687.

Hoffman, D. M. (2000a). Individualism and individuality in American and Japanese early education: A review and critique. *American Journal of Education, 108*, 300–317.

Hoffman, D. M. (2000b). Pedagogies of self in American and Japanese early childhood education: A critical conceptual analysis. *Elementary School Journal, 101*(2), 193–208.

Hoffman, D. M. (2009). Reflecting on social emotional learning: A critical perspective on trends in the United States. *Review of Educational Research, 79*(2), 533–556.

Holloway, S. (2000). *Contested childhood: Diversity and change in Japanese preschools.* New York: Routledge.

Kelly, W. W. (1991). Directions in the anthropology of contemporary Japan. *Annual Review of Anthropology, 20*, 395–431.

Kelly, W. W. (1998). Learning to swing: Oh Sadaharu and the pedagogy and practice of Japanese baseball. In J. Singleton (Ed.), *Learning in likely places: Varieties of apprenticeship in Japan* (pp. 265–285). New York: Cambridge University Press.

Kondo, D. K. (1990). *Crafting selves: Power, gender, and discourses of identity in a Japanese workplace.* Chicago: University of Chicago Press.

Kubota, R. (1999). Japanese culture constructed by discourses: Implications for applied linguistics research and ELT. *TESOL Quarterly, 33*(1), 9–33.

Lave, J., & Wenger, E. (1991). *Situated learning: Legitimate peripheral participation.* New York: Cambridge University Press.

LeTendre, G. K. (1999a). *Competitor or ally?: Japan's role in American educational debates.* New York: Routledge.

LeTendre, G. K. (1999b). The problem of Japan: Qualitative studies and international educational comparisons. *Educational Researcher, 28*(2), 38–45.

Lewis, C. (1995). *Educating hearts and minds: Reflections on Japanese preschool and elementary education.* Cambridge, U.K.: Cambridge University Press.

Peak, L. (1991). *Learning to go to school in Japan.* Berkeley: University of California Press.

Powell, K. (2006). Inside out and outside-in: Participant observation in *taiko* drumming. In G. Spindler & L. Hammond (Eds.), *Innovations in educational ethnography: Theory, methods, and results* (pp. 33–64). Mahwah, NJ: Lawrence Erlbaum.

Roesgaard, M. H. (2006). *Japanese education and the cram school business: Functions, challenges and perspectives of the juku.* Copenhagen, Denmark: NIAS.

Rohlen, T. P. (1984), *Seishin kyôiku* in a Japanese bank: A description of methods and consideration of some underlying concepts. *Anthropology & Education Quarterly, 15*(1), 17–28.

Rohlen, T. P., & LeTendre, G. K. (Eds.). (1996). *Teaching and learning in Japan.* New York: Cambridge University Press.

Ryang, S. (2004). *Japan and national anthropology: A critique*. New York: Routledge.

Sato, N. (2004). *Inside Japanese classrooms: The heart of education*. New York: Routledge.

Shimahara, N., & Sakai, A. (1995). *Learning to teach in two cultures: Japan and the United States*. New York: Garland Publishing.

Singleton, J (Ed.) (1998). *Learning in likely places: Varieties of apprenticeship in Japan*. New York: Cambridge University Press.

Sogen Hori, G. V. (1996). Teaching and learning in the Rinzai Zen monastery. In T. P. Rohlen & G. K. LeTendre (Eds.), *Teaching and learning in Japan* (pp. 20–49). New York: Cambridge University Press.

Tobin, J., Hsueh, Y., & Karasawa, M. (2009). *Preschool in three cultures revisited*. Chicago: University of Chicago Press.

Tsuneyoshi, R. (2001). *The Japanese model of schooling: Comparisons with the United States*. New York: RoutledgeFalmer.

White, M. (1988). *The Japanese educational challenge: A commitment to children*. New York: The Free Press.

Willis, D., Yamamura, S., & Rappleye, J. (2008). Frontiers of education: Japan as "global model" or "nation at risk"? *International Review of Education, 54*, 493–575.

PART II

Describing Japanese Education

School Context, Social Change,
and Global Perceptions

CHAPTER 3

Continuity and Change in Japanese Preschool Education

Akiko Hayashi & Joseph Tobin

Maintaining continuity in a program of early childhood education from one year or one era to the next requires as much effort and creativity as it does to change. If we think of change as being caused by external forces, like the movement of a small boat in a rushing stream, we can argue that it takes more energy to stay in place than to move with the flow. Absence of change over time in a preschool can reflect the inertia, stubbornness, or even laziness of the staff. But it can also reflect the resolution of teachers and directors to stand up to pressures to distort their practice in reaction to each education fad and demand from grandstanding politicians. The challenge for preschools in any country is to strike the right balance between continuity and change.[1]

Using the concept of "implicit cultural beliefs and practices" as an explanation for continuity in the face of pressure to change, we argue that cultural educational practices are more resilient and more resistant to change than is predicted by theories of economic determinism, modernization, and globalization. The economic decline in Japan from the boom times of the mid-1980s has affected preschools in direct and indirect ways, dropping the value of their land holdings, limiting the rate at which they can raise tuition, and changing patterns of women's work. There is a widespread feeling in Japan that the country modernized so quickly and thoroughly that core cultural values were compromised or lost. And yet, over the past 30 years, rather than change in reaction to these economic and social changes, Japanese preschools on the whole have remained largely the same in their curriculum and pedagogy.

To ameliorate the negative impacts of economic and social change, Japanese preschools have a mandate to pass on to young children the values, perspectives, and social skills that are believed to be at risk in the contemporary, hyper-modern society. Education reform movements in Japan put little pressure on preschools to rationalize or modernize their core practices because there is a general consensus that preschools have an inherently conservative function, which is to protect children from the negative effects of (post) modernization. In contrast to the reforms the government has mandated for primary and secondary education, the government ministries in charge of early childhood education have followed a hands-off approach that we describe and analyze using the Japanese emic pedagogical concept of *mimamoru*—guidance through watching and waiting rather than intervening.

USING MULTIVOCAL ETHNOGRAPHY
TO UNDERSTAND PRESCHOOL CHILDREN

Preschool in Three Cultures: Japan, China, and the United States (Tobin, Wu, & Davidson) was published in 1989, followed by its sequel, 20 years later *Preschool in Three Cultures Revisited: China, Japan, and the United States* (Tobin, Hsueh, & Karasawa, 2009). The new book foregrounds the question of historical continuity and change by analyzing preschools at two points in historical time, circa 1984 and 2004. This chapter draws on both those studies and on our more recent interviews with *yôchien* (nursery school/kindergarten) and *hoikuen* (day-care center) teachers and directors and with Ministry of Education officials.

The method we used in both Preschool in Three Cultures (PSin3C) studies is "video-cued multivocal ethnography." In this method we: 1) videotape a day in a preschool in each culture; 2) edit the videotape down to 20 minutes; 3) show this edited tape first to the teacher in whose classroom we filmed; 4) then show it to other staff at her preschool; 5) then show it to early childhood educators at other preschools around the country and in the two other countries in the study. The result is a video-cued multivocal conversation with early childhood educators in three countries discussing the same set of videos. In this method, the videotapes are not the data; rather, they are cues, stimuli, topics for discussion, interviewing tools.

In the new study we analyze processes of continuity and change in Japan in three ways. The first is by replicating the original study a generation later, once again videotaping a typical day at Komatsudani Hoikuen, and showing this video to our concentric circles of informants, from the classroom teachers to their counterparts in other regions of their country. The second is by showing the old videotapes to current and retired staff from Komatsudani and asking them to comment on what's changed, what's stayed the same, and why. The third is by videotaping in a second Japanese preschool, Madoka Yochien in Tokyo, and then conducting focus-group interviews about the video with cultural insiders and outsiders. Madoka Yochien is unlike Komatsudani in being a *yôchien* rather than a *hoikuen,* being private nonsectarian rather than Buddhist, and being in Tokyo rather than in Kyoto.

THE STRUCTURE OF JAPANESE EARLY CHILDHOOD EDUCATION

Since the early 1980s, demographic changes have led to some structural shifts in the provision in early childhood education, but the central goals and curriculum have remained largely consistent. Historically, the biggest difference between the two forms of provision is one of social class: *Hoikuen* historically have served the working classes, whose mothers could not afford to stop working to stay home with young children; *yôchien,* in contrast, have traditionally served middle-class *sarari-man* (salaried, white-collar) families (Wollons, 2000). Social change in Japan has worked to blur this distinction (Imoto, 2007).

With more professional women continuing to work when they become parents, there is an increasing need for full-day care for children from middle-class families. Some professional, middle-class parents choose to enroll their children in *hoikuen,* but because *hoikuen* are associated, accurately or unfairly, with day care rather than with education and also with working-class rather than middle-class values, some middle-class parents prefer *yôchien* for their children, even though their school hours are inconvenient for working mothers. In response, the Ministry of Education is working with *yôchien* to help them compete with *hoikuen* by diversifying their offerings and extending their school day with after-school enrichment classes.

To compete with *yôchien*, some *hoikuen* are adding frills and more academic emphasis to their curriculum. But Komatsudani and many other *hoikuen* see no need to make such adjustments. In contrast, *hoikuen* have less need to change than do *yôchien* because they have a built-in competitive advantage of taking infants and toddlers and remaining open all day. Once parents have enrolled their infant in a *hoikuen,* for reasons of schedule, convenience, trust, and a desire for continuity, they are unlikely to move him to a *yôchien* when the child turns 3 years of age. Many *yôchien* now have extended hours and afterschool enrichment plans, but their schedules and more frequent holidays still make them less convenient for working parents than the year-round, all-day service provided by *hoikuen.* With *yôchien* feeling pressure from parents to lengthen their school day and with some *hoikuen* feeling pressure to provide more academic preparation, programmatic and curricular differences between *hoikuen* and *yôchien* seem to have grown smaller over the years.

In 2006, the Ministry of Education and the Ministry of Health, Labour and Welfare introduced a "third alternative," a new kind of preschool: the *nintei kodomoen* (literally, "accredited children's garden") or, for short, *kodomoen* ("kindergarten"). With the aim of simplifying and rationalizing the system, and the hope that these new hybrid early childhood education and child-care programs might eventually replace the other two types of preschool, the government suggested that *kodomoen* can be created in these ways: merging *hoikuen* and *yôchien* operating in the same communities, *yôchien* taking on *hoikuen* functions or vice versa, and independent facilities that are currently unlicensed assuming the functions of both the *hoikuen* and the *yôchien* (that is, full-day care and early childhood education) and applying for licensure (Imoto, 2007). The number of *kodomoen* has gradually increased (to about 900 in 2012), but *yôchien* and *hoikuen* directors have not responded with enthusiasm to the opportunity to convert to *kodomoen*. We interpret their response as an indication of a general reluctance of stakeholders to make large-scale changes to a domain of education that they perceive as functioning well.

THE EFFECTS ON PRESCHOOLS OF DEMOGRAPHIC, ECONOMIC, AND SOCIAL CHANGE

When we asked Japanese early childhood educators to describe what has changed the most for them since 1985, most focused on the impacts of economic and demographic change. Japan has one of the lowest birthrates in the world. The birthrate, already low in 1984 at 1.8 children per woman of child-rearing age, fell to 1.2 in 2005. Many of the changes we observed at Komatsudani between 1984 and 2005 can be attributed to indirect and direct effects of Japan's falling birthrate. The shrinking birthrate is having similar effects on Madoka, and indeed on most Japanese preschools. The economic decline in Japan from the boom times of the mid-1980s has also made the business of running a preschool increasingly precarious, affecting programs in direct and indirect ways (e.g., dropping the value of their land holdings, limiting the rate at which they can raise tuition, and changing patterns of women's work). The career trajectories of teachers, too, have changed. Teachers are now less likely to take a leave from teaching during their childrearing years as they did a generation ago, when the strong economy made it possible for families to live on one income.

The most direct effect of the low birthrate on preschools is their having to compete more aggressively to maintain enrollments. A decline in student numbers can lead to cuts in programs that in turn make the preschool less attractive to potential customers. Enrollment drops also carry the risk of jeopardizing program reputations. To avoid downsizing in neighborhoods in Japan where birthrates are low, many private preschools are expanding their recruitment areas. Like fishing boats that go farther and farther from the homeport to fill their holds, many *yôchien* and *hoikuen* are sending their brightly colored fleets of buses greater distances in order to fill their classrooms. This strategy of recruiting outside their immediate neighborhood exacerbates the problem of competition as more and more preschools attempt to recruit from the same pool of children. It could be argued that this phenomena benefits families by increasing choice. But it carries the disadvantage of causing less well-funded programs without buses to close. The net result is fewer preschools serving children in their local communities and more children experiencing increasingly long bus rides. It also means that some *hoikuen* such as Komatsudani, which did not have buses 20 years ago, now spend money to provide bus service.

Another effect of declining birthrates on preschools is that many of them, particularly private *yôchien*, are distorting their curricula to attract prospective clients. Some preschools feel compelled to add trendy programs of little educational or social value. In neighborhoods where ambitious, nervous young parents are seeking an academic fast start for their children, preschools increasingly give in to the temptation to provide more explicit academic instruction. Computers, tennis, swimming, and English conversation are among the enrichment activities being added to the standard *yôchien* curriculum to attract customers.

From a consumer's point of view, competition has the advantage of compelling preschools to adjust to the desires of potential customers. But most Japanese early childhood experts and preschool directors we interviewed view the market effects on the curriculum negatively. Their view is that the market creates pressures that lead preschools to pander to the sometimes misguided desires of their potential clients and to lose sight of what is good for children. Other changes include extending the school day and running afterschool programs for primary school children, a service that Komatsudani now offers. A few preschools have responded to changing demographics by converting to eldercare centers.

The drop in the Japanese birthrate also means that preschools in Japan have had to adjust to the emotional and social needs of the "only child." In a society where young children have few siblings or cousins and live in urban settings that provide limited opportunities to interact with peers, Japanese preschools provide a range of social and emotional experiences that once occurred spontaneously at home and in the neighborhoods. Concern about the growing social isolation of Japanese children is widespread in Japan.

The precipitous economic decline Japan suffered in the 1990s has had a profound effect on the overall national mood, creating a climate of pessimism, blame, and recrimination. In this climate, for example, teachers and parents blame each other for what is widely perceived to be a decrease in young children's social, emotional, and cognitive competence. When a country's economy is going well, its social institutions—including schools—generally are viewed positively, and even receive partial credit for the nation's prosperity. When Japan's economy was booming in the 1980s, the whole world, including many Japanese, found much to praise about Japan's education system. Conversely, an economic crisis leads to harsher analyses of social institutions and to an eagerness to assign blame. In Japan, some of this blame has been placed on education.

Over the past 30 years or so, in response to the belief that the emerging information economy requires increasingly creative, flexible workers, the Ministry of Education has proposed making the primary school curriculum less structured and more student-centered. The recent decline in Japan's performance on international education tests has created a backlash that calls for MOE to follow America's lead and push for more emphasis on achievement and accountability in Japan's primary and secondary education (Bjork & Tsuneyoshi, 2005; Takayama, 2007), but so far such calls have not led to a shift away from the constructivist, play-oriented curricula found in a majority of Japanese preschools.

In 1998, the Ministry of Education issued its *National Curriculum Standards for Kindergartens*, which emphasizes the importance of facilitating the social and emotional development of children through play and social interaction. This document is consistent in emphasis and spirit with the Ministry's vision for elementary and secondary education outlined in *Education Reform for the 21st Century* (2001). The plan reflects a deep concern about the soul of Japanese society, and urges an appreciation for "education of the heart," critical thinking skills, and creativity, calling on teachers to make lessons more enjoyable, worry-free, and easy to understand. For preschools, these reform documents do not require a radical shift in approach, but rather an even stronger commitment to social-emotional development and avoidance of the kind of top-down academic curricular reforms pursued by the United States and many other nations.

THE CENTRAL GOALS OF JAPANESE EARLY CHILDHOOD EDUCATION

Although Japanese early childhood educators express concerns about the emotional health of contemporary young children, the quality of parenting, and the moral fiber of the nation, they do not call for radical changes in the preschool curriculum. Instead, these educators feel that they must hold firm in their approaches because now, even more than a generation ago, preschools must help children develop social skills not learned at home or in local neighborhoods. We find a striking similarity of points of view, and even some similar tropes, in the interviews we conducted. The director of Madoka suggested that children these days lack sufficient opportunities for complex social relations. When we asked him how he could explain our observation that there seemed to be a lot of incidents of children crying in the classroom, he replied, "Crying is not a problem. If there was no crying, that would be a problem." He suggested that when children cry at school, perhaps out of frustration at not being able to dress themselves or as an attempt to convince other children to follow their lead in play, this is a symptom of social inexperience, which offers an opportunity to learn. This explanation resonates with something the director of Komatsudani told us in 1985: "The world of young children has grown more and more narrow. Their parents protect them too much from playing roughly with other children without adult supervision, and from getting dirty from playing in the mud." In other words, one of the most important things that preschools can give young children is the opportunity to experience greater social complexity.

Dealing with tears, fights, and hardships are normal aspects of a healthy childhood that children in contemporary Japan are seen as being at risk of missing out on as a result of shrinking family size, a loss of opportunities to interact spontaneously with other children in neighborhood settings, and parents who are either anxiously overprotective or narcissistically too self-absorbed to give their children attention or opportunities for play with others. Today, as in 1985, Japanese preschools are asked to provide young children with the kinds of experiences and the traditional values they learned at home and in their neighborhood in an earlier era.

The majority of Japanese early childhood educators believe the following: Preschools should emphasize social and emotional development over academic preparation; collective play is more valuable than individual activities; and the overall mood should be easygoing rather than strict (Oda & Mori, 2006). Play-oriented *yôchien* such as Madoka and *hoikuen* such as Komatsudani have more in common with each other in curricular philosophy than they do with more academically oriented programs.

Some Japanese early childhood education experts we spoke with are concerned that preschool teachers are not doing enough to foster children's *chiteki hattatsu* (intellectual development). Some of these experts have introduced the ideas of Reggio Emilia and other project-oriented curricular approaches that emphasize the importance of teachers organizing cognitively stimulating activities and asking probing questions that support the intellectual development of young children. While we agree with the goal of providing children with cognitively stimulating experiences in preschool, we are not convinced that Japanese early childhood education will be improved by an increase in the explicit attention given to intellectual development. We would argue that in spite of the apparent lack of an academic curriculum or intellectual rigor at Komatsudani, the programs at these schools are in fact highly intellectually challenging for young children and reflect what we call the implicit cultural logic of Japanese early childhood education. The emphasis on free play, physicality, and social interaction with minimal teacher intervention are all practiced widely in Japanese preschools without often being explicitly taught.

MIMAMORU

The best-known finding from the Preschool in Three Cultures studies is the hesitancy of Japanese preschool teachers, compared to their counterparts in the United States and China, to intervene in children's disputes, a finding first reported by Catherine Lewis in her 1984 paper, and subsequently confirmed by studies by other scholars (Ben-Ari, 1997; Lewis, 1984; Walsh, 1991). A scene in the original PSin3C study showed a 4-year-old boy, Hiroki, stepping on his classmate Satoshi's hand, making him cry. As his teacher, Fukui-sensei, looks on from across the room, but does nothing to intervene, another classmate, Midori, comes over, and leads Satoshi away from Hiroki and advises him to avoid playing with Hiroki in the future. When asked later why she hadn't intervened, Fukui-sensei explained that by holding back she was providing children in the class with opportunities to experience emotions and deal with interpersonal conflicts they rarely experienced at home.

In *Preschool in Three Cultures Revisited*, there is a scene in which three girls pull and tug on a teddy bear until they fall into a struggling heap on the floor. During this struggle, the only visible and audible reaction of the classroom teacher Morita-sensei is to call out from across the room: "*Kora Kora, Kora Kora!*" (meaning something like "Hey, Hey!"). When asked about this scene, Morita-sensei explained that this is typical of her approach, i.e., letting children know that she is watching them, but avoiding intervention, in order to give them the opportunity to experience complex social interactions, and to work out their own solutions. Calling out "*Kora Kora*" let the children know that if the situation became too rough or chaotic the teacher would be there to help. Providing a sort of safety net for the children's interactions helps them develop the confidence and security they need to work things out on their own.

Morita-sensei as well as other teachers we interviewed used the term *mimamoru* to describe this strategy of supporting children's social-emotional development by holding back and watching without intervening. *Mi* literally means "to watch;" *mamoru* means "to guard." Together the words describe to a Japanese pedagogical strategy of child care that we translate as "teaching by watching and waiting." We suggest that *mimamoru* is an emic belief and practice employed by preschool teachers toward young children, by preschool directors toward young teachers, and by the Ministry of Education toward preschools themselves.

Mimamoru is a component of a larger pedagogical approach called *machi no hoiku* ("caring for children by waiting"). As a preschool teacher in Tokyo explained to us, "Japanese teachers wait until children solve their problems on their own. Children know their abilities, what they can do. So we wait. It could be said that we can wait because we believe in children."

In the preschool classroom this cultural logic of *mimamoru* takes the form of preschool teachers using a "hands-off" or low intervention approach to dealing with children's social interactions, especially with their disputes. Preschool directors described taking a similar approach to support the development of new teachers. A preschool director we interviewed in Kyoto commented on Morita's strategy of watchful nonintervention when she watched the video: "She can wait because she has three years' experience of working in a day-care center. A first-year teacher can't wait like this. It takes a long time." Yoshizawa-sensei, Komatsudani's recently retired director, said: "You have to be a real caring professional to tell the difference between a real fight and rough and tumble play. It takes at least 5 years." The directors' emphasis on the time it takes for teachers to develop skill in using *mimamoru* with children mirrors the similar strategy of *mimamoru* that they use with teachers, i.e., watching but not overly intervening as teachers over time develop their ability to hold back and scaffold children's social interactions.

When we asked how teachers come to be able to employ a strategy of *mimamoru* with their students, a preschool director in Tokyo responded: "By meeting a mentor (*onshi*). This sometimes happens before coming to the field, sometimes right after graduating from school, or sometimes in the middle of their career. Whenever, it's crucial for teachers to meet a mentor to develop their professionalism." This comment is consistent with a belief that directors need to take a long point of view on teacher development, giving each teacher time and space to develop in her own way at her own pace. Directors support this development through watching and waiting, and allowing young teachers to learn from their more experienced coworkers. This approach has much in common with the way teachers deal with the development of children's ability to handle social interactions. Morita-sensei explained her nonintervention in the fight over the teddy bear by saying, "It would be quick and easy if I intervened in their fight. But then, I would take away from children an opportunity to grow up."

Our argument is that *mimamoru* is a core cultural component of Japanese early childhood educational that cuts across contexts, giving young children, teachers, and directors space and time to work things out on their own. Where do preschool teachers and directors learn this idea? We might expect such a central pedagogical idea to be articulated in the kindergarten curriculum guidelines, or other documents produced by the Ministry. These guidelines, however, say nothing directly about *mimamoru*, or about how this approach can be put into practice either as classroom management or a strategy of staff development. When we asked Japanese preschool teachers and directors where the idea of *mimamoru* comes from, no one mentioned directives from the government ministries or from the early childhood education reforms. Japanese teachers and directors interviewed in the *Preschool in Three Cultures Revisited* study made very few mentions of the Ministry guidelines and no comments suggesting that any government agency or professional organization provides direct pressures or directives to guide preschool practice.

Mimamoru, then, is an example of an implicit cultural practice that serves as a source of consistency and continuity among preschool programs. Because it is implicit, in the sense of being passed on through apprenticeship learning and enculturation rather than taught systematically in schools of education or mandated in policy documents, it is largely immune to top-down reforms that address explicit aspects of curriculum and pedagogy. It contributes to a hands-off, yet observant style of management that we suggest characterizes how preschool teachers deal with students, directors with teachers, and government ministries with preschools.

GLOBALIZATION AND JAPANESE EARLY CHILDHOOD EDUCATION

Critics as well as proponents of globalization suggest that as goods, ideas, and people are exchanged among nations at an ever-increasing pace, nations are becoming more similar and cultural differences less salient. The world systems theory version of globalization suggests that as the world increasingly becomes one system, ideas from the most powerful, culture-exporting countries come to dominate those of other countries. This result is also the prediction of the modernization/rationalization version of globalization, which would suggest, following the logic of Social Darwinism, that over time the most rational, effective educational approaches spread, replacing tradition-bound, local approaches that have continued for reasons other than their rationality and functionality. The result is an ever-growing global convergence of education practices and ideas.

During the last 20 years, China has aggressively imported progressive ideas about early childhood education from the United States and Europe; the United States has borrowed ideas from Reggio Emilia and exported curricula to Third World nations. Over the same period, Japanese early childhood education, curiously, has stayed largely outside of this circuit of global borrowing and lend-ing, having relatively little apparent influence on the rest of the world, and been relatively little influenced by others. There are two questions here, which we will address one at a time: Why isn't the Japanese approach to early childhood edu-cation spreading globally? And why is Japanese early childhood education rela-tively impervious to influences from abroad?

Japanese early childhood education's lack of visible impact on other countries is all the more surprising considering Japan's growing role in the global circulation of cultural products and ideas. Japan became a major global exporter of manufac-tured goods in the 1960s. In the 1980s, as its economy boomed, Japan made the jump from exporting goods to exporting ideas and cultural products, and Japanese management practices provided models for the rest of the world. Japanese edu-cational approaches were also widely studied abroad. Envy of Japanese results on Trends in International Mathematics and Science Study (TIMSS) and other international measures of academic achievement led educators from Europe and the United States in the 1980s to attempt to imitate elements of Japanese primary and secondary school mathematics and science curricula, classroom organization, supplementary education programs such as Kumon math and *juku*, and teacher training and development (especially *kenkyû jugyô*, or "lesson study").

If the rest of the world has borrowed little from Japanese early childhood edu-cation in the last 20 years, it is not because of a lack of information about what goes on in Japanese preschools. Scholars from outside Japan have published books and articles that have pointed out some of the strengths of Japanese early childhood education. This scholarship has led to some questioning of taken-for-granted as-sumptions in the West about what is possible and desirable in preschools, but not to any borrowing of Japanese early childhood practices, nor opening of *yôchien* or *hoikuen* in the United States or Europe, nor calls from politicians to emulate the Japanese approach of 30 children with one teacher, nor workshops on how to implement the Japanese approach of nonintervention in children's fights, nor pilgrimages to Komatsudani.

Our general explanation for why Japanese early childhood educational ideas have had relatively little impact outside Japan is that Japanese early childhood education is deeply contextual. It is resistant to decontextualization and, there-fore, to global circulation. We suggest that early childhood education systems can be categorized as either self-consciously constructed or implicit. The constructed systems can travel abroad because they are readily packaged. Most have training manuals, or, if they don't favor manuals, they have a less didactic but nonetheless systematic approach to popularizing and marketing their program. In contrast, the core features of Japanese early childhood education have no author, no core text, and no mechanism for dissemination. For the most part, they are not explained in

Japanese teacher education textbooks and they are not taught systematically in pre-service teacher education programs. The core features of the Japanese pre-school are implicit, reflecting a deep cultural logic. Values such as social-minded-ness, liveliness, creativity, appreciation for nature, perseverance, and empathy are emphasized in government statements of goals for *yôchien* and *hoikuen*, but these statements lack clear directions on how to achieve them.

The characteristic qualities and strengths of the Japanese preschool system include alternating periods of chaos and order in the classroom (Sano, 1989), reluctance to intervene too quickly in children's disputes, high student–teacher ratios that encourage peer interaction, and emphasis on emotion and especially on the development of empathy. These are not spelled out in curriculum guides, found in training manuals, or much discussed by Japanese scholars in academic publications. They are passed on from one generation to the next not in principles taught in university courses and included in textbooks but instead through an apprenticeship model in which new teachers learn what to do from more experienced teachers. Because these key features of Japanese education are implicit and emergent, rather than constructed, they are for the most part unmarked and, from the Japanese perspective, unremarkable, not needing explanation, justification, or codification, and therefore not amenable to being packaged for export.

The cultural embeddedness of the Japanese approach to early childhood education also makes for little borrowing from outside. Because many people in Japanese society are concerned that their society has already changed too much and become too Westernized, Japanese preschools borrow few outside ideas. Japan looks to its preschools as a source of cultural continuity rather than as a source of change. Preschools, though not a traditional Japanese cultural institution, are viewed as sites where children growing up in a postmodern world acquire traditional values that are gradually becoming endangered. The more Japanese perceive their world as changing and the more their everyday lives are touched by globalization, the more pressure is exerted on preschools to stay the same.

Contemporary Japan is by no means a xenophobic or isolationist society. Japanese science, business, and other levels of education borrow ideas freely from other countries. Some Japanese professors of early childhood education attend international meetings and follow the international literature. But, for the most part, these external ideas result in minimal change in everyday preschool practice. Tellingly, there is little support for reducing student–teacher ratios to the levels found in Europe and the United States. Although a handful of Japanese preschools modeled on Montessori and other foreign approaches exist, these programs tend to think of themselves—and be thought of by others—as self-consciously non-Japanese alternatives to the usual Japanese approach.

Japanese early childhood education begins with core assumptions that are quite different from those programs in the United States, Europe, and China. Diane Hoffman (2000) argues that Japanese early childhood education is based on a notion of preserving and supporting the childishness of young children and not focusing on developmental outcomes. Japanese early childhood education also differs from the European and North American systems in viewing preschool as an institution not primarily of the mother, but of the traditional urban neighborhood or village square. It therefore emphasizes social complexity, not dyadic interactions. These fundamental differences in understanding childhood and the goals of early childhood education make it difficult for Japanese preschools to participate in the global exchange of ideas and practices.

Japanese early childhood education reflects an implicit cultural logic that is resistant to change as well as to borrowing and lending. This deep cultural logic makes Japanese early childhood education unique among world systems, and well attuned to the desire of contemporary Japanese parents and policymakers for institutions that can preserve cultural values in an era of rapid social transformation. Because so many other traditional Japanese institutions have been thoroughly modernized and postmodernized, preschools are looked to as islands of cultural continuity in a sea of social change.

NOTE

1. A portion of this chapter was published in Hayashi (2011), Tobin (2011), and Tobin, Hsueh, and Karasawa (2009).

REFERENCES

Ben-Ari, E. (1997). *Body projects in Japanese childcare: Culture, organization, and emotions in a preschool.* London, UK: Routledge.

Bjork, C., & Tsuneyoshi, R. (2005). Educational reform in Japan: Competing visions for the future. *Phi Delta Kappan, 86*(8), 619–626.

Hoffman, D. (2000). Individualism and individuality in American and Japanese early education: A review and critique. *American Journal of Education 108*(4), 300–317.

Hayashi, A. (2011). The Japanese hands-off approach to curriculum guidelines for early childhood education as a form of cultural practice. *Asian-Pacific Journal of Research in Early Childhood Education, 5*(2), 107–123.

Imoto, Y. (2007). The Japanese preschool system in transition. *Research in Comparative and International Education, 2*(2), 88–101.

Lewis, C. (1984). Cooperation and control in Japanese nursery schools. *Comparative Education Review, 28*(1), 69–84.

MEXT, Ministry of Education, Culture, Sports Science and Technology. (2001). *Education reform for the 21st century*. Tokyo: Author. Retrieved from http://www.mext.go.jp/b_menu/hakusho/html/hpac200101/index.html

MEXT, Ministry of Education, Culture, Sports Science and Technology. (1998). *National curriculum standards for kindergartens*. Tokyo: Author. Retrieved from http://warp.ndl.go.jp/info:ndljp/pid/286794/www.mext.go.jp/english/news/2001/04/010401.htm#01

Oda, Y., & Mori, M. (2006). Current challenges of kindergarten (yochien) education in Japan: Toward balancing children's autonomy and teachers' intention. *Childhood Education, 82*(6), 369–373.

Sano, T. (1989). Methods of social control and socialization in Japanese daycare centers. *Journal of Japanese Studies, 15*(1), 125–138.

Takayama, K. (2007). A nation at risk crosses the Pacific: Transnational borrowing of the U.S. crisis discourse in the debate on education reform in Japan. *Comparative Education Review, 51*(4), 423–446.

Tobin, J. (2011). Implicit cultural beliefs and practices in approaches to early childhood education and care. *Asia-Pacific Journal of Research in Early Childhood Education, 5*(2), 107–123.

Tobin, J., Hsueh, Y., & Karasawa, M. (2009). *Preschool in three cultures revisited: China, Japan, and the United States*. Chicago: University of Chicago Press.

Tobin, J., Wu, D., & Davidson, D. (1989). *Preschool in three cultures: Japan, China, and the United States*. New Haven, CT: Yale University Press.

Walsh, D. J. (1991). Extending the discourse on developmental appropriateness: A developmental perspective. *Early Education and Development, 2*(2), 109–119.

Wollons, R. (2000). The missionary kindergarten in Japan. In R. Wollons (Ed.), *Kindergarten and cultures: The global diffusion of an idea*. New Haven, CT: Yale University Press.

CHAPTER 4

School Guidance in Japanese Middle Schools

Balancing the Old and New Amidst Social Change

Christopher Bjork & Rebecca Erwin Fukuzawa

The social and moral development of children has always been a central component of the mission of Japanese schools (LeTendre, 1999; Shimahara & Sakai, 1995). In addition to providing a solid base of knowledge to their pupils, teachers are responsible for developing in students the attitudes and dispositions necessary to function as citizens, community members, and workers. Analyses of student guidance approaches (*seikatsu shidô*), therefore, can deepen our understanding of the values that anchor educational institutions, and clarify the characteristics considered most essential for success in Japanese society.

Scholarship published during the economic boom years explored in detail approaches to classroom management and student guidance. Previous accounts of the Japanese education system highlighted the serious attention devoted to establishing norms related to student comportment and dress in the schools (Cummings, 1980; Stevenson, Stigler, Lee, Lucker, Kitamura, & Hsu, 1985; White, 1987). Through a combination of well-established and strictly enforced discipline procedures, along with careful attention to group formation and the development of the "whole child" (Lewis, 1995), teachers in the 1980s created a balanced approach through what Rohlen (1983) called "intimacy coupled with severity" (p. 201). During the heyday of Japan's economic expansion, the foreign press, eager to explain the nation's ascension from vanquished debtor to global leader, drew attention to examples of orderliness and discipline in Japanese schools, but often ignored the more subtle ways that teachers orchestrated purposeful interactions between students. Images of adolescents in military-style uniforms standing obediently next to their wooden desks have proven difficult to erase from the popular imagination, regardless of how accurately they may have captured conditions in actual schools.

Outside of Japan, understanding of the practices teachers rely on to manage their pupils continues to be informed largely by research generated in the 1980s and 1990s. Yet, as we will show, much has since changed for students, teachers, and schools. Although many non-Japan specialists continue to assume that middle schools are highly regimented institutions filled with students who compliantly adhere to school rules, a visit to a Japanese secondary school today would likely dispel that notion. The architecture of the schools may have changed very little over the past 50 years, but that visible continuity obscures variation in the actors and activities within.

In the years since the collapse of Japan's economic bubble, the education system—and the larger society—has been transfigured. Expanding gaps between the haves and the have-nots and the adoption of a collection of reforms designed to reduce pressure in the schools (*yutori kyôiku*) have altered the context for teaching and learning. These reforms, which include reductions in curriculum and teaching hours, also stress diversity and flexibility through greater parent/student choice (Tsuneyoshi, this volume) and reductions in school-based club activities (Okano, 2008). At the same time, expanded access to mass media and independent social networks has weakened the ability of schools and parents to monitor student behavior. Challenged by these social changes and shifts in youth culture, teachers are revising their methods, searching for the appropriate mix of discipline and nurturance.

Although researchers have devoted a great deal of attention to the process of relaxed education policy formulation, they have largely ignored trends related to student guidance. In this chapter we take a close look at the evolution of the student guidance system in Japanese middle schools over the past 30 years. Drawing from ethnographic data collected over 3 decades, we examine changes in the practices deemed appropriate for guiding adolescents through this process of adjustment. In the 1990s, the Ministry of Education (MOE) prohibited teachers from using disciplinary measures that might be regarded as excessive or violent. As we will show, the combination of increasingly assertive students and the promotion of more accommodating guidance approaches has complicated the work of educators. Deterred from employing tactics that had proven effective in the past, many middle school teachers are struggling to maintain order in settings where their authority is frequently challenged.

PATTERNS IN SCHOOL GUIDANCE PRACTICES

The research methodology framing this study is rather unorthodox. In consideration of the themes that anchor this book, we sought to trace patterns in school guidance practices over time. Media reports as well as academic scholarship suggest that schools have experienced extensive modifications since Japan's economic boom years; yet, as we note above, debates about curricular change have overshadowed questions related to the strategies schools rely on to mentor their students in matters that fall outside of the formal curriculum. This is a notable oversight, given the strong emphasis placed on moral development in Japanese educational institutions.

To remedy this lack we collaborated in what might be described as an artificially constructed longitudinal ethnography, or a retrospective analysis of guidance practices. The institutions we studied were located in different geographical as well as temporal locations. Fukuzawa conducted fieldwork in three Tokyo middle schools between 1983 and 1986. Bjork studied three middle schools located in a rural area of northern Japan between 2005 and 2006.[1] Both of us employed ethnographic methods, spending extended periods of time (between 3 and 9 months) at each research site. Acting as participant observers, we adhered to the criteria for ethnographic research identified by Massey and Walford (Massey & Walford, 1998; Walford, 2001). Inside the schools, we employed comprehensive selection strategies, interviewing teachers and administrators at each site and observing each homeroom on multiple occasions. We took part in the broad range of activities that encompass middle school life. Our goal was to develop an understanding of "naturally occurring human behavior in context" (Moore, 2010, p. 87).

We acknowledge the limitations of this research methodology. First, the schools scrutinized in the 1980s differed from those examined in the 2000s in a number of respects. The most notable of those discontinuities relates to geographical setting. These schools served communities that differed in terms of employment patterns, income, proximity to social and entertainment activities, family structure, and many other factors. Second, we collected data independently, before deciding to collaborate on this chapter. Our conclusions would have been more convincing if we had established the data collection tools together, before heading into the field. Given the timing of the project, however, that was not possible, though we did study each other's field notes as we prepared this manuscript. Third, due to space constraints, we focus on conditions in two middle schools. We realize that events on those campuses do not represent standard practices in all of the schools we studied or in other parts of Japan, but they do lead us to important tentative conclusions.

Our objective was not to offer a set of findings that can be generalized to schools throughout Japan. Rather, we sought to take a close look at teachers' views about student guidance at two distinct points in time, and to analyze how and why the techniques for mentoring their pupils have changed. We chose to highlight certain conditions and events in this essay because they reveal how changes in pupil attitudes toward school and society have complicated the lives of teachers. As we will show, many contemporary educators are struggling to maintain order in the classroom while simultaneously conforming to the principles of relaxed education advocated by the MOE. The experiences of instructors at the two middle schools described in this chapter may be unique, but contrasts in their thinking about how to mentor adolescents underscore the extent of the changes that have shaken Japanese schools in the years between economic prosperity and the current, post-*yutori* reform era.

MIDDLE SCHOOL CLASSROOM MANAGEMENT

A number of studies of Japanese schooling have documented a basic core of organizational features and practices related to classroom management. Beginning with Lewis's study of strategies for social control in kindergarten, researchers have identified guidance strategies that deemphasize immediate compliance in favor of the nurturance of internal norms. Peak (1991) concluded that by minimizing the impression of teacher control, Japanese preschool teachers create a climate of cooperation. The major purpose of preschool was training children in specific routines and attitudes compatible with group life. Lewis (1995), Sato (1991), Tsuneyoshi (2001), and others have found parallel patterns in elementary schools. Fukuzawa and LeTendre (2001) and LeTendre (1994) document similar practices in middle schools.

These aspects of Japanese classroom culture are rooted in prewar classroom management routines (Sato, 1998). During the Taisho Period (1912–1926) classroom management incorporated the current form of autonomous classrooms in which students govern themselves through small groups. As part of a number of liberal education reforms, teachers developed a wide range of task-based small groups charged with cleaning, monitoring, news, and various subjects. These practices quickly diffused throughout the nation. Student guidance also has roots in the prewar juvenile policing and protection policies as well as wartime factory schools. Many of the carefully prescribed routines, dress codes, and surveillance techniques of lifestyle guidance were pioneered at this time (Ambaras, 2006).

Deeply rooted views about the inherent goodness of children also shape practices in contemporary Japanese schools. Especially in the early years of schooling, teachers "attempt to preserve and develop as much of the individual's original nature as possible" (Yamamura, 1986, p. 36). But this conception of the self is balanced by another set of values tied to the benefits of hard work. Nurturing children through the challenges that confront them, it is believed, will help them develop positive dispositions and relations with others; unchecked indulgence can produce egocentric, undisciplined individuals. White (1987) notes that in Japan there is "a notion that the child benefits from experiencing hardship. . . . *Kurô* (suffering or hardship) is believed to have a beneficial effect on the self, deepening it and maturing it, removing self-centeredness. Without *kurô* a person cannot be said to have grown up" (p. 29). As children progress through the education system, they are increasingly exposed to tasks designed to strengthen their character.

One mechanism for encouraging students to behave appropriately that has received a great deal of attention from foreign scholars has been the extensive rules (*kôsoku*) designed to control behavior in Japanese secondary schools. Teachers depend on rules to keep middle schools functioning smoothly, and to gauge the mental state of their pupils. Failure to adhere to school rules is often interpreted as a sign of deeper psychological issues, conflict with peers, or problems in the home (Fukuzawa, 1994). Enforcement of *kôsoku* is treated as a shared responsibility for all members of a school community. Ideally, pupil monitoring of personal behavior and that of their classmates will obviate the need for adults to step in and discipline children who break rules. Such school-sanctioned peer pressure endows students with extensive power over their classmates, an important aspect of Japanese schooling.

In summary, middle school represents a key transition point in the life of Japanese citizens, bridging the worlds of childhood and adulthood. Educators create social structures that encourage pupils, individually and in cooperation with their peers, to manage their own behavior (LeTendre, 2000). To increase the likelihood that pupils will meet the gradually narrowing definitions of acceptable behavior, an "intensive program of social control" (Fukuzawa, 1994, p. 83) is implemented. The key components of this program are daily routines designed to create order in school life, extensive rules related to student appearance and behavior, and activities designed to involve students in school life. In the past, if the system failed to produce its desired outcomes, teachers would step in and address transgressions as they saw fit; potent displays of authority communicated to all members of the community the importance of adhering to established rules.

In the following sections we present two case studies, one from the 1980s that illustrates the general patterns introduced here and one from the 2000s that suggests shifts in the application of this basic pattern. In the 1980s, not all classroom management was uniform. Individual teachers varied in how much they relied on empathy or authority to gain the respect of students. However, the approaches of all instructors did converge toward a basic pattern from the early to the mid-1980s. Moreover, teachers in the schools we visited at that time expressed confidence in the correctness and effectiveness of their classroom management and disciplinary strategies. In contrast, teachers today often lack both confidence and agreed-upon strategies. Our comparison of the two case studies highlights these changes.

CLASSROOM MANAGEMENT IN THE 1980S

In this section, we focus on guidance practices observed during the 1980s at Kita Middle School, an institution located in central Tokyo. The first reason we chose to highlight this particular case study was that *seikatsu shidô* practices at Kita most closely approximated the ideal of "intimacy coupled with severity." Members of the Kita faculty actively sought to involve students in daily activities and special events so as to reinforce their ties to the institution. These included activities designed to strengthen group cohesion and the extensive use of *han* (small groups of students) in classroom management. At the same time, disciplinary approaches at Kita were often severe: Physical punishment was common (until 1986), the number of school rules increased each year, and teachers enforced them vigorously.

The second reason we chose Kita was that the school's aggressive implementation of student guidance created a sense of unity and order in the school. Kita teachers remarked that the school could easily slide into chaos without their constant vigilance and efforts; in fact, Kita had experienced discipline problems in previous years. Instructors described the neighborhood surrounding the school as lower-middle-class, with a large number of "problem" residents. In other words, teachers did not feel that they could depend on all parents to support school policies. In this way, the Kita district in Tokyo resembled the community of our rural middle school in northern Japan, where a significant portion of students also held low educational expectations for their future.

In the 1980s, teachers at Kita thoroughly monitored student behavior, both in class and outside of school. The faculty placed a high priority on developing strong emotional ties between teachers and students. According to one young teacher interviewed during that period, "The starting point of all education is the love of teachers for students. Out of love and consideration, a heart-to-heart or close relationship of mutual trust can grow. Mutual trust means a relationship in which two individuals become indivisible or inseparable." Such intimacy was regarded as the basis for the empathetic, implicit side of discipline; the strength of students' connections to teachers and their involvement in the school community would lead them to behavioral rules.

To monitor out-of-school behavior, Kita teachers used both standard "Daily Life Notebooks" (*seikatsuchô*) and unstructured group diaries. The notebooks served as a place for students to write down assignments and lists of things to bring for the next day's classes. More important, they provided teachers with information about students' lifestyles and thoughts that might not be apparent during regular classroom activities. In a section of their notebooks labeled "record of daily life," students described their feelings and daily activities. At a glance, instructors could gauge students' attitudes toward school and their peers. In addition, to monitor afterschool life and personal feelings in more detail, homeroom teachers used unstructured group diaries, which they periodically collected to comment on.

Not only did Kita teachers closely scrutinize student behavior, but they also spent much time engineering an environment that systematically increased student/teacher interactions. According to the head of guidance,

> The school must make places for each and every student to play an active part. Thus we have developed special events and encourage participation in extracurricular activities, have teachers' aides, and promote an active student council and committees. When I came here, Kita had problems. We began to increase the number of special events and make those that existed into occasions for all students to participate. . . . We are always looking for more and better ways to involve students in school.

Although they invested extensive time and energy strengthening the emotional bonds that connected them to their students, teachers also recognized the benefits of maintaining a sense of discipline on campus. "At school, rules are like the constitution. Every group has rules, and students must learn the importance of rules in human society," observed one middle-aged teacher.

The use of physical punishment, or *taibatsu,* often lent a Spartan air to disciplinary procedures. In actuality, "physical punishment" at Kita rarely involved teachers striking students. More frequently, punishment meant sitting *seiza* (a formal position with legs folded underneath the thighs), often on a hard linoleum or wood floor in an unheated hallway or gym. On any given day, several students could be observed sitting *seiza* in the halls outside classrooms or the teachers' room. Kita teachers meted out this punishment for a number of chronic, but minor offenses, including talking in class or assembly, forgetting to bring books to class, bringing unnecessary items to school, running in the halls, and tardiness.

Teachers also used a bamboo rod (*shinai*) to discipline students, though infrequently. Only after repeated verbal reprimands and/or *seiza* had been tried with no apparent effect did teachers resort to using the long bamboo rods. An incident in a music class observed by Fukuzawa illustrates this approach. During a music rehearsal, students were particularly talkative and unfocused as they learned a song for the upcoming cultural festival. After warning a rambunctious male student to be quiet three times, the music teacher called him out of the class and whacked him on his buttocks three times. The teacher later explained that when all else fails, only physical punishment can bring students into line.

At Kita, physical punishment was coupled with extensive monitoring of student behavior in and out of school. Teachers regularly scrutinized students' appearance and the items they brought to school. Regulations concerning appearance comprised a major category of rules; the types of extra shoes, bags, and accessories students were allowed as well as hair length and shape, pant cuff width, and skirt length were all specified in detail. No nonacademic reading material, mirrors, jewelry, toys, or grooming equipment were allowed in school. Kita teachers vigilantly searched for such items (collectively labeled *fuyôbutsu*, or unnecessary items) by looking into students' desks and bags. They usually found quite a bit of "contraband," which they confiscated then returned to students after school, with a warning not to bring it again. At one faculty meeting, the first-year teachers even discussed restricting the number of colored pens and pencils students could bring to school in order to discourage drawing during classes.

As the following incident captured in Fukuzawa's field notes illustrates, teachers viewed violations of rules related to appearance and unnecessary items as indicators of serious problems:

> The sounds of Mrs. Iwasa, a P.E. teacher, yelling at a student outside in the cold hall in front of the teachers' room, can easily be heard from inside the warm teachers' room.
>
> "Why don't you work hard, huh? It's your irresponsible attitude, that's the problem. You're the one who is at fault. You have a twisted mind and I'm going to straighten it out for you. Look at me. What's wrong with you?"
>
> (Inaudible response)
>
> "You know why I have to discipline you. This is a big problem, bringing other things to school. Are you working part-time?"
>
> (Inaudible response)
>
> "You lie so much, how do I know you're telling the truth now? Huh? If you think you can fool me, you're mistaken."
>
> Mrs. Iwasa strides into the room and takes some paper out of her desk, then returns to the hallway. She gives the student, who is sitting *seiza* on the hall floor, the paper to write a reflection essay (*hanseibun*) about her transgression. When she returns to the teachers' room, Mrs. Iwasa explains that another teacher thought he noticed that the girl had faintly colored lips. A tinted lip gloss was found in her bag and the girl admitted to using it. "All lip gloss nowadays contains color," Mrs. Iwasa explained. "It's like wearing lipstick."

Teachers at Kita usually dealt with dress code violations and other precocious behavior in a similar manner. They were particularly concerned about girls who wore lipstick and other kinds of makeup to school. Akin to dyed hair or permanents, makeup signaled to teachers a student's inappropriate concern with physical appearance and the opposite sex.

For teachers during the 1980s, it was the combination of strictly enforced rules within close relationships that was effective. A web of activities nurtured student attachment to school and commitment to following school rules. When that type of "positive reinforcement" proved ineffective, teachers employed more direct and forceful means of eliciting student compliance. Verbal harangues, assignments of reflection essays, and meetings with parents were all standard practices. Rohlen's phrase, "intimacy coupled with severity," truly captures the style of student guidance found at Kita as well as the basic patterns at other middle schools we observed in the 1980s.

SHIFTING STUDENTS, PRACTICE, AND BEHAVIORS

The rules and rituals that organize life in Japanese middle schools have proven remarkably stable: Teachers continue to rely on traditional greetings to mark the beginnings and endings of lessons; all members of the community are still expected to participate in daily school cleaning activities (sôji); the focus and structure of special assemblies held each year have been altered only slightly, if at all; and students are still expected to adjust their language to convey their respect for individuals older than themselves. Anyone who has been educated in or spent extensive time in Japanese schools is familiar with these activities. Their continued prevalence suggests a dependable regularity to the rhythm of school life.

The durability of such routines, however, conceals underlying shifts in the relationships between teachers and pupils, and in the dynamics of student guidance practices. The rituals that organize daily life in middle schools may not have changed significantly, but their implementation has. Adults continue to depend on tried-and-true strategies to manage the behavior of adolescents, but not all middle school students are choosing to follow the "scripts" (LeTendre, 2000, p. 95) that have been delivered to them. Many are engaging in revisions and improvisation rarely displayed by their predecessors. With increasing frequency, the carefully choreographed exchanges between school actors are culminating in unpredictable endings.

One factor that led to this shift was heightened concern about the methods used to control students. In the 1990s, responding to criticism that middle schools were excessively rigid and pressure-filled sites for learning, the MOE encouraged teachers to exhibit more empathy toward their students. In May 1994, the Ministry issued a directive that spelled out implications of the UN Convention on the Rights of the Child for schools (MEXT, 1994). Using the rhetoric of international human rights, the Ministry emphasized the need to ban the use of any form of physical punishment in schools.[2] The shift toward more compassionate approaches to student guidance was regarded as one way of reducing bullying and in-school violence.

This attention to the affective aspects of learning meshed with the curricular revisions that formed the core of the relaxed education reform movement. Regulations related to hair length were not eliminated, but responding to transgressions with harsh remedies was discouraged. As the incident from Bjork's field notes below illustrates, the revised student guidance practices often created spaces for students to assert their individuality and to challenge institutional norms.

During the first month of the 2005–2006 school year at Hama Middle School, an institution located in a small city in northern Japan, approximately 75 third-year students straggle in and spread across the gym.[3] All of the students are wearing warm-up suits, but most of the outfits have been altered. Several girls have cut lines in their pants, starting at the ankle and continuing up to the knee, creating flaps that hang like curtains in a window; others have removed the elastic cuffs from their sleeves. It is rare to spot a boy whose pants or shorts reach his hips. The current fad is for boys to pull their pants down to their thighs, just covering the bottom hem of their shirts. All of the young men don the requisite sweatpants, but several are not wearing the matching jacket.

Mr. Hori stands in front and informs the group that today they will practice bowing and saying *"onegai shimasu"* (a greeting, loosely translated as "Please teach us," that students typically recite in unison to begin all formal lessons). After demonstrating the proper bowing technique, he divides the class into groups of four and tells them to rehearse the action he just modeled. At this point Mrs. Sakamoto, another P.E. teacher who has been observing from the opposite side of the gym, joins Mr. Hori in inspecting students as they practice bowing. Mrs. Sakamoto tells one girl to hold her buttocks together more tightly as she bows. Both instructors pay close attention to the angle of students' backs as they bend forward. The adults are assisted by a student who moves through the gym and reads a set of directions printed on a piece of paper she carries in her right hand. At first glance, this person seems like an unusual choice to hold this position: Her lower lip is pierced by a large silver ball and a swath of pink hair punctuates her black bangs. But the girl carries out her role dutifully, displaying none of the rebelliousness hinted at by her appearance.

During these inspections, most of the participants listen carefully to the suggestions shared by their teachers, and modify their performances accordingly. But as soon as a teacher moves on to another group, students tend to lose interest in the bowing exercise. One group of boys moves to a basketball hoop and takes turns trying to jump up and touch the rim; the members of another *han* initiate a shadow boxing match; a combination of boys and girls run across the floor and slide on their knees, seeing who can propel themselves the farthest.

The teachers continue to conduct the inspections, but begin to look frustrated by the antics occurring around them. Thirty minutes into the period, Mr. Hori announces that the independent practice time has ended. He calls a group composed of two boys and two girls to the front of the gym and tells them to perform the ritual for the rest of the class. One of the boys yells out a command and the group forms a straight line, bows, and calls out *"onegai shimasu"* in unison. After a short pause, everyone turns to the right, creates a new line, and crisply repeats the set of steps. The audience applauds.

Mr. Hori calls a second group, all boys, to the front of the gym. This foursome is not nearly as impressive as the first. It follows the correct procedure, but with little enthusiasm. When the group finishes, Mr. Hori announces that their posture was poor, and makes them repeat the act. The second performance does not look noticeably better than the first, but Mr. Hori offers no additional criticism, and allows the students to return to their spots on the floor. The next group, all girls, is even sloppier. Two of the performers giggle throughout, and the other two make no attempt to bow. Mr. Hori, looking increasingly irritated, releases the four girls. The members of the audience who are chatting among themselves now outnumber those who are paying attention.

When only 5 minutes of the period remain, Mr. Hori returns to the front of the room and calls the class to attention. He instructs everyone to check if the person sitting next to them is sitting straight. Upon hearing this, most of the third-year students sit up; a few do not respond. Mrs. Sakamoto walks over to four girls who are lying on the floor and tells them to pull their legs up against their chests. Two of the girls follow this direction; the other two ignore it.

Mr. Hori informs the students that he thinks they did a really good job and thanks them for their effort. After pausing briefly, he adds, "But you can do better. I would give you a score of 20 out of 100." He then demonstrates improvements they could make, such as holding their hands straight at their sides when they bow. Mr. Hori informs the group that it will continue to practice bowing and stretching the next time they meet.

UNDERSTANDING GUIDANCE PRACTICES

This third-year P.E. lesson captures the tensions that middle school teachers are experiencing as they attempt to adapt to changes in both their students and the approaches to guidance employed in their schools. Following a secondary school model commonly used for decades, Mr. Hori and Mrs. Sakamoto sought to establish a dependable routine that would create order in their class and instill in students a sense of seriousness that they would display throughout the year. As LeTendre (2000) has observed, Japanese teachers tend to believe that, "given proper routines, young adolescents [can] control their behavior and organize themselves quite effectively in groups" (p. 119). Yet the power of such routines has always depended on a delicate balance of clearly communicated behavioral expectations, student obedience, an established system of peer monitoring, and the presence of teachers willing to assert their authority when necessary.

In the physical education class, however, students appeared to realize that misbehavior would not generate any serious consequences. The most obvious sign of nonconformity was communicated visually. In the past, students who did not conform to a school's dress code or rules on appearance could face serious disciplinary consequences, as the incident from Fukuzawa's field notes illustrates. In the contemporary setting, however, teachers are prohibited from applying the severe punishments commonly administered at Kita in the 1980s.

Commitment to controlling unnecessary items has also waned in the succeeding years. This was true at all of the middle schools we visited in the years since the introduction of *yutori kyôiku* policies. Although the rules governing student presentation and possessions remained in place, they were rarely enforced with vigor. Not only did Hama pupils come to class without some of the standard pieces of the physical education uniform, but many of them went to great lengths to alter the items that they did wear. Yet neither Mr. Hori nor Mrs. Sakamoto commented on such infractions. They did not reprimand students with long or dyed hair, makeup, or pierced body parts.

Also notable was the lackadaisical attitude displayed by many individuals. Several of the third-year students did take this activity seriously, and capitalized on the opportunity to hone their bowing skills. Pupils who invested minimal effort in the activity, however, outnumbered these more serious students. Some participants followed their teachers' directions at a surface level, but socialized with their friends when not being observed by a teacher. Others made no attempt to disguise their lack of interest in the proceedings. Even when asked to perform before their peers, several individuals continued to display an attitude of defiance. Through silence, refusal to follow directions, and verbal comments, they expressed a critique of the lesson.

The two teachers, both veteran educators who were well liked by students, appeared unsure about how to respond to the student resistance. It is quite possible that in a pre-*yutori* environment, the instructors would not have tolerated such displays of disrespect; students who refused to follow instructions would have been sternly reprimanded. But Mr. Hori and Mrs. Sakamoto avoided exercising their authority in a heavy-handed manner, a response that contrasted sharply with the actions taken at Kita a generation earlier. At Hama, the instructors did not raise their voices or punish individuals who did not take the activity seriously. Instead, they encouraged and cajoled misbehaving pupils, to little effect. The difficulties they experienced during this lesson are illustrative of the challenges faced by contemporary educators, regardless of their subject area specialty. The teachers we observed and interviewed understood the rationale driving the shift to more student-friendly approaches to mentoring adolescents, but very few at Hama Middle School had figured out how to follow such advice while maintaining order in their classrooms.

SOCIAL REINFORCEMENT OF EDUCATIONAL PRACTICE

The balance of nurturance and punishment traditionally found in Japanese schools appears to have been recalibrated. Rather than admonish or discipline pupils who cross the line of acceptable behavior, educators like Mr. Hori gently encourage students to follow school rules and procedures, presenting themselves as allies rather than authority figures. Of course, there is great variety in the personas displayed by educators. Many veteran teachers we observed created classroom environments that were highly ordered and formal. But even the most assertive instructors were careful not to use disciplinary tactics that could be construed as harsh or abusive.

A 2011 revisit to one of our 1980 research schools in Tokyo evidenced similar soft, counseling-based disciplinary approaches. When minor dress code violations occurred, homeroom teachers talked to the offender. If the problem persisted, the parents were called in for a meeting. If that failed, the principal himself talked to the student individually. According to the principal,

> The most important way to change students is to let them know how important they are, to cherish them. I try to get them to see how important they are as well as how important others are. The point of discipline is for them to live happily with others. Wearing clothes that offend other people (e.g., falling down pants, overly short skirts) shows lack of consideration for others. . . . Dressing neatly preserves social cohesion. If I can convey this and my sense of respect for them as individual human beings to them, they change.

Teachers at this school now deal with forgotten and forbidden items, tardiness, and other minor issues with individual checklists. For students who habitually forget to bring the things they need, teachers call the parents. If the problem continues, they refer the student to the school counselor, a position introduced in the early 1990s. The rationale for this approach is that "students who constantly forget things and whose families are unable to do anything about the problem usually have deeper psychological problems that we teachers cannot handle," explained the principal.

This trend toward more psychological and individualized approaches to student guidance meshes with the great value attached to maintaining harmony at the interpersonal level in Japanese society (Krauss, Rohlen, & Steinhoff, 1984). The teachers we observed went to great lengths to avoid conflict with students. On a daily basis, they attempted to diffuse potential clashes. Consistent with the framing of the middle school as a site of transition from childhood to adulthood, instructors emphasized to pupils that they ultimately needed to take responsibility for their own actions. This message does not represent a departure from the ideas that have traditionally anchored student guidance in Japanese middle schools, but in the contemporary setting students have greater freedom to apply that advice as they see fit. The balance of "intimacy" and "severity" has been disrupted.

Teachers continue to seek to strengthen their bonds with students through activities such as Daily Life Notebooks. As was true at Kita, members of the Hama faculty depended on small groups of students to support and monitor each other. For example, following a long-established tradition, daily homeroom meetings at Hama included *hanseikai* (meetings that focus on self-reflection). During these group discussions, which were led by students, members of the class were encouraged to reflect on positive accomplishments as well as things they could be doing better. In theory, such collective brainstorming would lessen the pressure placed on teachers to act as authority figures. The Hama faculty also organized a number of special activities designed to build class cohesion. The members of each grade level, for instance, participated in an annual overnight excursion. Students worked in groups to plan all aspects of the trips, including scheduling, budgets, and meals. Adults explained that these activities—daily rituals as well as the special events—were designed to make students feel more connected to their classmates and to the school. In practice, however, these strategies did not always produce their intended results. In most 2nd- and 3rd-grade classrooms, a handful of individuals chose not to participate in, or disrupted, the proceedings.

Relaxed enforcement of school rules has enhanced the autonomy experienced by students, who in the past were required to adhere to school rules, or face serious consequences. They realize that rules about acceptable behavior and dress are not consistently enforced. Capitalizing on the mismatch between official school policies and their implementation on campus, adolescents are questioning, criticizing, and resisting behavioral directives with increasing boldness. Many treat school rituals designed to serve an integrative function as "empty formalities"

(Geertz, 1960) that have little connection to their immediate needs. Teachers may feel compelled to avoid conflict whenever possible, but students do not necessarily place a high priority on preserving group harmony.

Middle school pupils have learned that ignoring school rules about dress is not likely to provoke the harsh reprisals that were common in the past. In the schools we visited in northern Japan, second- and third-year students unapologetically adjusted their body and possessions to assert their individuality. Boys as well as girls grew their hair longer than was officially permitted; they also dyed it a variety of shades. Boys' sideburns sometimes extended below their cheeks. Girls wore makeup and jewelry that often was quite flashy. Individuals of both genders pierced their ears, lips, and eyebrows. Students shortened the hems of their uniforms, removed the cuffs, added additional layers, and left pieces (such as neckties) at home. They also modified accessories and physical spaces to fit their personalities. Backpacks were frequently covered with stickers, ornaments, and decorative patches. Some students invested a great deal of energy in decorating their desks, placing objects (tape dispensers, stuffed animals, plastic and metal figurines) on top of their desks to create a sort of portable personal office space.

To someone educated in other school systems, these examples of resistance may not seem noteworthy. Teachers in other parts of the world face challenges to authority far more serious than dyed hair or graffiti-covered desks. In the Japanese context, however, acceptance of these acts represents a sharp detour from previous practice. The tendency to accommodate rather than reprimand individuals who do not follow school rules reduces the risks associated with misbehaving in class. This ambiguity creates opportunities for students to augment their autonomy and power.

Of course, not all adolescents take advantage of opportunities to challenge school authority. Factors such as an individual's socioeconomic status, ethnicity, linguistic abilities, and family background can shape his/her attitudes toward educational institutions and authority figures (Banks, 2007; Lee, Murphy-Shigematsu, & Befu, 2006; Ogbu, 2008). In a comparative study of children's performance in school, D'Amato (1993) observes that structural as well as situational rationales shape a child's orientation toward school. Students who find structural reasons for investing in their education, such as links between academic achievement and future educational and occupational opportunities, "tend to construct their peer cultures around the politics of school, organizing themselves in terms of teacher standards and teacher indications of relative peer standing" (D'Amato, 1993, p. 192). Pupils may also find intrinsic value in the schooling process. D'Amato (1993) concludes that youngsters who are not motivated by either of these forces often "appear free to confront the premises and politics of schools openly and directly" (p. 197). Children who face socioeconomic or academic challenges are especially likely to display such resistance.

Students as well as teachers come to school with distinct attitudes toward each other and the purpose of education, motivations for investing in their work, and opinions about what constitutes appropriate behavior at school. As one would expect, pupils with a record of academic success tended to accept the authority of the school and to comply with school rules—in the 1980s as well as today. Children who struggle academically, in contrast, have begun to rebel against structures that do not serve their own interests. School rules that previously deterred even adolescents who earn low marks in school do not exert the same power to shape behavior that they did 30 years ago. The paucity of meaningful short- as well as long-term penalties for insubordination has expanded the autonomy enjoyed by pupils. Instructors can no longer depend on their pupils to compliantly adhere to the expectations of adults.

Teachers are also modifying their actions to fit contemporary realities in schools. Many veteran educators are attempting to reconcile their experiences with student guidance prior to adoption of the relaxed education policies with current conditions in schools. Challenged to mentor children whose needs they often find have grown more extensive over time, and constrained by limits to the practices deemed acceptable by the MOE, they question their ability to instill in students the values and attitudes necessary to succeed in contemporary society.

We do not mean to suggest that middle school classrooms are the anarchic sites of youth rebellion that media reports on classroom collapse (*gakkyû hôkai*) sometimes suggest. Nor did we witness any secondary teachers who completely lost control of a group of pupils. In most classrooms we observed, the majority of students sat quietly at their desks and performed the assigned tasks. For a variety of reasons, the absence of negative consequences for misbehavior did not tempt such students to challenge teachers. Those with promising academic futures tended to focus on lessons regardless of the instructor's class management skills. With a track record of academic success, they appeared eager to protect their reputation as good students. Another carrot that good students chased was the possibility of receiving a recommendation (*suisen*) to a high school from the faculty based on grades. Third-year students who were awarded recommendations were not required to take written high school entrance examinations.

CONCLUSION

The changes between Tokyo in the 1980s and schools in northern Japan after 2000 are truly striking. Teachers currently feel challenged by a combination of more extensive pupil needs and inconsistent support for education in the home. Of course, Japanese classrooms have always included students who tested the authority of teachers and institutions. Instructors we studied in the 1980s also voiced their frustration with unruly members of their classes. However, the consensus among the educators we interviewed in the 2000s was that adolescents today lead more complicated lives than their predecessors, which has expanded the range and intensity of the demands placed on schools. Demographic data as well as qualitative research supports this view (Bjork, 2009; Gordon, 2005; Kariya, 2010). The following comment by a middle school teacher underscores the disequilibrium that perceived changes among adolescents have created for instructors:

> Every day at this school I ask myself, "Is there some common reason students should be like this?" There are established ideas about what students should be like and what they should do. Since I came here, many of those preconceptions have been broken. For example, my fixed ideas have become very unstable. In education, there should be some fixed things and some things we should try based on students' needs. That border is shifting.

Feelings of frustration, confusion, anger, self-doubt, and disappointment pervaded the comments of interviewees as they reflected on their work. For most, the classroom was a different place from what it had been when they began their careers, and responding to new conditions presented a seemingly unending set of trials for them.

Over a long period of time, teachers used a stable set of familiar yet flexible practices to mentor pupils that had roots in prewar traditions of juvenile protection and classroom management. The various threads of those traditions were woven together to form systematic classroom management practices that spread throughout schools nationwide, homogenizing approaches to *seikatsu shidô* by the mid-1980s. Observers often found fault with some of those practices, especially those that involved physical punishment, but they did enhance instructors' ability to maintain order in their classrooms.

Over the last 20 years, the programmatic guidance approaches of the 1980s have steadily eroded. The Ministry of Education has prohibited teachers from using the "strict" tactics common in the 1980s—without supplying them with a new set of practices. As Okano (2008) suggests, the Ministry seems unwilling to push one vision of school management on schools, but "leaves room for a wide range of interpretations and further negotiations among the different lower level parties, by for example, framing the policies in vague language open for diverse interpretation" (p. 252).

The teachers we interviewed in northern Japan had received a barrage of information about what not to do, but thirsted for more tangible advice about how to engage and mentor students who resisted their authority. Many found that broad proclamations about the need to adopt more "friendly" approaches to student guidance were difficult to translate into concrete action. The absence of a detailed set of procedures designed for use in a relaxed school environment left many instructors feeling unmoored; they approached student guidance with trepidation, often in isolation. Lacking specific policy guidelines or models introduced in conjunction with *yutori kyôiku*, teachers tended to use pieces of the student guidance system that were effective in previous decades, such as Daily Life Notebooks. However, in many cases, partial implementation of what had been considered an effective web of practices no longer produced the expected outcomes. In those situations, the options available to teachers who were no longer permitted to resort to actions that might be considered "physical punishment" were inadequate. Cognizant of the limits to adult authority, less constrained by pressure to accede to the power of the group, and not concerned about the consequences of resisting authority, disaffected adolescents "reengineered the environment" to fit their immediate personal needs. In this context, the comprehensive guidance approaches of the 1980s seem to have fallen apart.

NOTES

1. We also conducted follow-up visits to our research sites after the primary period of data collection had ended. Fukuzawa made multiple follow-up visits as an assistant language teacher from 1987 to 1989 and again in 2011 for follow-up interviews. Bjork returned to the schools in his sample in 2009 to conduct additional interviews with key informants.

2. We thank Mark Langager for pointing out the significance of this directive and sharing with us his experiences of its impact on middle school guidance while he was working in schools in the Tokyo area at this time.

3. At this school, two homeroom classes were usually combined for P.E. lessons. This is why the number of students participating in this activity is so large with two teachers present.

REFERENCES

Ambaras, D. R. (2006). *Bad youth: Juvenile delinquency and the politics of everyday life in modern Japan*. Berkeley: University of California Press.

Banks, J. A. (2007). *Diversity and citizenship education: Global perspectives*. San Francisco: Jossey-Bass.

Bjork, C. (2009). Local implementation of Japan's integrated studies reform: a preliminary analysis of efforts to decentralize the curriculum. *Comparative Education, 45*(1), 23–44.

Cummings, W. (1980). *Education and equality in Japan.* Princeton, NJ: Princeton University Press.

D'Amato, J. (1993). Resistance and compliance in minority classrooms. In E. Jacob & C. Jordan (Eds.), *Minority education: Anthropological perspectives* (pp. 181–207). Westport, CT: Ablex.

Fukuzawa, R. E. (1994). The path according to Japanese middle schools. *Journal of Japanese Studies, 20*(1), 61–86.

Fukuzawa, R. E., & LeTendre, G. (2001). *Intense years: How Japanese adolescents balance school, family and friends.* New York & London: RoutledgeFalmer.

Geertz, C. (1960). *The religion of Java.* London: The Free Press.

Gordon, J. (2005). The crumbling pedestal: Changing images of Japanese teachers. *Journal of Teacher Education, 56*(5), 459–470.

Kariya, T. (2010). *Education reform and social class in Japan.* New York & London: Routledge.

Krauss, E. S., Rohlen, T. P., & Steinhoff, P. G. (Eds.). (1984). *Conflict in Japan.* Honolulu: University of Hawaii Press.

Lee, S., Murphy-Shigematsu, S., & Befu, H. (2006). *Japan's diversity dilemmas: Ethnicity, citizenship, and education.* Lincoln, NE: iUniverse.

Lewis, C. (1995). *Educating hearts and minds: Reflections on Japanese pre-school and elementary education.* Cambridge, U.K.: Cambridge University Press.

LeTendre, G. K. (1994). Disruption and reconnection: Counseling young adolescents in Japanese schools. *Educational Policy, 9*(2), 169–184.

LeTendre, G. K. (1999). Community-building activities in Japanese schools: Alternative paradigms of the democratic school. *Comparative Education Review, 43*(3), 283–310.

LeTendre, G. K. (2000). *Learning to be adolescent: Growing up in U.S. and Japanese middle schools.* New Haven & London: Yale University Press.

Massey, A., & Walford, G. (1998). Children learning: Ethnographers learning. In G. Walford & A. Massey (Eds.), *Children learning in context: Studies in educational ethnography* (Vol. 1) (pp. 1–18). Stamford, CT: JAI Press.

MEXT, Ministry of Education, Culture, Sports Science and Technology. (1994). *Concerning the treaty on the rights of the child (Publication No. 149)* (in Japanese). Tokyo: Author. Retrieved from http://www.mext.go.jp/b_menu/hakusho/nc/t19940520001/t19940520001.html

Moore, F. (2010). Case study research in anthropology. In A. J. Mills, G. Durepos, & E. Wiebe (Eds.), *Encyclopedia of case study research* (pp. 86–92). Thousand Oaks, CA: Sage Publications, Inc.

Ogbu, J. (2008). *Minority status, oppositional culture, and schooling*. New York: Routledge.

Okano, K. (2008). Educational reforms in Japan: Neoliberal, neoconservative and "progressive education." In D. Hill (Ed.), *The rich world and the impoverishment of education* (pp. 238–258). London: Routledge.

Peak, L. (1991). *Learning to go to school in Japan*. Berkeley and Los Angeles: University of California Press.

Rohlen, T. P. (1983). *Japan's high schools*. Berkeley: University of California Press.

Sato, M. (1998). Classroom management in Japan: A social history of teaching and learning. In N. Shimahara (Ed.), *Politics of classroom life: Classroom management in international perspective*. New York: Garland.

Sato, N. E. (1991). *An ethnography of Japanese elementary schools: Quest for equality*. Unpublished doctoral dissertation, Stanford University, Palo Alto, CA.

Shimahara, N., & Sakai, A. (1995). *Learning to teach in two cultures: Japan and the United States*. New York & London: Garland.

Stevenson, H. W., Stigler, J. W., Lee, S., Lucker, G.W., Kitamura, S., & Hsu, C. (1985). Cognitive performance of Japanese, Chinese, and American children. *Child Development*, *56*, 718–734.

Tsuneyoshi, R. (2001). *The Japanese model of schooling*. New York & London: RoutledgeFalmer.

Walford, G. (2001). *Ethnography and educational policy*. Oxford, U.K.: Elsevier Science.

White, M. (1987). *The Japanese educational challenge: A commitment to children*. New York & London: The Free Press.

Yamamura, Y. (1986). The child in Japanese society. In H. S. Stevenson, H. Azuma, & K. Hakuta (Eds.), *Child development and education in Japan* (pp. 28–38). New York: Freeman.

CHAPTER 5

Student–Teacher Relationships and *Ijime* in Japanese Middle Schools

Motoko Akiba & Kazuhiko Shimizu

Ijime, school bullying, has been a major problem in Japan since the 1980s. Mass media attention to student suicides related to *ijime* and several subsequent lawsuits during the 1990s uncovered the seriousness of *ijime* and created a sense of urgency among educators and policymakers to take action. More recently, two student suicides in 2005 and 2006 led the Ministry of Education (MOE) to organize the Committee of Citizens for Protecting Children (CCPC) in 2007. The CCPC has produced several reports, emphasizing the need for greater collaboration between schools and community members to overcome the problem of *ijime* (MEXT, 2006, 2007a). In 2007, a 24-hour national *ijime* hotline for victims was established (MEXT, 2007b). In the same year, the suicide of a high school student due to cyber bullying led the committee to produce a report on the prevention of cyber bullying (MEXT, 2007c).

Although many studies have examined the characteristics of bullies and victims in Japan and discussed the possible causes of *ijime*, few empirical studies have examined the reality of *ijime* from the student perspective. Even less is known about the relationship between student–teacher interactions and student involvement in *ijime*. In Japanese schools, homeroom teachers provide guidance for student psychological and social development, in addition to academic development (Bjork & Fukuzawa, this volume; Fukuzawa & LeTendre, 2001; LeTendre, 1994, 1995, 2000). Homeroom teachers spend a significant amount of time counseling students, visiting their families, and developing a community where students come to a sense of belonging. When *ijime* occurs in a homeroom, the homeroom teacher is responsible for resolving the case by discussing the situation with students and seeking a group decision on how to solve the problem. This intervention is based on the widely held assumption that problem behaviors emerge as a result of detachment from the homeroom, and the belief among Japanese teachers that a homeroom as a group can most effectively deal with student problems (LeTendre, 2000; Lewis, 1995).

Teachers are generally perceived as playing a central role in identifying and intervening when *ijime* occurs. To fully understand their role, however, it is also important to examine how their relationships with students in daily educational activities and interactions may potentially influence student involvement in *ijime*. This chapter, based on two empirical studies conducted during the past decade (Akiba, 2004; Akiba, Shimizu, & Zhuang, 2010), examines the way student–teacher relationships influence the dynamics of *ijime*. Specifically, we explore the following questions:

1. How do Japanese students perceive and experience *ijime*?
2. How do student–teacher relationships influence student involvement in *ijime*?

To address the first research question, we compared student perspectives of *ijime* with information presented in official reports. Drawing from an extended case study of 30 students in one classroom (Akiba, 2004), we examined how *ijime* starts, escalates, and ends, along with the reasons students give for bullying others. For the second research question, we conducted a survey of 2,999 students in seven middle schools in one district to examine the association between student involvement in *ijime* and three types of student–teacher relationships: 1) teacher bonding, 2) student guidance, and 3) instructional support (Akiba, Shimizu, & Zhuang, 2010).

RESEARCHING *IJIME*

These two empirical studies (the case study and the student survey) were conducted in Ibaraki prefecture, which, among Japan's 47 prefectures, has an average student and teacher population size (Government Statistics, 2011a) and an average student achievement level (National Institute for Educational Policy Research, 2011). The case study was conducted in 2000, and the survey was administered in 2006. Haruno Middle School[1] was chosen for the case study site because of the first author's longstanding professional relationship with Mr. Suzuki, the homeroom teacher in charge of the 30 9th-grade students included in the case study. The study focused on one homeroom because *ijime* tends to occur among homeroom classmates (Morita & Kiyonaga, 1996; Takekawa, 1993). A 9th-grade class was selected for the study because these students can speak of their prior experience during their 3 years of middle school.

The following data collection methods revealed Japanese student perspectives on and experiences with *ijime*: 1) participant observations, 2) student diaries, and 3) in-depth individual interviews. The first author (Akiba) spent 1 month with the members of Mr. Suzuki's homeroom. She observed daily lessons and co-taught English for 45 minutes every day with the homeroom teacher. Students in the class were given a notebook and invited to share their experiences related to *ijime*, as well as any other concerns or problems. At the end of the fieldwork period, in-depth interviews with all the students were conducted. During those conversations, which lasted approximately 1 hour each, students were asked open-ended questions that followed up on comments made in their diaries. Approximately 200 pages of diaries and 30 hours of interviews from these 30 students were collected during the visit to Haruno Middle School. Additional data came from a series of phone interviews with the homeroom teacher and email communications with students over the course of 1 year.

The authors used a multistage sampling method to select students for the survey, randomly selecting seven middle schools from another district. They then invited all 3,161 students in these schools to participate and received a 95% return rate. Overall, the school district served 5,269 students in 14 middle schools (grades 7 through 9). Three of the schools that were selected are located in urban centers, two schools are in suburban areas, and two schools are in rural areas. Teachers administered the survey during the spring of 2006 with instructions to: 1) explain to the students that the survey participation was voluntary, 2) give students sufficient time to complete the questionnaires, and 3) collect the questionnaires immediately after completion. Teachers then returned the questionnaires to the school administrator, who sent them to the second author (Shimizu). The questionnaire included questions that investigated three dimensions of student–teacher relationships: teacher bonding, student guidance, and instructional support.

DEFINITION AND FREQUENCY OF *IJIME*: OFFICIAL REPORTS VERSUS STUDENT PERSPECTIVES

What is *ijime*? How frequently does it happen? These questions can be addressed using two types of data: official reports and student perspectives. An official definition of *ijime* brings together various perspectives into a consensus description that allows for systemic collection of *ijime* statistics. This approach, however, does not necessarily reflect variations in student perspectives or experiences. In addition, the official statistics come from reports of cases made by principals. Because students do not always report *ijime* to teachers or principals, these reports underestimate the total number of cases. Therefore, it is important to examine both the official definition and accompanying statistics along with student perspectives and experiences regarding *ijime* based on student interviews.

The Ministry of Education defines *ijime* as "continuous physical and psychological aggression inflicted upon someone weaker, which causes the victim serious pain. It includes aggression that occurs both inside and outside of school" (MEXT, 2006). This definition is similar to the definition used widely in Europe.[2]

Students who participated in the current study perceived any type of harassment, including physical as well as psychological actions, as *ijime*. The four most common types of *ijime* among the surveyed students were: 1) ostracism; 2) verbal abuse; 3) stealing, hiding, and damaging personal belongings; and 4) physical violence. Such behaviors were always conducted by a group of perpetrators targeting one student. *Ijime* perpetrated by one student toward another does exist, but such cases are considered minor, given the social support that the victim can receive from other students. All of the cases that the first author observed and received information about were collective *ijime*—one student experiencing *ijime* from a group of students. Most cases occurred within a single gender group: girls bullying girls or boys bullying boys. The only exception is when the entire homeroom student population joins in ostracizing one student.

In addition, the authors observed some gender differences in behavior. Minor *ijime* by girls may involve ostracism and verbal abuse by a few students, but serious cases involve multiple harassments, including both verbal and physical threats as well as ostracism by all of a victim's classmates. The latter case is illustrated by the experience of a student named Miho, a thin 14-year-old girl who wrote in her diary that all her classmates had ostracized her since elementary school and frequently stole her possessions. They took her notebook and returned it severely damaged and filled with scribbling such as "Die!," "Ugly!," and "Feel sick to be with you!" These acts of *ijime* led her to miss school for 1 year.

Ijime among boys involves physical violence in addition to verbal abuse, ostracism, and theft. Hiroki, a 15-year-old boy, often experienced physical violence during recess time in his homeroom. A group of students dragged him by his hair, kicked, and punched him. He reported that his possessions, such as bags or bikes, were often stolen or damaged and that he found his shoes frequently missing or with pushpins inside them. He also became a victim of aggravated assaults. For example, a small group of students took him to a storage room adjacent to an art classroom, where they kicked and punched him. This happened because of a false rumor generated by students that Hiroki was saying, "I will kill the bullies."

Most boys believed that physical violence and ostracism by all classmates each qualified as *ijime*, but verbal abuse or ostracism by only a few people did not. Such perceptions about whether a certain behavior constituted *ijime*, however, varied based on the personalities and attitudes of victims. Although Hiroki was ostracized by all his classmates during the 7th and 8th grades, some boys thought that it was not *ijime*. They viewed it as Hiroki being punished for his negative attitude. The actions taken against him were perceived to be something he deserved. Such situation-specific definitions were less common among girls. This finding is supported by Hara's (2002) survey of 100 students in two middle schools that indicated boys were more likely than girls to blame *ijime* victims.

HOW FREQUENTLY DOES *IJIME* HAPPEN?

The Ministry of Education collects annual data on the number of *ijime* cases reported by school principals. According to these national statistics for 2010, the number of cases reported was 34,766 in elementary schools, 32,111 in middle schools, and 5,642 in high schools (Government Statistics, 2011a). The number of cases per school is 1.6 for elementary schools, 2.9 for middle schools, and 1.0 for high schools. Official reports, however, do not accurately capture the number or rate of *ijime* because many cases are not reported to school administrators. Therefore, it is important to look at student reports to accurately understand the frequency of *ijime* in schools.

All the 30 students interviewed by Akiba shared firsthand experiences with *ijime*, either as a bully, a victim, or an observer. They stated that it happens on a daily basis and is so widespread that it has become a regular part of classroom life. To understand more accurate rates of *ijime*, Akiba conducted a secondary analysis of the 2007 Trends in International Mathematics and Science Study (TIMSS), in which a nationally representative sample of 4,263 Japanese 8th-graders reported being victims of school bullying.

Based on the question, "In school, did any of these things happen during the last month?," 24.9% responded that they were "made fun of or called names," 18.8% were "hit or hurt by other student(s) (e.g., shoving, hitting, kicking)," 6.2% were "left out of activities by other students," and 8.6% were "made to do things they didn't want to do by other students." These percentages, based on a secondary analysis of the TIMSS data, show that approximately one in four 8th-grade students (seven to eight in a classroom of 30 students) is a victim of *ijime* at least once a month and that government statistics may severely underreport cases of bullying. According to the students in our research, *ijime* sometimes occurs on the way to and from school, but less frequently than during school hours, which confirms prior research that *ijime* occurs predominantly on school grounds (Morita, Taki, Hata, Hoshino, & Wakai, 1999). None of the students in Mr. Suzuki's homeroom described observing instances of *ijime* outside of school. Most bullying occurred among classmates or club mates during recess time, lunch break, and club activities, i.e., times when teachers were not supervising the students.

GROUP DYNAMICS: HOW *IJIME* STARTS AND ESCALATES

A typical response to the question of how *ijime* starts is that, at first, a group of two or three students in the same homeroom starts to pick on one classmate. The situation then starts to involve other students, and finally all the classmates get involved. Yoshiko, a cheerful 14-year-old girl, explained how she started bullying one girl with her friends.

> I was in the same club (with her). She wasn't serious about the club activity when everyone was practicing hard. I really hated it. So I asked others around, saying, "Isn't she annoying?" and "Do you want to do it (*ijime*)?" Then, we decided to ostracize her. We also harassed her and she stopped coming to school.

A case of *ijime* perpetrated by a group of bullies can last from 1 month to 1 year. One case involving ostracism and verbal abuse of a girl ended after 1 month, when another girl became the new victim. However, most cases lasted longer; for example, the *ijime* of another girl continued for almost 1 year starting immediately at the beginning of the academic year and ending at homeroom reorganization in the next academic year, when she had less contact with the bullies.

Ijime usually begins when one student targets a member of his or her peer group, and then spreads to a larger group, or an entire homeroom or club. Always a collective behavior focused on a single student, it can last as long as the relationship between bullies and a victim continues. *Ijime* often ends when the group dynamic is changed—when the bullies in the same peer group are separated into different classrooms at the beginning of each academic year or when victims choose to avoid the bullies by staying away from school or quitting a club.

WHY DO STUDENTS BULLY THEIR PEERS?

Eight out of the 30 students in Mr. Suzuki's homeroom confessed that they had bullied someone. In his diary, Haruki, a high achiever, described his experience of bullying a classmate.

> I bullied someone before. At that time, I knew it was wrong but I just couldn't stop it. When I bullied him, he was a bit weird, and followed people around and everyone hated him. So I hated him and bullied him. I don't think *ijime* is necessarily the bullies' fault. Surely, *ijime* behavior is bad, but like in my case, when bullied students don't stop something everyone hates, I think they have the problems.

During a follow-up interview, Haruki explained how he and two of his classmates had kicked and punched one of their classmates. When asked why he did this, Haruki said that the victim "was too *shitsukoi* (obstinate or annoying)."

Students often considered these purportedly selfish, overtly persistent, and noisy students as incapable of understanding how to behave appropriately. They also saw them as different from others, which resulted in their standing out in the classroom or on club teams. Students who instigated *ijime* did so mainly because they believed that everyone hated the victims. Yoshiko bullied one girl because she thought "everyone hated her personality." This perception of "bullying on behalf of everyone else" was commonly shared among *ijime* perpetrators.

Another reason that students engaged in *ijime* was to protect their own reputations. When Akiba asked why they supported *ijime* perpetrators, many students answered, "I just didn't want them to think I am a friend of the victim." Most students did not feel that they were forced by bullies to join them, yet they agreed that if they tried to stop the bullies, they would likely have become the next victims. This concern, however, did not seem so important. Rather, they felt that it was just natural for most of them to follow the *ijime* perpetrators. They either thought it was fun to join or believed, as noted above, that the victims deserved to be bullied. Kouji, who is actively engaged in the soccer club and is popular among classmates because of his cheerful personality, described *ijime* as fun.

Q: Why did you join in the *ijime*?
Kouji: If I didn't, I would be bullied.
Q: Were you scared of the bullies?
Kouji: No, I was not.
Q: Then why did you get involved? Can't you just not
    get involved at all?
Kouji: Well, it's fun to bully someone.

Sachiko, an athletic and high-achieving student, explained how one of her friends became a victim.

Sachiko: We were a group of six students. When I arrived at school one
    morning, I found that one of the group members was totally isolated
    from the others. Then my friends told me that they had decided to
    ostracize her, so I joined too.
Q: Why did she get ostracized?
Sachiko: Well, I am not sure, but they said a lot of bad things about her like
    she was "selfish" and never listened to people, or talked bad about us
    behind our backs. So I thought she should be bullied.

All the students we interviewed appeared quite sensitive to what others thought and how they acted. They used this dominant group dynamic to rationalize acts of *ijime*, regardless of individual feelings of morality or justice. Following others was the main reason—sometimes the only reason—why students became involved in bullying. Resisting such pressure was extremely difficult. Students who attempted to stop the *ijime* were considered "strange," "stupid enough to risk their own victimization," or "trying to get credit from teachers."

Some students were victimized because they had personality traits that were considered different from "normal" students, such as being "selfish" or "noisy." Other pupils were bullied because of physical characteristics, such as being short, fat, or having some amount of gray hair. As a result of the broad range of characteristics that could provoke bullying, almost all students faced the possibility of becoming victims. In fact, more than one-third of the students who participated in the study reported that they had been victims of *ijime* at least once during their middle school years.

STUDENT–TEACHER RELATIONSHIPS AND *IJIME*

To examine the question, "How do student–teacher relationships influence student involvement in *ijime*?," we analyzed survey data collected from 2,999 students in seven middle schools. The survey included a series of questions related to three dimensions of student–teacher relationships: 1) teacher bonding, 2) student guidance, and 3) instructional support. Students were asked to respond to 30 statements about their relationships with their homeroom teachers based on three aspects of teacher bonding: trust, respect, and fairness. The items on trust included "I feel that my teacher sees me as important" and "I think my teacher always cares about me." The items on respect included "My teacher is knowledgeable" and "My teacher is well respected." The items on fairness included "My teacher clearly communicates what is right and wrong" and "My teacher favors some group of students over others." The responses were coded from 1 = strongly disagree to 4 = strongly agree. Due to the high correlations of above .70 among three subscales,[3] the mean of the three subscales was computed as a composite measure of teacher bonding (Cronbach's alpha = .95).

Figure 5.1 shows the level of teacher bonding reported by victims and bullies compared with other students. We can see that victims felt stronger bonds toward their teachers than other students did. The difference was statistically significant for victims of verbal abuse and physical violence. In contrast, bullies felt weaker bonds with their teachers than the other students did, and the differences were all statistically significant.

Figure 5.1. Level of Teacher Bonding Reported by Victims and Bullies

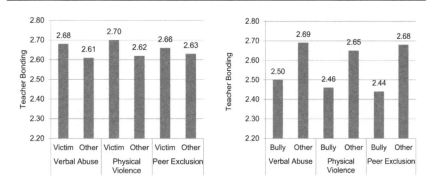

Student guidance is an important responsibility of homeroom teachers in Japanese middle schools. To measure student perceptions of student guidance, another question on the survey asked respondents, "How much do you agree or disagree with each of the following statements about your homeroom teacher?" The question was followed by statements such as "I feel that I can talk to my teacher if I have a problem," "My teacher can protect me if I become a victim of bullying or violence at school," and "My teacher works hard to keep a safe environment." The responses were coded from 1 = strongly disagree to 5 = strongly agree, and the mean was computed as a composite of student guidance (Cronbach's alpha = .72).

Figure 5.2 shows the level of student guidance reported by victims and bullies compared with other students. The differences in ratings from victims and other students were not statistically significant. However, bullies rated student guidance provided by their homeroom teachers more negatively than other students. Those differences were all statistically significant.

Students were also asked how much they agreed with the following statements about their teachers: 1) My teachers give extra help when students need it; 2) Most teachers continue teaching until the students understand; and 3) When I work hard on schoolwork, most of my teachers praise my efforts. The responses were coded from 1 = strongly disagree to 5 = strongly agree, and the mean was computed as a composite of instructional support (Cronbach's alpha = .77).

Figure 5.3 indicates that the level of instructional support reported by victims and bullies was similar to those of other students across the three types of *ijime*. Bullies' ratings of instructional support, however, were generally lower than that of other students. For bullies who engage in verbal abuse and peer exclusion, the difference was statistically significant.

Figure 5.2. Student Guidance Reported by Victims and Bullies

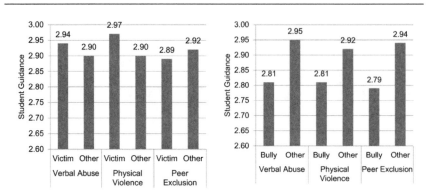

Figure 5.3. Instructional Support Reported by Victims and Bullies

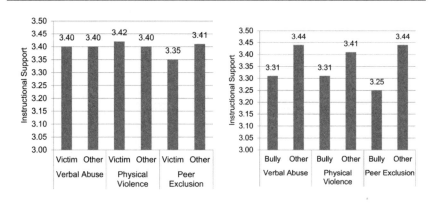

These figures show that whereas victims have stronger teacher bonding than other students, bullies tend to have weaker bonds with their teachers than other students do. Bullies also rated the guidance and instructional support provided by teachers less positively than other students did. They were less likely to indicate that they trusted and respected teachers, or thought their teachers were fair. They did not believe that their homeroom teachers could create a safe classroom environment or protect them from bullying or violence. Furthermore, they were less likely to indicate that teachers provided them extra instructional support, ensured that students understood subject matter, or praised students who worked hard. In contrast, victims were more likely to rate their teachers positively in these areas. They appeared to have stronger bonds with their teachers, trust and respect instructors, and believe that instructors treated pupils fairly.

UNDERSTANDING *IJIME*

What happened to the cultural ideal of homeroom communities in Japanese schools where students develop a sense of belonging as explained in the previous studies (LeTendre, 2000; Lewis, 1995)? The current study suggests that homeroom is no longer a place where students feel safe. Mr. Suzuki observed that homeroom teachers rarely bring their students together to seek collective solutions to *ijime* cases anymore because of negative attitudes among students toward those who display behaviors considered desirable by teachers.[4] Changes in homeroom group dynamics reflect the families and neighborhoods where the students come from. Urbanization and a flow of people from various regions into cities have weakened the social ties that anchored many communities. When parents become strangers and do not trust one another, it becomes difficult for their children to develop trusting relationships with their peers. The same applies to the relationship between parents and teachers. Gordon (2005) reported, based on interviews of teachers and parents, that Japanese teachers no longer enjoy the high social status and respect they had in the past, mainly due to increased parental education levels and shifting perspectives toward teachers and schools. The media have also reported on "monster parents" who openly accuse teachers of any problem such as their child's minor injury during a physical education class. When parents do not respect teachers, it is not surprising that students do not respect them either.

The survey data presented in this chapter indicate that bullies have weaker bonds with teachers, and negative views about the quality of guidance and instructional support provided by teachers. The absence of trusting relationships between many students and their teachers is a reflection of the lack of trust among parents and community members, which further exacerbates the situation. In schools where such distrust is commonplace, it follows that students will succumb to peer pressure and take part in *ijime*. The goal of emulating model students no longer motivates many middle school students, which makes it difficult for homeroom teachers to resolve *ijime* cases through collective problem-solving activities. In contrast, victims tend not to have negative views about their teachers. They often develop strong bonds with their homeroom teachers, respecting and trusting them. Yet displaying such positive attitudes toward their instructors may actually make students targets of *ijime* by peers who have negative attitudes toward teachers.

Analysis of interview and survey data sheds light on the factors that influence student involvement in *ijime*. In the past, when students were bullied, homeroom communities could usually solve the problems with the guidance of teachers, who were trusted and respected by their pupils. Morality and justice could be reinstalled in the homeroom without punishing or removing bullies from the classroom. Over the past 25 years, the homeroom as a community has lost its capacity to solve problems. One reason for this is the gradual breakdown of parental (or external) communities. Another is the strong criticism of teachers by parents and the media.

In addition to these relational factors, structural realities also make it possible for *ijime* to proliferate. Japanese schools are organized so that students remain unsupervised during recess, lunchtime, breaks between classes, and cleaning times, based on the belief that students can and should supervise one another. When the homeroom can no longer solve problems, these unsupervised periods provide bullies with frequent opportunities to openly engage in *ijime* without fear of being caught.

Japanese approaches to discipline also make it difficult to solve *ijime* cases. Bullies are rarely punished in Japanese schools, due to the cultural belief that punishment and exclusion will exacerbate behavior problems. Traditionally, teachers dealt with behavior issues through intensive consultation and remediation. Identification of bullies can also be difficult because multiple students often become involved. Homeroom teachers usually talk with victims first and ask them what can be done to help them. Afraid of possible retaliation, victims usually do not want teachers to speak with the bullies. This can result in long-term isolation inside the classroom or long-term absenteeism from school.

When homeroom communities lose the capacity to control and resolve behavior issues internally, bullies take advantage of these conditions. They become aware that they are unlikely to be punished for their behavior, that students have plenty of unsupervised time, and that victims are stuck in their homeroom classes the entire school year.

POLICY AND PRACTICE IMPLICATIONS FOR *IJIME* PREVENTION AND INTERVENTION

How can Japanese schools reduce *ijime*? There are three possible approaches: 1) reinstate the capacity of homeroom communities to control and resolve student problem behaviors, 2) restructure school organizations by increasing supervised time and introducing a flexible homeroom configuration, and 3) implement school-wide *ijime* prevention and intervention programs, sending a clear message that *ijime* is not tolerated.

Reinstating the capacity of homeroom communities is the most effective yet most difficult to accomplish. If homeroom capacity can be enhanced, there is no need to change the school structure or the inclusionary disciplinary approaches currently used by Japanese teachers. Yet accomplishing this goal is quite difficult, considering recent deterioration of parent–teacher and student–teacher relationships. Even if the homeroom environment can be improved, such a change will require significant time and resources.

Restructuring school organizations by reducing unsupervised time and introducing a flexible homeroom configuration is more feasible, and more likely to quickly reduce the prevalence of *ijime*. Because Japanese teachers are already overworked,[5] it is important to involve volunteers (college students, community members) to monitor students during recess time and report to homeroom teachers. School districts can hire and supervise these volunteers with minimal costs. In addition, the yearlong configuration of homerooms can be made more flexible. Most *ijime* cases stop when new homeroom classes are formed. If this could occur every semester, bullies will be separated from victims more frequently and fewer students will suffer from long-term isolation or verbal and physical abuse. To reduce the additional work associated with frequent homeroom reconfiguration, schools could assign two homeroom teachers to work as a team, supervising two groups of students together.

The last approach to school-wide *ijime* prevention and intervention is important. The data collected for this project suggest that students consider *ijime* the norm in many homerooms, and that bullies openly engage in bullying because they know there are no consequences for their behavior. Schools need to send a clear message to all students that *ijime* is not allowed, perhaps through a school-wide prevention program. Teachers could work with students to develop a system of confidential reporting, and identify ways of developing a safe school environment. When *ijime* does occur, teachers and counselors need to work with bullies while protecting victims. Survey data show that bullies have negative perceptions of teachers. Therefore, school districts could employ counselors to talk with bullies about the sources of negative perceptions, as well as to identify possible strategies for improving student-teacher relationships.

Japanese teachers are known for their professionalism and collaboration. Instructors regularly work together to improve their practice through activities such as lesson study (Lewis, 2002; Lewis, Perry, & Hurd, 2009). In the past, cases of *ijime* were viewed as a sign of failed homeroom management. As a result, many homeroom teachers are reluctant to ask for help from other teachers, administrators, or counseling professionals. It is important for schools to realize that bullying occurs in every classroom. When teachers and school administrators begin to take collective responsibility for resolving *ijime* cases, and start to share their prevention and intervention practices, they will be able to develop a better knowledge base for creating safe homeroom and school environments for students.

NOTES

1. Pseudonyms are used throughout the text when referring to schools and individuals.

2. Olweus (1999) defined bullying as "1) aggressive behavior or intentional harm doing 2) which is carried out repeatedly and over time 3) in an interpersonal relationship characterized by an imbalance of power" (p. 11).

3. Pearson r correlation coefficients were .74 between trust and respect, .71 between respect and fairness, and .84 between respect and fairness.

4. The number of *futôkô* students—defined as students who are absent for more than 30 days—increased from 54,172 (1.0%) in 1991 to 100,105 (2.8%) in 2009 (Government Statistics, 2011b).

5. National statistics indicate that Japanese middle school teachers are spending an average of 11 hours each day at school (MEXT, 2007d).

REFERENCES

Akiba, M. (2004). Nature and correlates of *ijime*—Bullying in Japanese middle school. *International Journal of Educational Research 41*, 216–236.

Akiba, M., Shimizu, K., & Zhuang, Y. (2010). Bullies, victims, and teachers in Japanese middle schools. *Comparative Education Review, 54*(3), 369–392.

Fukuzawa, R. E., & LeTendre, G. K. (2001). *Intense years: How Japanese adolescents balance school, family, and friends*. New York: RoutledgeFalmer.

Hara, H. (2002). Justifications for bullying among Japanese schoolchildren. *Asian Journal of Social Psychology*, 5, 197–204.

Government Statistics. (2011a). *Number of schools with* ijime *and number of* ijime *cases* (in Japanese). Retrieved from http://www.e-stat.go.jp/SG1/estat/eStatTopPortal.do

Government Statistics. (2011b). *Statistics on long-term absenteeism in elementary and middle schools* (in Japanese). Retrieved from http://www.e-stat.go.jp/SG1/estat/eStat-TopPortal.do

Gordon, J. A. (2005). The crumbling pedestal: Changing images of Japanese teachers. *Journal of Teacher Education, 56*, 459–470.

LeTendre, G. K. (1994). Guiding them on: Teaching, hierarchy, and social organization in Japanese middle schools. *Journal of Japanese Studies, 20*(1), 37–59.

LeTendre, G. K. (1995). Disruption and reconnection: Counseling young adolescents in Japanese schools. *Educational Policy, 9*(2), 169–184.

LeTendre, G. K. (2000). *Learning to be adolescent: Growing up in U.S. and Japanese middle schools*. New Haven, CT: Yale University Press.

Lewis, C. C. (1995). *Educating hearts and minds: Reflections on Japanese preschool and elementary education*. Cambridge, U.K.: Cambridge University Press.

Lewis, C. C. (2002). *Lesson study: A handbook for teacher-led instructional change.* Philadelphia: Research for Better Schools, Inc.

Lewis, C. C., Perry, R., & Hurd, J. (2009). Improving mathematics instruction through lesson study: A theoretical model and North American case. *Journal of Mathematics Teacher Education, 12*(4), 285–304.

MEXT, Ministry of Education, Culture, Sports, Science, and Technology. (2006). Urgent recommendations on *ijime* prevention (in Japanese). Tokyo: Author. Retrieved from http://www.mext.go.jp/b_menu/shingi/chousa/shotou/040/toushin/06120713.htm

MEXT, Ministry of Education, Culture, Sports, Science, and Technology. (2007a). Development of a system for early detection and effective intervention of *ijime* (in Japanese). Tokyo: Author. Retrieved from http://www.mext.go.jp/b_menu/shingi/chousa/shotou/040/toushin/07030123.htm

MEXT, Ministry of Education, Culture, Sports, Science, and Technology. (2007b). 24-hour *ijime* hotline (in Japanese). Tokyo: Author. Retrieved from http://www.mext.go.jp/a_menu/shotou/seitoshidou/130698 8.htm

MEXT, Ministry of Education, Culture, Sports, Science, and Technology. (2007c). Urgent recommendations on cyber bullying preventions (in Japanese). Tokyo: Author. Retrieved from http://www.mext.go.jp/b_menu/shingi/chousa/shotou/040-2/toushin/071227.pdf

MEXT, Ministry of Education, Culture, Sports, Science, and Technology. (2007d). *Teacher working condition survey* (in Japanese). Tokyo: Author.

Morita, Y., & Kiyonaga, K. (1996). *Bullying-pathology in classroom* (in Japanese). Tokyo: Kaneko Shobo.

Morita, Y., Taki, M., Hata, M., Hoshino, K., & Wakai, S. (1999). *Bullying in Japan* (in Japanese). Tokyo: Kaneko Shobo.

National Institute for Educational Policy Research. (2011). 2010 national student achievement and learning assessment report: Results (in Japanese). Tokyo: Author. Retrieved from http:/www.nier.go.jp/10chouskekkahoukoku/index.htm

Olweus, D. (1999). Sweden. In P. K. Smith, Y. Morita, J. Junger-Tas, D. Olweus, R. Catalano, & P. Slee (Eds.), *The nature of school bullying: A cross-national perspective* (pp. 7–27). New York and London: Routledge.

Takekawa, I. (1993). *Sociology of bullying and absenteeism* (in Japanese). Kyoto: Hôritsu Bunkasha.

PART III

Minority Groups and Educational Reform

The Intersection of Domestic Reform, Policy, and Global Forces

CHAPTER 6

Ethnic Schools and Multiculturalism in Japan

Kaori H. Okano

This chapter examines the roles that ethnic schools[1] play in educating immigrant children in contemporary Japan. Drawing on fieldwork conducted in the Kansai and Nagoya regions from 2006 to 2010, I examine how ethnic schools operate in the context of national and local government policies and mainstream school practices. I argue that ethnic schools currently take on significant roles, offering what mainstream schools have not been able to, but that there have been some negative consequences for individual students and society as a whole. Finally, I identify specific factors that should be considered in assessing the current roles and future operations of ethnic schools.

The chapter starts with four premises. First, Japan has become more ethnically diverse in the last 2 decades, with the addition of newcomer immigrants to the old-timer ethnic minorities of former colonial subjects. Subsequent interactions among individuals have redrawn the boundaries of ethnic groups and old-timer and newcomer categories, with increasing hybridity (Graburn, Ertl, & Tierney, 2008). Second, mainstream schools have become more inclusive and tolerant of diversity, partly in response to both old-timer minority movements since the 1970s and to the immediate needs of newcomer ethnic groups. Schools now provide Japanese as a Second Language (JSL) programs and assistance with the "cultural adaptation" of immigrant children. Third, while some new immigrant students succeed in moving up the school ladder, a substantial number of them have found the acquisition of academic language a demanding process, and schooling beyond compulsory education via competitive entrance examination difficult, if not impossible. For immigrant children who lack a high school diploma (which 98% of Japanese students obtain), prospects in the mainstream employment market are bleak, given that high school completion is considered a prerequisite for full participation in adult Japanese society (Miyajima & Oota, 2005; Sakuma, 2006). Fourth, several ethnic communities, concerned about the behavior of their children who were not attending school, established full-time ethnic schools (Gekkan Io, 2006; Haino, 2010; Sekiguchi, 2003). While these schools do not grant school qualifications, they do keep children under supervision.

The chapter directs attention beyond studies of mainstream schooling (e.g., Shimizu, 2008; Shimizu & Kojima, 2006; Shimizu & Shimizu, 2001; Tsuneyoshi, Okano, & Boocock, 2011; Watado & Kawamura, 2002), and redresses a critical lack of literature on ethnic schools. Approximately 300 ethnic schools in Japan, each offering full-time schooling in a particular ethnic language, operate outside of the mainstream system of schooling. These schools, labeled "miscellaneous schools" (*kakushu gakkô*) or small private tutoring schools, are granted relative autonomy in terms of curriculum design and language of instruction, but they do not grant qualifications recognized in mainstream Japanese society. They are an essential component in understanding immigrant communities, especially their perceptions of Japan's education system and employment market and their desires for their children's futures.

MULTICULTURALISMS AND MAINSTREAM SCHOOLING

Multiculturalism is an overused term. Diverse interpretations by various players compete with each other in the public discourse, resulting in some confusion in public debates. It is often unclear just which definition of multiculturalism underpins the discussion at any particular time. Japan is no exception. I see multiculturalism both as a normative interpretation by governments and organizations and as a description of the actual conditions that people understand and experience.

There are many multiculturalisms in contemporary Japan that are variously understood, practiced, and experienced by different players in different parts of the country (e.g., Graburn, Ertl, & Tierney, 2008; Tsuneyoshi, Okano, & Boocock, 2011). In this chapter, I focus on the contexts and implications of this diverse range of views about, and experiences of, multiculturalism in education. Variations exist between and within ethnic groups, institutions, nonprofit organizations, local governments (regional variations), and the national government. The concept of "multicultural co-living" (*tabunka kyôsei*), a current buzzword, is similar to that of liberal multiculturalism pursued by Western liberal democracies, but is specific to Japan, reflecting its own history and immediate conditions. The term emerged through multiethnic interactions in the aftermath of post-earthquake Kobe in 1995, and has gradually gained popularity in grassroots activism, public debates, and local governments. Even the national government now uses the term.

The two official categories commonly used by the Japanese government in describing the increasing diversity of the student population are "foreign nationals" (non-Japanese citizens) and "students who require instruction in Japanese as a Second Language." The two categories do not necessarily match: Fifth-generation Korean nationals living in Japan typically have Japanese as their sole language, while many children of Japanese citizens (of mixed marriage or otherwise) require JSL support. Because the government does not collect the data, Japanese citizens of diverse ethnic heritage are invisible in the public discourse. In recognition of this, some local governments and professional bodies have adopted more nuanced categories, such as "students with foreign roots" and "students with special relationships with foreign countries." I refer to them simply as "migrants,"[2] regardless of citizenship.

Japan's central government has yet to articulate a comprehensive national policy to address the cultural and ethnic diversity of the student population, only issuing a range of ad hoc "notices" regarding the treatment of foreign nationals (Okano, 2011). Current law requires Japanese citizens to attend mainstream schools, and the expectation is that noncitizens will do the same. The postwar government's fundamental "principle of simple equality" (treating everyone in the same way) still remains, although it has recently been softened, as discussed below.

The recent national curriculum guidelines (MEXT, 1998a, 1998b, 1999, 2003a, 2003b, 2003c) show a clear departure from the simple equality principle. These documents advocate special treatment for immigrants, including more concerted efforts to build on their prior overseas experiences. The new national curriculum, scheduled for implementation in 2013, maintains this emphasis. In 2008, for the first time, the guidelines acknowledged that experiences shared by foreign students will benefit Japanese students, and that schools should consider providing foreign students opportunities to learn their own languages and cultures (MEXT, 2008a, 2008b). While these documents adopt the category of "foreigners," the category is arbitrarily interpreted at local and school levels.

The most significant change to immigrant education in mainstream schooling brought by the national government has been the structural reform to senior high schools in the late 1990s (Okano, 2012). Although the reform was not intended to address new immigrants in particular, there have been positive consequences for immigrant education, which are elaborated below.

Some local governments have taken more initiative in creating multicultural education policies (Okano, 2006). In 2007, approximately 80 local governments maintained "policies for the education of foreign nationals in Japan" (Zenkoku Zainichi Gaikokujin Kyôiku Kenkyû Kyôgikai, 2007, pp. 26–28). It is difficult to assess, however, how effective these policies are in affecting school-level practices. One tangible impact is the provision of local government funding for support of policy goals or projects that a school can justify as relevant for immigrant students. Teachers can now take leave to attend professional development workshops on immigrant education. To date, many of these local policies focus on mainstream schools without referring to ethnic schools.

School-level practices for immigrant education have been ad hoc, rather than guided by systematic multicultural education policies from national authorities. The most basic arrangements, JSL classes and "cultural adaptation classes" (often called "international classes"), were initially set up by individual schools in response to their immediate needs. Later, the Ministry of Education oversaw the JSL curriculum. More recently, primary schools began teaching immigrant languages, out of a concern that the loss of first languages would have negative consequences for learning Japanese. Given that no mention is made regarding immigrant first-language teaching in the national curriculum guidelines, individual primary schools often find strategic ways to make use of available institutional resources and programs not specifically designed for such language classes.

Absenteeism remains a major concern (Miyajima & Oota, 2005; Sakuma, 2006), and a significant number of new immigrant children do not make it to postcompulsory schooling. The percentage of immigrant children who enter senior high schools is estimated to be about half of the 98% of majority Japanese students who enter high school (Shimizu, 2008). It is difficult to estimate the national ratio, however, given that some immigrant students drop out before completing middle school, never attend a Japanese school, or enroll in a "school for foreigners." Local retention rates of immigrant children to senior high schools provide some understanding: 53% in Hyogo Prefecture (Hyôgo-ken Zainichi Gaikokujin Kyôiku Kenkyû Kyôgikai, 2007), 76.6% in Toyota (Gaikokujin Shûjûtoshi Kaigi Yokkaichi, 2005), and 84.5% in Osaka (Shimizu, 2008).

Local education boards have used a variety of strategies to address the low retention rate to post-compulsory schooling. One is special consideration (or concessions) for entrance examinations for new immigrants, such as extension of examination time, provision of phonetic readings of kanji characters, and permission to take language dictionaries into examination venues. The other is separate entrance procedures for immigrant children (Okano, 2012). Fourteen prefectures and five municipalities offered a separate entrance examination procedure for immigrant children (Chûgoku Kikokusha Teichaku Sokushin Sentâ, 2011).

In senior high school, immigrant students are assisted by a more flexible curricular structure, introduced in the late 1990s. In these credit-based senior high schools (*tan'isei gakkô*) and integrated studies courses, individual students can create their own curricula by selecting from a wide range of school-based subjects that reflect local needs and conditions. As of April 2010, 349 integrated courses and 928 credit-based high schools were operating (MEXT, 2010a). The number of such schools cannot accommodate all immigrant children aspiring to post-compulsory education (e.g., Zenkoku Zainichi Gaikokuin Kyôiku Kenkyû Kyôgikai, 2011), even considering similar practices in mainstream schools. As a result, some immigrant families choose full-time ethnic schools.

ETHNIC SCHOOLS IN JAPAN: "SCHOOLS FOR FOREIGNERS"

In the government and public discourse, full-time ethnic schools are collectively designated as "schools for foreigners" (*gaikokujin gakkô*), although their enrollments include a substantial number of Japanese nationals. Japanese researchers who study ethnic schools also use this term, typically in a descriptive rather than analytical manner (Gekkan Io, 2006; Pak, 2008). The officially used collective term *schools for foreigners* suggests both the categorization of "others" based on nationality and a reluctance to acknowledge the diverse ethnicities of Japanese nationals.

At least 24,000 students studied at over 200 ethnic schools in 2006 (Gekkan Io, 2006; see Table 6.1). Because small-scale schools for Brazilians often emerge in places of employment and then disappear when the community disperses, the exact number is difficult to estimate. In fact, the number of Brazilian schools has declined in the last 5 years as substantial numbers of Brazilians returned home, due to the recession in manufacturing. Schools for foreigners include: 1) schools for long-existing ethnic minorities, 2) schools for new immigrants (Brazilian and other South Americans), 3) Anglophone international schools, 4) European schools, and 5) the Amerasian School in Okinawa, which caters to children of American military men and local women.

Full-time ethnic schools in Japan are not approved by the national Ministry of Education as mainstream schools (*ichijôkô*) as defined by the School Education Act. While their ambiguous status allows individual schools greater autonomy in terms of language of instruction, curriculum, and school hours, it also limits employment options for graduates of these schools. The establishment of ethnic schools was initially driven by the ethnic community's belief that mainstream schools did not sufficiently meet the needs of its children. These specific needs vary by ethnic groups and change over time as the circumstances of the groups shift.

These schools are also diverse in terms of legal status, level of resources, and mission. Legal status determines eligibility for government subsidies and tax exemptions. The most privileged status (*ichijôkô*) is granted to only three South Korean schools, while "miscellaneous school" status (*kakushu gakkô*)

Table 6.1. Number of Schools for Foreigners

Types	Number	Legal Status
North Korean schools	73	All "miscellaneous schools"
South Korean schools	4	3 "mainstream schools" 1 "miscellaneous school"
Chinese schools	5	All "miscellaneous schools"
Schools for Brazilians	96	No school status
Schools for other South Americans	3	1 "miscellaneous school" 2 no school status
International schools (including one French and two German)	26	23 "miscellaneous schools" 3 no school status
Indonesian school	1	No school status
Indian international school	1	No school status
School for children of overstayers	1	No school status
Amerasian school Okinawa	1	No school status

Source: Gekkan Io, 2006, pp. 224–235

is granted to North Korean schools, Chinese schools, and some Anglophone international schools. Numerous small schools for Brazilians have not yet been granted even this status, and operate as private tutoring schools while they attempt to gain miscellaneous school status. Most ethnic schools receive no support from the central Ministry of Education, but they may obtain financial assistance from local governments.

Ethnic Chinese schools have the longest history, dating back to 1897. They are well resourced and perceived by the general public to offer trilingual schooling of a high academic standard, which allows many of their graduates to enter mainstream senior high schools (Qiu, 2004). North Korean schools, which initially sprang up in the late 1940s to prepare students for repatriation to the homeland, differ from other ethnic schools in that they are run by *Chôsôren* (Association of North Korean Residents in Japan), a national body that oversees the content of the curriculum for such schools across Japan. Brazilian schools were established by ethnic communities to support students who do not succeed in mainstream Japanese public schools or who intend to return to Brazil.

Schools for foreigners have historically had little contact with mainstream schools. For instance, their legal status did not initially allow them to participate in major interschool events and competitions. In response to petitions, North Korean schools were first included in the national high school baseball association in 1991 and the national high school sports association in 1994, enabling North Korean school students to compete against their peers from mainstream schools. Around this time, North Korean school students also became eligible for student discounts on public transport. In 2003, Brazilian schools formed the Association of Brazilian Schools in Japan in order to protect their interests in Japan and to lobby Brazilian government authorities (Taminzoku Kyôsei Kyôiku Forum, 2008 Osaka Jikkôiinkai, 2008).

Interactions among schools serving different ethnic groups, although somewhat limited, became more common after the Hanshin-Awaji earthquake in January 1995. Nineteen schools (including 14 North Korean schools, a Chinese school, three Anglophone international schools, and a German school) formed the Hyogo Prefecture Association of Schools for Foreigners in July 1995. The group lobbied local and central governments collectively for funding assistance. The first formal event to demonstrate nationwide interaction among schools for foreigners was the Multiethnic Education Forum, held in Kobe in 2005. Additional forums were organized in Nagoya (2006, 2010), Tokyo (2007), and Osaka (2008).

The Hyogo Prefecture Association has played an important role in mobilizing ethnic schools across the country. Encouraged by this success, similar associations were formed in Kanagawa, Saitama, and Shizuoka. The collective action of national organizations, such as the Australian Federation of Ethnic Schools, facilitates negotiation with national education authorities. One body that may develop into a national organization is a network focused on realizing an institutional guarantee for foreigners and ethnic schools. The group, which consists of academics, lawyers, activists, and practitioners, has been actively involved in organizing the annual Multiethnic Education Forum, and has a strong influence on many discussions about ethnic schools.

Another notable interaction took place in 2003 when the Ministry of Education granted students at most Anglophone international schools (but not other ethnic schools) eligibility to take entrance examinations for national universities. North and South Korean schools, Chinese schools, and South American schools all questioned the Eurocentric nature of this decision, forcing the Ministry to grant some non-Western ethnic schools the same eligibility.

A current debate involving ethnic schools is the central government's new policy of extending free schooling through the upper secondary level (grades 10 through 12). In 2010, the Ministry included 31 "schools for foreigners" under this policy, using eligibility criteria that included recognition from the government in their home country and recognition by one of the organizations of international schools in Japan. Because North Korean and many Brazilian schools did not qualify, they have appealed the decision.

CHOICES AND CONSEQUENCES FOR
STUDENTS, PARENTS, AND COMMUNITIES

Minority students and their parents face many considerations when they choose ethnic schools over mainstream schools. This section includes a list of benefits and disadvantages, both immediate and long-term, and the consequences of choices made by individual students, their ethnic communities, and Japanese society as a whole.

Securing an Alternative Place for Children at Risk

Ethnic schools offer alternative schooling for children who are at risk of leaving education altogether. They perform a welfare function by supervising children from 7:00 A.M. until 9:00 P.M., when their parents are away from home.

The number of "overseas" Brazilian schools operating in Japan increased from 14 in 2000 to 90 in 2007. A variety of reasons points to the need for the establishment of full-time Brazilian schools. First, mainstream schools do not usually accommodate newcomer minority students successfully. Children often have difficulty adjusting to and keeping up with their studies in mainstream Japanese schools, due to the character-based writing system, differences in school culture, and bullying. These difficulties manifest despite the availability of various support measures, such as JSL classes or counselors (Castro-Vazquez, 2009; Haino, 2010). In addition, many Brazilian parents have trouble supervising their children's homework, due to their lack of sufficient Japanese language proficiency or the necessary time, given their long work hours. When school-age children are idle and unoccupied, rather than enrolled in school, they are at greater risk of unemployment and delinquency in the future (Miyajima & Oota, 2005; Sakuma, 2006).

Seeking a "Comfort Zone"

Ethnic schools offer a "comfort zone" and social networks for new arrivals (both children and adults) by catering to the specific needs and desires of those with limited or no knowledge of the host society and its language. Japan's new immigrants, such as South Americans, often come to feel inadequate in mainstream schools. This situation may lead to low self-esteem and loss of confidence, which subsequently undermine academic achievement and hinder the development of healthy relationships with peers. Children often can regain confidence if they receive instruction in their native language.

Deliberate Transnational Strategy:
Expanding or Restricting Life Chances

Choosing an ethnic school can be a deliberate strategy used by immigrant families who are uncertain about how long they will remain in Japan. If they only plan to stay in the country for a few years, they may reason, it is more beneficial for their children to remain in a Portuguese-speaking environment and to study the Brazilian curriculum. In addition, parents worry that children who adjust to Japanese schools will lose their Portuguese language and ability to communicate within the family and community (Gordon, this volume).

The perceived attraction of these schools became more prominent in 1999, when the Brazilian government began to provide official approval for some schools and to administer an examination to Brazilian students who complete their compulsory education in Japan (Haino, 2010). Japan is the only country outside Brazil where such an examination is offered (Ishikawa, 2003). By attending these Brazilian schools, children can make a smooth return to local schools in Brazil and also gain Brazilian qualifications while living in Japan. Furthermore, when the Japanese government designated the mother country government's approval as a criterion for exemption from the high school completion qualification examination, these schools gained more respectability (Haino, 2010).

Although this option seems to provide flexibility, it does restrict employment prospects for graduating students to unskilled labor as long as they stay in Japan. Haino's study (2010) reveals that occupational choices contemplated by students attending Brazilian schools in Japan are to: 1) receive tertiary education and pursue a career if they are returning to Brazil; 2) choose the kind of jobs that do not require higher education, if they are staying in Japan; 3) work in factories in Japan for the time being; and 4) return to Japan to work in unskilled jobs, if their plans do not include living in Brazil.

Lifestyle Choices: Maintenance of Ethnic Language and Cultures

Concerns about the acquisition and maintenance of ethnic languages and cultures initially mobilized ethnic Korean schools and Chinese schools in Japan. Given that almost all mainstream schools choose to teach English for their foreign language option, there are very few opportunities at mainstream schools to learn ethnic languages.

A large pool of the existing research concludes that heritage language maintenance (in the form of "additive bilingualism") creates academic and personal benefits for minority students. In addition to providing the immediate benefit for facilitating child–parent communication, it also aids acquisition of the dominant language,
fosters cognitive development, and contributes to high self-esteem and a stronger
sense of identity (e.g., Cummins, 1986; Fishman, 2001; Lee & Oxelson, 2006).

Lifestyle Choices: Sharing and Identity

Parents send their children to ethnic schools so that they will share a similar
background and culture, which contributes to positive identity development. This
affective or emotional benefit for marginalized ethnic minority students comes
from their feeling comfortable with peers who relate to similar experiences and
from the value, respect, and encouragement to excel that they receive from ethnic
schools (e.g., Nelson-Brown, 2005). These benefits are especially important for
newly arrived immigrants who lack a social network (e.g., South Americans). It is
also important for established minorities, when members no longer reside in close
geographical locations, and the school is one of the few ethnic community institutions in which they participate.

The Ethnic Community's Sense of Empowerment
and Demonstration of Agency to Outsiders

Maintaining ethnic schools for the direct benefit of their offspring often gives
community members a sense of pride, achievement, and empowerment. To outsiders, this effort signals that marginalized ethnic communities are taking the initiative to promote their own interests and expand educational opportunities for
their children, rather than passively receiving "welfare multiculturalism" policies
or simply appealing to the mainstream system of education to act on their behalf
(Nelson-Brown, 2005). Finding the right balance between the benefits (financial
assistance) of being a mainstream school and the consequent disadvantage (con-
formity to various rules and regulations), however, remains a challenge.

Social Integration of Minority Groups

Critics argue that ethnic schools might isolate a particular community by exclud-
ing minority children from meaningful interactions with mainstream children,
thereby hindering their integration into the host society (Karsten, Felix, Ledoux,
Mejinen, Roeleveld, & van Schooten, 2006; Resnik, Sabar, Shoham, & Shapira,
2001). The chance of integration is further reduced when separation from the
mainstream reinforces parents' critical views of the host society (Portes & Zhou,

1993). In contrast, others argue that ethnic schools may create a protective environment and shield students from teasing, bullying, and discriminatory comments. But this arrangement also reduces opportunities for students to learn from such interactions, and to understand and appreciate "others." Research suggests that Koreans at North Korean schools do not regularly interact with people outside the North Korean ethnic community (Okano & Tsuchiya, 1999; Ryang, 1997). Brazilians attending Brazilian schools also follow this pattern, making it more difficult for them to integrate into the mainstream host society (Haino, 2010).

Other observers counter isolationist arguments by emphasizing the positive long-term effects of attending ethnic schools. By raising self-esteem of individuals and empowering communities, ethnic schools often contribute to the academic success of their students, which in turn enables them to participate and succeed in the mainstream society (Asanova, 2005). This eventually supports their integration into the host society, while at the same time fostering change in the host society that accommodates them.

Public discussion about multicultural co-living has continued, and a number of reports have been presented in the last several years.[3] Only two national government reports, however, have touched on schools for foreigners. In one, the Ministry of Internal Affairs and Communications suggested that schools for foreigners be granted "miscellaneous schools" status with less stringent requirements (Sômushô, 2006). The other is a Ministry of Education report on measures for education of foreign children (MEXT, 2008c), which proposed providing JSL in the nonformal education sector and offering more flexible options to students interested in transferring from ethnic schools to mainstream schools. The most extensive report on ethnic schools was prepared by the study group of Members of Parliament from the Liberal Democratic Party and Komei Party to support the education of foreign children. The group drafted a proposal that advocated national government support for schools for foreigners (*Gaikokujin Gakkô Shienô*, literally translated as "Assistance for Schools for Foreigners Act") and suggested that small-scale ethnic schools be funded by the national government (Taminzoku Kyôsei Kyôiku Forum 2008 Osaka Jikkôiinkai). The group views the issue in relation to Japan's economic prosperity and responsibilities, rather than in terms of the human rights of children, which is often the focus of other supporters of ethnic schools.

CONCLUSIONS

In the last 3 decades, individual schools and local governments have tried to accommodate new immigrants in the context of mainstream schooling. In the initial stages, such practices included conventional JSL classes and cultural adaptation classes; later, they included multicultural co-living education, bilingual JSL class-es, immigrant languages as high school subjects, and special senior high school entrance examination schemes for immigrants. In most cases, schools and local education boards proposed the initiatives, which the Ministry of Education later took up at the national level. Ethnic schools have rarely been discussed in aca-demic debates on multiculturalism or in official policy discourse.

Ethnic schools currently play a significant role in immigrant education, of-fering what mainstream schools have not been able to provide. This has been pos-sible because they maintain the autonomy to design curricula and offer schooling in ethnic languages. On the other hand, the schools neither provide educational qualifications useful for the mainstream employment market in Japan, nor receive central government funding. Ethnic schools carry out five important tasks: 1) pro-viding education for immigrant children who might not otherwise attend school, 2) equipping these students to make lifestyle choices by teaching their ethnic lan-guages and nurturing self-identity, 3) enhancing (and restricting) children's life chances through transnational strategies, 4) empowering ethnic communities, and 5) promoting social integration of immigrants through interethnic interaction.

My research indicates that immigrant children and their parents consider at least some of these points when making decisions about schools. Educational practitioners and administrators also are aware of them. Finding a balance among them is a challenge that requires collaboration among ethnic schools, mainstream schools, and mediating agencies. When mainstream schools begin to offer educa-tion that responds to the needs and desires of immigrants, ethnic schools are likely to evolve into a different form, perhaps becoming a supplementary school rather than an alternative.

NOTES

1. Ethnic schools have not been discussed in the context of multicultural education policies and practices as widely as mainstream school systems (Nelson-Brown, 2005). Seen in the global context, ethnic schools vary in their mission, form, and place in the national system of schooling; level of national and local host government recognition and financial support; and their relationship with their "motherland" country governments. Ethnic schools can be full-time schools or operate outside school hours as supplementary institutions. Among full-time schools, some are licensed as "regular" mainstream schools by the authorities, entitling them to financial support, but requiring them to conform to government regulations on curriculum and other conditions. The terms used to describe ethnic schools vary and reflect local contexts. For example, they are referred to as "ethnic schools" or "community language schools" in Australia, and "supplemental ethnic schools or programs" or "heritage schools" in the United States (Hornberger, 2005).

2. A reliable estimation of the number of "migrant" children is difficult to ascertain. According to the Ministry of Education, there were 28,575 foreign students who required JSL in primary and secondary schools in 2008, a 12.5% increase from the previous year. Their major first languages are Portuguese (spoken by 11,386), Chinese (5,831), and Spanish (3,634). Enrollments decline considerably as they proceed from primary school (3,791) to middle school (2,028) and on to senior high school (342) (MEXT, 2009). The data, however, are problematic because the assessment of JSL needs at the individual school level is quite arbitrary. For example, even within a single school, disagreements often emerge when reporting the number to the authorities. One area of contention is whether the number should include Japanese citizens (since many JSL students hold Japanese nationality). The other is the level of Japanese language competence below which students have "JSL needs." Students who possess native-like conversational language competence may not have the academic language competence required to keep up with classes. A 2010 census shows that there were 74,219 foreign national students in government schools (MEXT, 2010b), which included old-timer fourth- and fifth-generation Koreans whose first language is Japanese. The number of foreign nationals in government schools had slowly declined until 2005, due to the decreasing number of old-timer Korean children, the majority of whom now have a Japanese parent and hold Japanese citizenship from birth. In 2006, with rising numbers of newcomer children, the number began increasing.

3. The reports include: *Tabunka kyôsei no suishin ni kansuru kenkyûkai hôkokusho 2006* (Sômushô, March 2006); *Tabunka kyôsei no suishin ni kansuru kenkyûkai hôkokusho 2007* (Sômushô, March 2007); *Tabunka kyôsei no suishin ni kansuru kenkyûkai hôkokusho 2010* (Sômushô, March 2010); *Shôshi kôreika kyôseishakai ni kansuru chôsa hôkokusho* (Sangi'in, June 2008); *Jimin Kômei-tô Gaikokujingakkô-hô oyobi gaikokujin shitei no kyôiku o shiensuru gi'in no kai no chûkan hôkoku* (Jimin Kômei-tô, June 2008); *Gaikkujin rôdôsha ukeire no aritaka ni kansuru hôkokusho* (Nihon Shôkô Kaigisho, June 2008); *Gaikokujin jjidô seito kyôiku no jujitsu hôsaku nit suite* (MEXT, June 2008).

REFERENCES

Asanova, J. (2005). Educational experiences of immigrant students from the former Soviet Union: A case study of an ethnic school in Toronto. *Educational Studies, 31*(2), 181–195.

Castro-Vazquez, G. (2009). Immigrant children from Latin America at Japanese schools: Homogeneity, ethnicity, gender and language in education. *Journal of Research in International Education, 8*(1), 57–78.

Chûgoku Kikokusha Teichaku Sokushin Sentâ. (2011). *The 2010 survey results on special consideration for the 2011 senior high school entry examinations for Chinese returnees and foreign national students according to prefecture* (in Japanese). Tokorozawa, Japan: Author. Retrieved from http://www.kikokushacenter.or.jp/shien_joho/shingaku/kokonyushi/other/2010/koko-top.htm

Cummins, J. (1986). Empowering minority students: A framework for intervention. *Harvard Educational Review, 56*(1), 18–36.

Fishman, J. (Ed.). (2001). *Can threatened languages be saved? Reversing language shift, revisied: A 21st century perspective*. Clevedon, U.K.: Multilingual Matters.

Gaikokujin Shûjûtoshi Kaigi Yokkaichi. (2005). *In pursuit of multicultural society: For the sake of the children who are the future* (in Japanese). Yokkaichi, Japan: Author.

Gekkan Io. (2006). *Schools for foreigners in Japan* (in Japanese). Tokyo: Akashi Shoten.

Graburn, N. H. H., Ertl, J., & Tierney, R. K. (Eds.). (2008). *Multiculturalism in the new Japan: Crossing the boundaries within*. New York: Berhahn Books.

Haino, S. (2010). *Children in Brazilian schools in Japan* (in Japanese). Tokyo: Nakanishiya.

Hornberger, N. (2005). Heritage/community language education: U.S. and Australian perspective. *International Journal of Bilingual Education and Bilingualism, 8*(2&3), 101–108.

Hyôgo-ken Zainichi Gaikokujin Kyôiku Kenkyû Kyôgikai. (2007). *The report of the 2007 meeting of the Hyogo Prefectural Association of Research on Education of Foreign National Students in Japan* (in Japanese). Kobe, Japan: Author.

Ishikawa, E. A. (2003). Brazilian immigrants and the process of immigration policy formulation: Diverse overseas communities and support measures for them (in Japanese). In H. Komai (Ed.), *Imin seisaku no kokusai hikaku* (pp. 245–282). Tokyo: Akashi Shoten.

Karsten, S., Felix, C., Ledoux, G., Mejinen, W., Roeleveld, J., & van Schooten, E. (2006). Choosing segregation or integration? The extent and effects of ethnic segregation in Dutch cities. *Education and Urban Society, 38*(2), 228–247.

Lee, J., & Oxelson, E. (2006). It's not my job: K–12 teacher attitudes toward students' heritage language maintenance. *Bilingual Research Journal, 30*(2), 453–427.

MEXT, Ministry of Education, Culture, Sports, Science, and Technology. (1998a). *Course of study for primary schools* (in Japanese). Tokyo: Author. Retrieved from http://www.mext.go.jp/a_menu/shotou/youryou/main4_a2.htm

MEXT, Ministry of Education, Culture, Sports, Science, and Technology. (1998b). *Course of study for middle schools* (in Japanese). Tokyo: Author. Retrieved from http://www.mext.go.jp/a_menu/shotou/youryou/main4_a2.htm

MEXT, Ministry of Education, Culture, Sports, Science, and Technology. (1999). *Course of study for senior high schools* (in Japanese). Tokyo: Author. Retrieved from http://www.mext.go.jp/a_menu/shotou/youryou/main4_a2.htm

MEXT, Ministry of Education, Culture, Sports, Science, and Technology. (2003a). *Course of study for primary schools* (in Japanese). Tokyo: Author. Retrieved from http://www.mext.go.jp/a_menu/shotou/youryou/main4_a2.htm

MEXT, Ministry of Education, Culture, Sports, Science, and Technology. (2003b). *Course of study for middle schools* (in Japanese). Tokyo: Author. Retrieved from http://www.mext.go.jp/a_menu/shotou/youryou/main4_a2.htm

MEXT, Ministry of Education, Culture, Sports, Science, and Technology. (2003c). *Course of study for senior high schools* (in Japanese). Tokyo: Author. Retrieved from http://www.mext.go.jp/a_menu/shotou/youryou/main4_a2.htm

MEXT, Ministry of Education, Culture, Sports, Science, and Technology. (2008a). *Course of study for primary schools* (in Japanese). Tokyo: Author. Retrieved from http://www.mext.go.jp/a_menu/shotou/newcs/youryou/index.htm

MEXT, Ministry of Education, Culture, Sports, Science, and Technology. (2008b). *Course of study for middle schools* (in Japanese). Tokyo: Author. Retrieved from http://www.mext.go.jp/a_menu/shotou/newcs/youryou/index.htm

MEXT, Ministry of Education, Culture, Sports, Science, and Technology. (2008c). *Report on measures to improve the education of foreign students* (in Japanese). Tokyo: Author. Retrieved from http://www.mext.go.jp/b_menu/shingi/chousa/shotou/042/houkoku/08070301/htm

MEXT, Ministry of Education, Culture, Sports, Science, and Technology. (2009). *Results from a 2008 survey of foreign children enrolled in Japanese schools requiring Japanese language education* (in Japanese). Tokyo: Author. Retrieved from http://www.mext.go.jp/b_menu/houdou/21/07/1279262.htm

MEXT, Ministry of Education, Culture, Sports, Science, and Technology. (2010a). *Progress in senior high school reforms* (in Japanese). Tokyo: Author. Retrieved from http://www.mext.go.jp/b_menu/houdou/22/11/1298797.htm

MEXT, Ministry of Education, Culture, Sports, Science, and Technology. (2010b). *Basic school survey results 2010* (in Japanese). Tokyo: Author. Retrieved from http://www.mext.go.jp/b_menu/toukei/chousa01/kihon/1267995.htm

Miyajima, K., & Oota, H. (Eds.). (2005). *Foreign children and education in Japan: the problem of school non-attendance and challenges to multicultural co-living* (in Japanese). Tokyo: Tokyo University Press.

Nelson-Brown, J. (2005). Ethnic schools: A historical case study of ethnically focsed supplemental education programs. *Education and Urban Society, 38*(1), 35–61.

Okano, K. (2006). The global-local interface in multicultural education policies in Japan. *Comparative Education, 42*(2), 473–491.

Okano, K. (2011). Ethnic Koreans in Japanese schools: Shifing boundaries and collaboration with other groups. In R. Tsuneyoshi, K. Okano, & S. Boocock (Eds.), *Minorities and education in multicultural Japan: An interactive perspective* (pp. 100–125). London, U.K.: Routledge.

Okano, K. (2012). Languages and citizenship in education: Migrant languages in government schools. In Nanette Gottlieb (Ed.), *Language and citizenship in Japan* (pp. 58–78). New York: Routledge.

Okano, K., & Tsuchiya, M. (1999). *Education in contemporary Japan: Inequality and diversity*. Cambridge, U.K.: Cambridge University Press.

Pak, S. (2008). *Schools for foreigners: From international schools to ethnic schools* (in Japanese). Tokyo: Chûkô Shinsho.

Portes, A., & Zhou, M. (1993). The new second generation: segmented assimilation and its variants. *Annals of the American Academy of Political and Social Science, 530*, 74–96.

Qiu, X. (2004). The education of overseas Chinese in Japan: Fulltime ethnic schools (in Japanese). *Waseda Daigaku Daigakuin Kyôikugaku Kenkyûka Kiyô, 12*, 215–226.

Resnik, J., Sabar, N., Shoham, E., & Shapira, R. (2001). Absorption of CIS immigration into Israeli schools: a semipermeable enclave model. *Anthropology and Education Quarterly, 32*(4), 424–446.

Ryang, S. (1997). *North Koreans in Japan*. Boulder: Westview Press.

Sakuma, K. (2006). *School non-attendance among foreign national children: In search of schools open to other cultures* (in Japanese). Tokyo: Keisô Shobo.

Sekiguchi, T. (2003). *Japanese-Brazilian children living in Japan: Identity formation of children growing up across cultures* (in Japanese). Tokyo: Akashi Shoten.

Shimizu, K. (Ed.). (2008). *Newcomer children at senior high schools: Educational assistance offered by Osaka prefectural senior high schools* (in Japanese). Tokyo: Akashi Shoten.

Shimizu, K., & Shimizu, M. (Eds.). (2001). *Newcomers and education* (in Japanese). Tokyo: Akashi Shoten.

Shimuzu, M., & Kojima, A. (2006). *Curriculum-making for foreign students* (in Japanese). Tokyo: Sagano Shoin.

Sômushô, Ministry of Internal Affairs and Communications. (2006). *Community-based multicultural co-living plans* (in Japanese). Tokyo: Author.

Taminzoku Kyôsei Kyôiku Forum 2008 Osaka Jikkôiinkai. (2008). *Multicultural Co-living Forum 2008* (in Japanese). Osaka, Japan: Korea NGO Centre.

Tsuneyoshi, R., Okano, K., & Boocock, S. (Eds.). (2011). *Minorities and education in multicultural Japan: a interactive perspective*. London, U.K.: Routledge.

Watado, I., & Kawamura, C. (Eds.). (2002). *Multicultural education in Japan* (in Japanese). Tokyo: Akashoshoten.

Zenkoku Zainichi Gaikokujin Kyôiku Kenkyû Kyôgikai. (2007). *The 28th conference of the national association of research on education of foreign nationals living in Japan* (in Japanese). Kyoto: Author.

Zenkoku Zainichi Gaikokujin Kyôiku Kenkyû Kyôgikai. (2011). How schools ensure learning and post-school destinations for foreign children (in Japanese). *Zengaikyô Tsûshin* [newsletter of the National Association of Research on Education of Foreign Nationals Living in Japan], *121*, 3–8.

CHAPTER 7

Ainu Schooling
Self-Determination and Globalization

Christopher J. Frey

This chapter explores developments within Ainu education over the last 2 decades in an attempt to better understand why there are currently no ethnic schools for Ainu youth, as well as how the emerging global Indigenous rights movement might create new opportunities for culturally relevant educational institutions in Japan. Reflecting global trends, Japan has expanded its public education system toward universal access, and in the process new institutional models of schooling have proliferated. Human rights discourses of the post–World War II era, along with global movements for civil and human rights, have meant universal access for minority children and those with disabilities, though children who are not citizens are not required to attend school.

For Japan's Indigenous Ainu, access to public schooling is complicated by the uniformly *Japanese* character of public education, and by official resistance to culturally relevant schooling for Ainu children. Although the Japanese government has only recently officially acknowledged the Ainu as an Indigenous people, policies distinguishing their unique status in relation to other Japanese have existed since at least the early 19th century (Emori, 2007), including segregated schools and classrooms throughout much of the Meiji era (1868–1912) (Frey, 2007; Ogawa, 1997). For Ainu people, there is a tension between recognizing their unique status and insisting on equal access to public schooling and other services. In theory, as Japanese citizens, Ainu have the same access as other Japanese to all levels of public education. Nevertheless, Ainu students continue to report social discrimination within schools, and higher rates of economic poverty among Ainu families have historically limited their access to secondary and postsecondary education (Ishikida, 2005).

In this chapter, I analyze how the tension between assimilation and self-determination has manifested in policy and practice over the last 2 decades, and how the emergence of global Indigenous self-determination movements are complicating and transforming discourses about education for the Ainu. As I will show, the intersection of Indigenous, national, and global agendas remains contested, as many actors inside and outside of Japan approach these crossroads and negotiate new directions for the education of people who identify as Ainu.

Decades of assimilation policies and practices, as well as intermarriage with other Japanese, make it difficult to define who is Ainu. If a "blood quantum" definition is applied, perhaps a half million people have some Ainu heritage. In contrast, using a "full blood" definition, by which many Japanese define themselves, there may be no Ainu at all. The most common estimates are based on membership in the Hokkaido Ainu Association, and put the population of Ainu in Hokkaido at about 24,000. If we include the number of Ainu who refuse to self-identify because of discrimination, along with a substantial population in Tokyo, the number of Ainu people doubles or triples (Maher & Yashiro, 1995).

Cultural and linguistic dissimilation policies in the 17th and 18th centuries reified status distinctions and boundaries between the Ainu and the Yamato Japanese population that continued into the Meiji era (1868–1912) (Frey, 2007). The expansion of state schooling in the early 20th century, the rapid colonization of Ainu lands in the Meiji era, and the breakdown of many Ainu communities in Hokkaido across the 20th century all contributed to the rapid decline in the number of Ainu language speakers. Today, there is a concerted effort to preserve and reinvigorate Ainu cultural practices and the Ainu language, in part supported by the 1997 Cultural Promotion Act[1] (Maher, 2001; Sjöberg, 1993; Yamada, 2001). These efforts, however, are complicated by the weight of Japanese colonialism in Hokkaido, a lack of economic resources, and a wide range of opinions among Ainu themselves about whether cultural and linguistic revitalization is in their best interests.

WELFARE COLONIALISM, STATE POLICIES AND PRACTICES, AND AINU SCHOOLING

For Ainu and other Indigenous peoples, government provisions for public schools were part of an attempt to break the cycle of welfare dependency that developed in the 19th century, and to fully integrate the Indigenous populations into the colonizing culture. The state's desire to limit welfare to Indigenous peoples has been framed as necessary to reduce the financial burden on the state and to "free" welfare recipients from government dependency.

This strong impulse to liberate the Ainu from state aid is analyzed here through the conceptual framework of "welfare colonialism" (Paine, 1977; Siddle, 1996) and dependency (White, 1983). This concept posits that the welfare and social support systems of modern states have replaced the more explicit colonial appropriation policies, particularly among internally colonized people like the Ainu, by maintaining dependency on state aid. Funding for assimilationist education is part of this settlement, because schooling for Ainu children has long focused on graduating productive citizens who would not make claims to state resources. Similarly, the social education of Ainu children attempted to inculcate a Japanese identity, while extinguishing Indigenous knowledge, and thus the foundation for claims to an independent Ainu identity.

In a sense, welfare and other government support can be seen as an attempt to compensate for the unilateral confiscation of Ainu lands during the Meiji era. Thus, continued government support for the Ainu, while engendering dependency, is part of an exchange that acknowledges Ainu claims against Japan's colonization of Hokkaido and a unique relationship between the Japanese and Ainu that is different from any other in Japan. The challenge for educators, then, is to create publicly funded learning environments where government funding is not channeled into schooling that seeks to extinguish Ainu identity.

Ainu schooling developed following the confiscation of Ainu lands by the Japanese government in the 19th century. In 1899, the Japanese government enacted the Hokkaido Former Aborigines Protection Act, which included welfare, land reform, and education measures. In 1901, education provisions were detailed in the Regulations for the Education of Former Aborigine Children, which established two dozen segregated schools and classrooms for Ainu children in Hokkaido (Ogawa, 1997). By the early 1920s, most Ainu children attended integrated schools, although they continued to experience discrimination and isolation (Kaizawa, 1993). Pressure and desire to assimilate intensified during World War II, and by the early 1950s, most young Ainu had little knowledge of their grandparents' language or culture.

Influenced by other domestic and international movements, Ainu of the "baby boom" generation began openly questioning the political settlement of Japanese colonialism in the 1960s (Yûki, 1997). These challenges to assimilationist policies, as well as the rapid expansion of the Japanese economy and national focus on *Burakumin* issues, led to new large-scale welfare programs for Hokkaido Ainu. These measures, implemented in the 1970s, addressed Ainu poverty, but also reinforced the dependency of many Ainu on the government.

Modeled after the *Dôwa* Special Measures Law, the 1974 Hokkaido *Utari* (Ainu) Welfare Countermeasures flooded Ainu communities with nearly 12 billion yen (approx $140 million) in grants and loans for business development, training, housing, and education. Administered through the *Utari* Association, the successor of the Hokkaido Ainu Association, these measures led to a rapid expansion in membership in the Association, but deepened its obligation to cooperate with the Japanese government. Without the ability to establish an independent economic base, Ainu remained dependent on Tokyo, yet defiant about government claims to the colonized resources of Hokkaido, reflecting the tensions between assimilation and self-determination.

The current Ainu welfare policy is the sixth iteration of the 1974 Hokkaido *Utari* Welfare Measures (Hokkaidô-chô, 2011). Under the plan, Ainu welfare measures target income stability, school completion, employment security, industrial promotion, and encouragement of nongovernmental organization (NGO) activities. Directives for education include "raising academic standards for children" and subsidizing secondary and tertiary school fees (Hokkaidô-chô, 2011). The government of Hokkaido and five different central government ministries support funding for these five policy arenas.

Taken together, these policies illustrate the ways that the Japanese government supports Ainu through welfare, community development, and educational aid. Historically, Ainu education started with the presumption that Ainu are first and foremost Japanese citizens. The assumption is that all Ainu should be treated the same as other Japanese citizens, though continuing gaps in academic performance between Ainu and Japanese students are framed in ways that deflect away from historical and structural inequalities. Instead, academic achievement gaps are generally framed as emanating from financial problems within Ainu families and from social discrimination by individual Japanese. This is evident from recent surveys of Ainu communities, and in the remedies proposed to alleviate those problems.

The Achievement Gap and the Ainu Family

One dominant discourse around the education of Ainu youth is their low rate of matriculation to secondary and tertiary educational institutions. A 2004 government survey found that upon graduation from junior high school, 93.5% of Ainu students and 98.3% of Japanese students from the same communities enrolled in high school, an increase from 41.6% and 78.2% respectively since 1972. However, a wider gap emerges after high school. Half (49.9%) of Ainu high school graduates in 2004 entered the job market, compared to only 18.8% of Japanese high school graduates living in the same communities. Similarly, only 17.4% of Ainu high school graduates enrolled in postsecondary institutions, compared to 38.5% of their Japanese counterparts. These rates may reflect the wishes and experiences of Ainu parents, who themselves attended high school and college at much lower rates than their Japanese counterparts. The different responses among Ainu parents might be explained by family income. The same 2004 study found that families engaged in fishing and crafts were less likely to receive welfare assistance than Ainu living in urban and farming areas. The surveys also suggest that the independent livelihoods of some Ainu families, those who are less reliant on welfare, lead to lower school achievement (Hokkaidô Kankyô Seikatsubu, 2006). Physical isolation from urban centers and universities may also help explain the gap.

The government's current education support measures focus solely on financial barriers to secondary and postsecondary education, and do not address culturally relevant education for Ainu youths. For example, the Hokkaido prefectural government began providing stipends to Ainu high school students in 2009 (Hokkaidô-chô, 2011); the following year, public school tuition was eliminated nationwide, and Hokkaido began offering tuition waivers for private high school to low-income households (Japan Today, 2010). In Hokkaido, 20-year interest free loans are available to Ainu university students (Hokkaidô-chô, 2011). These support measures are similar to other measures for *Burakumin* children, and reflect a deeper ideology of promoting access to Japanese educational institutions rather than providing financial support for culturally relevant education.

Social Discrimination and the Ignorance of Individual Japanese

The same studies also suggest that social discrimination and inequality is the result of social discrimination by unenlightened Japanese individuals. This viewpoint leads to educational programs focusing on teaching Japanese about Ainu, rather than on initiatives *for* the Ainu. The 2004 survey referred to above confirms that discrimination in schools remains a problem. Among recent graduates, about a fifth reported being discriminated against or knowing someone who was in the past 7 years. Overall, reports of discrimination in schools and in the selection of marriage partners are decreasing, although reports of workplace discrimination are increasing. Most respondents noted that when faced with discrimination, they "persevered" or did nothing; one-fifth responded that they confronted the discrimination, sometimes with physical force. The survey data suggest that few Ainu talk about the discrimination, either with family members or teachers (Hokkaidô Kankyô Seikatsubu, 2006).

Findings such as these frame social discrimination as a problem between individuals, not as the result of policy, government-sanctioned discrimination, or colonialism. The 1997 Cultural Promotion Act maintains this focus on the ignorant individual by promoting "knowledge and awareness" about Ainu language and culture to "the nation" (*kokumin*) (Ainu Bunka Shinkô Kenkyû Kikô, 2012). This illustrates how official problematizing of Ainu education, and human rights education in general, deflects attention from deeper structural problems like land claims and Indigenous rights, and toward the "human rights consciousness in each citizen," which presumes "that human rights violations are a problem caused by citizens with an inadequate understanding of the subject" (Jones, 2008).

In practice, the emphasis placed on financial support and the focus on changing Japanese opinion about the Ainu are reflected in the activities sanctioned under the 1997 Cultural Promotion Act and its official arm, the Foundation for Research and Promotion of Ainu Culture (FRPAC). While some Ainu have been able to utilize FRPAC funds to promote and hone their traditional arts and crafts, many others have been critical of the focus on traditional culture and the control that Japanese bureaucrats have maintained over how Ainu culture is defined and promoted (Siddle, 2002; Winchester, 2009).

It could be argued that this *laissez-faire* approach to cultural education by the government protects the autonomy of Ainu individuals to determine the content and process of educating their children about Ainu culture. On the other hand, very little money is available to support the development of culturally relevant models of education for Ainu youth. To a great degree, the responsibility to develop programs for Ainu children has been left to Ainu communities. The centralized structure of public education in Japan suggests that any initiative in culturally relevant schooling for the Ainu will likely be constrained by the policy patterns already established by other minority groups in Japan.

DISCOURSES OF MINORITY SCHOOLING IN JAPAN AND THE AINU

The dominant discourse around minority education in Japan remains assimilationist. The foundations of this approach, however, have evolved from a postwar grounding in monoculturalism (embodied in *Nihonjinron* theories, which posited that all Japanese are equal because of their shared ethnic, cultural, and biological heritage) to one based on global human rights discourses of equality in which Japanese citizens share legal rights and duties as Japanese. One relevant example is the educational programs that target the nearly 3 million *Burakumin*. *Dôwa* (or "social integration") education that developed in the 1960s and 1970s, focused on teaching *Burakumin* children about their culture in order to confront and eliminate discrimination, and ultimately, to erase lingering caste distinctions altogether. Non-*Burakumin* Japanese were also taught about human rights in an effort to reduce mistreatment.

Although some Ainu desire assimilation, *Burakumin* have more generally sought integration into Japanese society because they are culturally and linguistically indistinguishable from other Japanese. As Okano (2011) notes, educational initiatives for *Burakumin* children emphasize the importance of nondiscrimination and equality of opportunity through human rights language to argue for "equal treatment because they are also 'Japanese'" (p. 36). Efforts to teach *Burakumin* children about their history may be more politically palatable than those teaching Ainu children about Ainu history, given that one goal of *Dôwa* education was to foster integration (Gordon, 2006). In contrast, a possible outcome of cultural and political education for Ainu could be to foster political orientations that conflict with state interests, particularly those connected to land and resources.

On the surface, the group in Japan that seems to have the most in common with the Ainu is the Okinawans, or Ryukyuans (United Nations, 2008). However, the U.S. military occupation complicates comparisons between these two groups (Minority Rights Group International, 2008). After World War II, the U.S. government promoted a distinct Ryukyuan identity as a way to separate Okinawa from the Japanese mainland and maintain American military control of the islands (Heinrich, 2005). Evidence suggests that in 1946, U.S. Occupation authorities met with Ainu leaders to discuss possible independence from Japan, but found no interest in separation (Takemae, 2002). Rather, Ryukyuans have tended to rally around standard Japanese language and culture, rather than the unique culture of Okinawa, as symbols of struggle against the American Occupation and for the return of Okinawa to Japan. Educational self-determination in Okinawa has been complicated by the overlay of American military power in ways that are not comparable in Hokkaido.

Like the Ainu, Japan's resident (*zainichi*) Koreans also experienced Japanese colonization and resettlement, and their educational situation has reflected similar tensions around autonomy and exclusion. Akiba (2000) notes that Japan's educational policies toward Koreans in public schools have been "based on an ideology of belief in a homogenous nation" (p. 601). In general, this approach has meant that policies have advocated treating Koreans the same as Japanese students, with limited regard for cultural differences. Although policies at the national level and practices at the school level have liberalized somewhat in the last 2 decades, social discrimination, particularly in employment, remains a significant problem for Korean students (Okano, 2004), as it does for the Ainu.

Emerging discourses for Ainu educational self-determination are likely to draw, at least implicitly, on the experiences of Koreans, who have over time been able to maintain schools that are grounded in an ethnic identity and language, and not the *Burakumin* or Okinawan approaches, which are grounded in assimilation. In addition to the domestic discourses, the emerging global Indigenous rights movement has radically changed the policy landscape for Ainu people in the last decade.

THE GLOBAL INDIGENOUS RIGHTS MOVEMENT
AND NEW DOMESTIC LEGISLATION

Like other activists who have engaged international connections to further their domestic agenda (Chan, 2008), Ainu have forged connections to Indigenous groups and international organizations since the 1970s to leverage policy changes inside Japan. These new networks have connected Ainu with Indigenous people in the United States, Canada, New Zealand, Taiwan, and China. One of the earliest contacts occurred in 1971, when a group of Alaska Natives traveled to Hokkaido to meet with Ainu representatives. During a 1974 visit to autonomous minority regions of China, Ainu participant Tokuhei Narita was "plunged into thought on the various problems that are involved in our inheriting and perpetuating Ainu traditional culture" (Hokkaidô Ainu Chûgoku Hômondan, 1975, p. 7, quoted in Siddle, 1996, p. 177). Ainu delegations began attending the World Conference of Indigenous Peoples in 1983, and have continued to participate in international forums on Indigenous rights.

Efforts to apply new models of educational self-determination that Ainu were learning abroad were generally resisted inside Japan. Concerned about the rapid decline in the number of speakers of the Ainu language, Ainu activist Shigeru Kayano offered Ainu language classes in Nibutani in the 1970s. In 1979, his plan for an Ainu-language kindergarten was thwarted by the Ministry of Welfare, because it violated laws requiring that instruction be provided in Japanese. Kayano rallied community members to back the school, which opened in 1982 (Kayano, 1994). Although no other schools emerged, many communities began hosting regular Ainu language classes during the 1980s. These courses, often staffed by Japanese educators, both inspired young Ainu to devote energy to cultural revitalization, and created opportunities for Japanese to develop an interest in Ainu culture (Gayman, 2011).

In the early 1980s, international connections, and the development of a new consciousness about the frailty of Ainu culture and language, increased pressure to revise the 1899 Former Aborigines Protection Act, which was still the official policy of the Japanese government. The Ainu Association wrote a draft proposal in 1984, which drew heavily from examples from the United States, Canada, Australia, and New Zealand, where Indigenous people were experimenting with varying degrees of educational self-determination.

The reports of the Ainu researchers reflected their interest in new forms of schooling, by documenting how spaces for Indigenous education abroad included several years of Indigenous language instruction, courses in Indigenous and dominant languages, the inclusion of elders in teaching traditional knowledge, Indigenous control of schools, university courses in Indigenous studies, teaching about Indigenous people in public schools, and inclusion and support within the secondary and tertiary education systems (Hokkaidô Ainu Kyôkai, 1994). However, those reports also noted several concerns, including problems with standardizing language for formal teaching, a problem they noted with the many dialects of spoken Māori, and the poor quality of instruction, curriculum, training, and extracurricular activities among Aborigines in Australia, where Ainu representatives observed that supplementary programs for Australian Aborigines consisted of "drawing pictures or going to a center for industrial training" (Hokkaidô Ainu Kyôkai, 1994, p. 1321). Though encouraged by the emerging forms of Indigenous education they observed, the poor quality of the schools they visited abroad, as well as discriminatory policies inside Japan and the lack of an independent funding base, likely convinced the crafters of the 1984 Draft Proposal to avoid pushing for culturally relevant educational institutions for the Ainu.

EMERGING LEGAL ENVIRONMENTS IN JAPAN: THE 1997 CULTURAL PROMOTION ACT AND BEYOND

The Ainu Association's 1984 Draft Proposal was the starting point for negotiations that eventually led to adoption of the 1997 Cultural Promotion Act. Several domestic and international factors contributed to its passage, including the United Nations Decade of Indigenous Peoples (1995–2004), an international forum in 1993 on Indigenous issues held at Nibutani, and the election of Ainu activist Shigeru Kayano to the Diet in 1994. In the days before the Act was ratified, the Sapporo Circuit Court ruled that land confiscated from Ainu landowners in 1989 to build a dam on the Saru River in Nibutani violated their rights as Japanese citizens and as Indigenous people. This was the first ruling that Ainu had internationally recognized rights as Indigenous people that the Japanese government was obliged to protect. Nevertheless, the government refused to reintroduce language into the Act recognizing Ainu as an Indigenous people (Dietz, 1999).

The conservative approach to education about Ainu that targeted Japanese people in the 1997 Cultural Promotion Act likely helped create a broader base of support for official recognition. Japan's assent to the United Nations (2007) Declaration on the Rights of Indigenous Peoples (UN DRIP), and the international spotlight focused on Hokkaido when it hosted the G8 Summit in 2008, created a unique environment that pushed the Japanese Diet to recognize Ainu as an Indigenous people under the UN definition on June 6, 2008. Although the policy changes in Japan have been impressive in light of the 2007 UN DRIP, the early policy formation process continued long-established practices of minimizing Ainu voices. When Chief Cabinet Secretary Nobutaka Machimura established the Ainu Policy Expert Panel to recommend additional policies a month after the passage of UN DRIP (Office of the Prime Minister, 2008), Japanese members dominated. The eight members included only one Ainu, Takashi Katô, the chair of the Ainu Association. The current iteration of the policy panel includes four Ainu members, but as of December 2012 has yet to issue a formal report (Office of the Prime Minister, 2012).

POSSIBILITIES AND CHALLENGES FOR AINU SCHOOLING

Transformation of the political environment since 2007, as well as emerging international recognition of Indigenous self-determination in education, may create new opportunities for the development of culturally relevant, Indigenous-led educational programs and institutions. Recent reforms have decentralized, democratized, and privatized public education; extended university entrance to graduates of ethnic schools (Okano, this volume); and enhanced the growth of private schools in Tokyo (Tsuneyoshi, this volume). Despite this changing landscape, officials, particularly at the national level, have shown little willingness to support educational programs that are not explicitly *Japanese* in nature.

Local efforts to develop culturally relevant education have multiplied in the last decade across Hokkaido. At least two after-school programs (*juku*) provide Ainu children help with school lessons and teach them about Ainu history and culture. The branch in Obihiro, founded in 1990, has sent students and volunteers to Canada and Taiwan to meet with other Indigenous youth (Tokachi Shimbun, 2010). In 2009, Kushiro Meiki High School became the first high school to offer a course in Ainu culture as an elective, rather than embedding a few lessons in an existing Japanese history course (47 News, 2009).

At the university level, Sapporo University initiated the Ureshipa Project[2] in 2009, which aims to foster a multicultural, interdisciplinary environment for Ainu college students (Sapporo University, 2011a). The university has committed almost 10 million yen (approximately $120,000) to scholarships for Ainu students to study Ainu history, culture, and language. Also, as part of the project, students create outreach programs and offer symposia in local schools (Sapporo University, 2011b). In addition, a group led by an Ainu former principal from Ebetsu, Shimizu Yûji, began work in 2010 with a group of Japanese and international scholars to study the possibility of an ethnic school for Ainu children in Hokkaido (Gayman, 2011; Hokkaidô Shimbun, 2010). Ethnic schools are one of five policy proposals in the first platform of the Ainu People's Party, established in 2011 by Shiro Kayano, the son of Shigeru Kayano. The proposal demands the recognition of Ainu as an official language, and the creation of ethnic schools from kindergarten to university (Asahi Shimbun, 2012; Yomiuri Shimbun, 2012). The grassroots development of education initiatives for and about Ainu reflects an incredibly rich educational environment, one that may support the development of new forms of ethnic schooling in the near future.

The rapid development in the past 5 years of new policies and legal frameworks, both globally and in Japan, that recognize and support Ainu have created new opportunities for the expansion of culturally relevant schooling. To many people, the pace of change has been startling, but much difficult work remains. Unlike in other multiethnic and settler-colonial countries, there are no clear models in Japan for what an Ainu school might look like in this new era of expanding Indigenous self-determination. While official recognition is a necessary starting point for greater Ainu autonomy, Tokyo's reluctance to recognize Ainu also signals that rights that may have been legally "granted" still must be fought for. The relationship between Ainu and Japanese is rapidly changing, and the definition of Ainu educational self-determination remains in flux.

NOTES

1. The full name of the 1997 act is *Ainu bunka no shinkô narabi ni Ainu no dentô nado ni kansuru chishki no fukkyû narabi ni teihatsu ni kansuru hôritsu,* or The Law for the Promotion of the Ainu Culture and for the Dissemination and Advocacy for the Traditions of the Ainu and the Ainu Culture.

2. *Ureshipa* can be translated from Ainu as "to raise together."

REFERENCES

47 News. (2009, February 23). *One Hokkaido high school is the first to establish "Ainu Culture" as a school subject* (in Japanese). Retrieved from http://www.47news.jp/CN/200902/CN2009022301000010.html on 1 April 2011

Ainu Bunka Shinkô Kenkyû Kikô. (2012). About the Organization (in Japanese). Retrieved from http://www.frpac.or.jp/prf/index.html.

Akiba, M. (2000). Educational policy for Korean students in Japan. *International Journal of Educational Research 33*(6), 601–609.

Asahi Shimbun. (2012, January 15). *Ainu People's Party announces five major platforms* (in Japanese). Retrieved from http://mytown.asahi.com/hokkaido/news.php?k_id=01000001201160007

Chan J. (2008). *Another Japan is possible: New social movements and global citizenship education in Japan.* Palo Alto: Stanford University Press.

Dietz, K. (1999). Ainu in the international arena. In W. Fitzhugh & C. Dubreuil (Eds.), *Ainu: Spirit of a northern people* (pp. 359–365). Washington, D.C.: Smithsonian.

Emori, S. (2007). *A history of the Ainu people* (in Japanese). Tokyo: Sôfukan.

Frey, C. J. (2007). *Ainu schools and education policy in nineteenth-century Hokkaido, Japan.* Unpublished doctoral dissertation, Indiana University.

Gayman, J. (2011). Ainu right to education and the Ainu practice of "education": Current situation and imminent issues in light of indigenous education rights and theory. *Intercultural Education 22*(1), 15–27.

Gordon, J. A. (2006). From liberation to human rights: challenges for teachers of the *Burakumin* in Japan. *Race, Ethnicity and Education 9*(2), 183–202.

Heinrich, P. (2005). Language loss and revitalization in the Ryukyu Islands. *Japan Focus.* Retrieved from http://japanfocus.org/-Patrick-Heinrich/1596

Hokkaidô Ainu Chûgoku Hômondan (ed.) (1975). *A record of the Hokkaido Ainu China travel group* (in Japanese). Sapporo: Author.

Hokkaidô Ainu Kyôkai. (1994). *Ainu history: A history of activities* (in Japanese). Sapporo: Hokkaidô Shuppan Kikaku Sentâ.

Hokkaidô-chô. (2011). *Policy for improvement of Ainu livelihoods* (in Japanese). Retrieved from http://www.pref.hokkaido.lg.jp/ks/ass/suisin.htm

Hokkaidô Kankyô Seikatsubu. (2006). *Summary report of the 2004 survey of the conditions of the Hokkaidô Ainu* (in Japanese). Sapporo, Japan: Author. Retrieved from http://www.pref.hokkaido.lg.jp/file.jsp?id=56318

Hokkaidô Shimbun. (2010, January 2). *Discussions on an Ainu school: Research group proposes curriculum* (in Japanese). Retrieved from http://www.hokkaido-np.co.jp/news/education/208243.html

Ishikida, M. Y. (2005). *Japanese education in the 21st century.* Lincoln, NE: iUniverse.

Japan Today. (2010, May 17). 37 prefectures make private high school tuition free. Retrieved from http://www.japantoday.com/category/national/view/37-prefectures-make-private-high-school-tuition-free

Jones, C. P. (2008, July 15). Human rights—strictly personal, strictly Japanese? *The Japan Times.* Retrieved from http://search.japantimes.co.jp/cgi-bin/fl20080715zg.html

Kaizawa, T. (1993). *Ainu: My life (in Japanese).* Tokyo: Iwamani Shôten.

Kayano, S. (1994). *Our land was a forest: An Ainu memoir.* Boulder, CO: Westview Press.

Maher, J. C. (2001). Akor Itak—Our language, your language: Ainu in Japan. In Fishman, J. A. (Ed.), *Can threatened languages be saved?: Reversing language shift, revisited: A 21st century perspective* (pp. 323–349). Clevedon, UK: Multilingual Matters.

Maher, J. C., & Yashiro, K. (1995). *Multilingual Japan.* Clevedon, UK: Multilingual Matters.

Minority Rights Group International. (2008). *World directory of minorities and indigenous peoples—Japan : Ryukyuans (Okinawans).* Retrieved from http://www.unhcr.org/refworld/docid/49749cfdc.html

Office of the Prime Minister. (2008, July 1). *Regarding establishment of expert panel for Ainu policy. Chief cabinet secretary decision* (in Japanese). Retrieved from http://www.kantei.go.jp/jp/singi/ainu/konkyo.pdf

Office of the Prime Minister. (2012, November). *Synopsis of Ainu policy* (in Japanese). Retrieved from http://www.kantei.go.jp/jp/singi/ainusuishin/policy.html

Ogawa, M. (1997). *Research on the history of the modern Ainu education system* (in Japanese). Sapporo: Hokkaidô Daigaku Toshokan Kôkai.

Okano, K. (2004). Koreans in Japan: A minority's changing relationship with schools. *International Review of Education 50*, 119–140.

Okano, K. (2011). Long-existing minorities and education. In R. Tsuneyoshi, K. Okano, & S. S. Boocock (Eds.), *Minorities and education in multicultural Japan: An interactionist perspective* (pp. 29–43). New York: Routledge

Paine, R. (1977). *The white Arctic: Anthropological essays on tutelage and ethnicity*. St. John's NL, Canada: St. John's Memorial University of Newfoundland: Institute of Social and Economic Research.

Sapporo University. (2011a). *Sapporo University Ureshipa Project begins* (in Japanese). Retrieved from http://www.sapporo-u.ac.jp/soryo/no120/no120-01.html

Sapporo University. (2011b). *Sapporo University: Hopes for a school for Ainu elementary children* (in Japanese). *Mainichi Shimbun*. Retrieved from http://mainichi.jp/select/opinion/eye/news/20090813k0000m070126000c.html

Siddle, R. (1996). *Race, resistance and the Ainu of Japan*. New York: Routledge Press.

Siddle, R. (2002). An epoch making event? The 1997 Ainu Cultural Promotion Act and its impact. *Japan Forum 14*(3), 405–423.

Sjöberg, K. (1993). *The return of the Ainu: Cultural mobilization and the practice of ethnicity in Japan*. Chur, Switzerland: Harwood Academic Publishers.

Takemae, E. (2002). *The Allied occupation of Japan*. New York: Continuum International Publishing Group.

Tokachi Shimbun. (2010, January 7). *Children from the Ainu juku "Eteke no kai" travel to Taiwan* (in Japanese). Retrieved from http://www.tokachi.co.jp/news/201001/20100107-0003915.php

United Nations. (2007). United Nations Declaration on the Rights of Indigenous Peoples. Retrieved from www.un.org/esa/socdev/unpfii/documents/DRIPS_en.pdf

United Nations. (2008). Consideration of reports submitted by states parties under Article 40 of the covenant, Human Rights Committee, Ninety-fourth session, Geneva, October 13–31, 2008.

White, R. (1983). *The roots of dependency: Subsistence, environment, and social change among the Choctaws, Pawnees, and Navajos*. Lincoln: University of Nebraska Press.

Winchester, M. (2009, October 12). On the dawn of a new national Ainu policy: The "Ainu as a situation" today. *Japan Focus*. Retrieved from http://www.japanfocus.org/-mark-winchester/3234

Yamada, T. (2001). Gender and cultural revitalisation movements among the Ainu. *Senri Ethnological Series, 56,* 237–257.

Yomiuri Shimbun. (2012, January 16). *Protecting rights and promoting revitalization: Policy proposals announced by "Ainu people's party"* (in Japanese). Retrieved from http://www.yomiuri.co.jp/e-japan/hokkaido/news/20120114-OYT8T00033.htm

Yûki, S. (1997). *Debate* (in Japanese). Tokyo: Sofukan.

CHAPTER 8

Nikkei and Japan's Enduring Cultural Inequities

June A. Gordon

This chapter attempts to demonstrate ways in which enduring patterns of discrimination, once directed predominantly against *Burakumin*, Koreans, and Okinawans, have evolved to envelop *Nikkei,* the "immigrants" who, after two to three generations of living in Latin America, returned "home" to Japan during the 1980s to participate in its late 20th century economic success. My argument is that the line between these two apparently discrete groups, the historically stigmatized and the recently arrived, is not so distinct. Predispositions toward *Nikkei* may in fact be based on the realities and the assumptions surrounding their identities, their status prior to departing Japan, and their reasons for leaving Latin America.

Social attitudes and government policies have created a precarious condition for adult *Nikkei* migrant workers and for their children, both those brought along on the journey and those born in Japan (Ninomiya, 2002; Tsuda, 2003). The situation is complex and growing in urgency, as *Nikkei* who perceive their time in Japan as temporary do not, and often cannot, return to South America due to a host of factors (Higuchi & Tanno, 2003; Linger, 2001; Yamanaka, 2003). The resulting ambivalent state has led to a lack of commitment both by parents and the Japanese government toward the education of *Nikkei* youth (Gordon, 2006a; Shimizu, 2000). One recent response to Japan's inability to incorporate *Nikkei* into their society, their ancestral home, is to pay them to leave. To encourage the process, the government offered unemployed *Nikkei* a severance package of 300,000 yen (approximately \$3,600), with an additional 200,000 yen (approximately. \$2,400) for each family member, if they agree to return to their "country of origin" and surrender the right to reenter Japan.

My interest in this quandary was sparked while conducting research in sections of Hiroshima and Osaka historically known as the *buraku*, districts to which the so-called *Burakumin* have traditionally been restricted (Gordon, 2008b). The longstanding marginal status of *Burakumin,* legalized by the Tokugawa regime of 17th- and 18th-century Japan, set in place status demarcations: nobility, samurai, farmers, artisans, and merchants. All others whose lives were marked by impure work with animals or death, such as hunters, guards, tanners, or refuse disposers, were placed outside and beneath these categories. In spite of efforts to remove the outcaste status of *Burakumin* through various reforms, starting with the Meiji Restoration in the late 19th century and continuing to today, discrimination in work, schooling, residence, and marriage remains a reality in much of Japan (Ikeda, 1999; Nabeshima, 2010).

During my years of research in schools and historically demarcated *Burakumin* communities, I became aware of changes in the composition of the *buraku* as a growing number of immigrants, including *Nikkei*, began to move into these districts (Gordon, 2009). Given the lower cost of housing in these areas, due in part to stigma and in part to location, these districts appealed to the newly arrived, who were not as aware of the legacies of these communities as were local Japanese. Gradually, the population shifted as socioeconomic class began to influence residency more than ascribed identity. These communities embraced a mixture of peoples from around the world, although hierarchical status remained important. Schools that had been set up in the early 1960s as part of a national effort to alleviate discrimination toward *Burakumin* (called *Dôwa kyôiku*, or education for integration), began to see children from South America, China, Vietnam, and Korea fill chairs vacated by *Burakumin.* This shift occurred as some *Burakumin*, who by the 1990s had gained a degree of wealth, began to leave their communities—and often their identities—behind in an attempt to move into mainstream society and "pass" as citizens free of stigma (Gordon, 2008b). This mélange led me to begin an inquiry into ways in which discrimination against a traditionally marginalized people could be transferred onto families and their children through identification with a particular location. I was also interested in how *Dôwa* education could encompass, and be transformed by, the presence and demands of newly arrived residents (Gordon, 2009).

ENTERING COMMUNITIES

In this chapter I focus on the identities of *Nikkei* and Okinawans who traveled to South America in the early 1900s. Specifically, I am interested in how, three generations later, their descendants are haunted by those identities as they return to their ancestral home. I am not asserting that all *Nikkei* or Okinawans have a questionable past. My point is that some are viewed as having one, which creates an unspoken shadow or a question mark over them, enhanced perhaps because most Japanese shun the work they have returned to Japan to do.

In Japan these topics remain largely taboo, making it difficult to access these communities. A discussion with an informant about immigration comes fairly easily, but broaching issues pertaining to *Burakumin* could result in the loss of a friend or contact (Gordon, 2006b). People willing to discuss these issues usually take a distant historical view or hold onto the assumption that identifiable *buraku* communities may exist in the Kansai region around Osaka, Kyoto, and Hiroshima, but not in the Kanto or Tokyo areas. I knew this was not true from my work in low-income communities and *konnankô* ("difficult schools") spread throughout the Kanto region that included *Nikkei* immigrants from South America (Gordon, 2008a).

My original research intentions had nothing to do with the *Burakumin* or with newcomers. Rather, I wanted to better understand how resistance to education played out among low-income youths. My professional colleagues and contacts, however, insisted that such an inquiry must include reference to *Burakumin*. Even though I disagreed, I followed their suggestions into areas I might not otherwise have pursued.

My entrée to a remarkable and intriguing community of scholars and activists also came unexpectedly. Based on my reputation as an ethnographer and researcher on marginalization in urban contexts in America and Britain (Gordon, 2000, 2003), a professor invited me to teach a graduate course on Ethnographic Research Methodology at the University of Tokyo. The seminar was composed of young scholars from South Korea and China, as well as Japanese nationals who were committed to comprehending the "other" Japan, mostly the schools and communities that support the education of low-income children living in difficult circumstances. This opportunity led to my exploration of the interface between historical discrimination against *Burakumin* and contemporary attitudes toward and treatment of immigrants, known generally as newcomers (Shimizu, 2000).

Focusing on the districts of urban Kanagawa to the east of Tokyo, my research revealed that *Burakumin* had not disappeared from the Kanto area. In fact, as I entered deeper into the lives of newcomer families, and in particular those of the South American *Nikkei*, I discovered some historical relationships and ancestral linkages between the *Nikkei* and the *Burakumin*. Additionally, the work brought to my attention the distinctive place of Okinawans in the transnational lives of *Nikkei* now living and working in urban Japan.

MISLEADING APPEARANCES

One sunny Saturday I received an invitation from a social worker to an event that had been billed as a *Nikkei* community gathering. The all-day celebration appeared to offer me the opportunity to talk to several people who had made the journey from South America to Japan for work and presumed wealth. Thanks to the social worker's introductions, I was able to interview 15 people, all of whom had university degrees and worked as professionals in Brazil. The majority, however, claimed that they were currently working in factories that, while offering wages 10 times higher than what they could earn in Brazil, Peru, or Bolivia, trapped them in one of the most expensive cities of the world. Unable to move into mainstream Japanese society due to weak language skills, the demands of their employers, and restrictive contracts, they felt that they were forfeiting their futures in exchange for an unfulfilling present. Most were temporary, nonregular employees with few, if any, benefits. Unable to save money or send remittances "back home" as promised, they and their families were locked into a cycle common to many South American *Nikkei*. Their children, growing up with little familial or financial security, lacked the education needed to survive in a society that viewed *Nikkei* as foreign rather than Japanese.

Not long into the day of interviews, I realized that the event, which featured music, dancing, eating, and skits, was in fact an Okinawan festival. I was sitting in an auditorium among 7,000 individuals, nearly a quarter of the 30,000 Okinawans living in the Yokohama area. My mind reeled as I tried to make sense of who composed this group called *Nikkei*. Who were these people whose ancestors left Japan in the early 1900s for a presumed better life in Brazil, only to return to Japan two to three generations later to work in jobs perceived as undesirable? How can we understand their willingness to put up with blatant discrimination in a place they are supposed to see as their ancestral "home"? What was the relationship between the past treatment of Okinawans and present view of Latin American immigrants?

Further conversations that day with *Nikkei*, as well as Japanese labor brokers and community organizers, made me aware that *Nikkei* hold strong ties to Okinawans as well as to *Burakumin*, two historically stigmatized groups. I then began to wonder whether these enduring identities have impeded the social acceptance and academic success of *Nikkei* youths as they struggle to survive in Japan's homogeneous school system. Could it be that the qualities and images so often attributed to *Nikkei* in Japan are actually an extension of Okinawan or *Burakumin* heritage? Conversely, could these qualities, along with experiences as Japanese outsiders, in fact, be a source of their success in South America? Later, I took questions that arose that day on research trips to Okinawa and Brazil.

THE *NIKKEI* PERSPECTIVE INSIDE BRAZIL

A year later, back home in California, an invitation arrived from a Japanese Brazilian social worker/colleague named Maria whom I had worked with in Kanagawa. She asked me to join her and her daughter on a visit to her family in

São Paolo, where I could further my research on the cycle of *Nikkei* migration to Brazil and back to Japan as migrant workers (*dekasegi*). In total we completed approximately 35 interviews in São Paolo with clergy, immigration officers, museum curators, social workers, government officials, teachers of both Brazilian and Japanese schools, psychologists, and politicians. All had experience working with *dekasegi*, and most had at least one family member who had attempted the journey to Japan for economic gain.

In addition to these interviews, we traveled away from urban areas to visit several *colonias* (agricultural communities established by Japanese immigrants), where we interviewed 16 leaders representing three generations of *Nikkei*. These were people, now living adjacent to the *colonias,* who opted to stay in the countryside to continue to work their productive farms and send their children to the university. Meeting them in the context of their Brazilian towns enabled us to see the breadth of their influence, something that probably would not have been visible to us in conversations with their counterparts who had chosen to live in Japan. As guests in the home of the elder spokesperson for the *colonias*, whose daughter was a colleague of Maria's in Kanagawa, we were able to enter into substantive conversations on complicated, often avoided topics. These included the value of retaining Japanese traditions while living in Brazil, the transfer of status and prejudice from Japan to South America, and ways that social stratification continues to play out in Brazil, as well as among the *Nikkei* from different South American countries, such as Peru, Bolivia, Colombia, and Cuba (Masterson & Funada-Classen, 2004).

TEMPORAL AND GEOGRAPHIC TRAJECTORIES

This research project, spanning Japan, Okinawa, and Brazil, demonstrates that many of the qualities ascribed to *Nikkei* as Brazilian are, in fact, linked to Okinawan culture (Mori, 2003). The festival mentioned earlier is an example of this complex identity formation. The *Nikkei* returned to Japan with their Okinawan heritage and recent Brazilian identity to a country that has never accepted them but is now dependent on their labor (DeCarvalho, 2003b). The tight-knit village orientation of the Japanese, even as they dispersed throughout the world, enabled people to be identified by region of origin, dialect, name, and even caste. Although the men were less inclined to reveal status differentiation ("We all suffered; we do not see differences anymore."), the women, as I spoke with them in their home kitchens on the Brazilian *colonias*, easily identified with those who were *Burakumin* when they left Japan generations ago (DeCarvalho, 2003b). They had not forgotten which families they had prevented their children from entering into through marriage, or whom they entrusted with certain types of work. I found similar awareness of origins and networks in the Tokyo cafés run by Okinawan women married to *Burakumin* whose main clientele are *Nikkei*. Such enclaves, along with Japanese adherence to age-old customs of insider/outsider, have enabled people to know where people of certain "backgrounds" live, work, and survive in the shadows.

Nikkei came to Japan in the late 1980s when Japan was at its pinnacle of production and wealth and when Brazil, along with other Latin American countries, was struggling to feed its people. Unable to provide the labor force needed to meet the demands of industry and leery of immigrant workers from the Middle East, the Japanese government decided to focus on the *Nikkei*. They assumed that their Japanese ancestry would allow them to understand and fit into the cultural landscape (Befu, 2001; DeCarvalho, 2003a).

Responding to an economic pull from Japan and a push from Brazil, the two governments devised legal means to provide access to these new immigrants through a complex and often corrupt system facilitated by labor brokers who recruited and financed the process (Takenaka, 2003). Soon, many thousands of young *Nikkei* were convinced that work in Japan could solve their financial problems and, in the future, enable them to return to Brazil better off than when they left. The *Nikkei* communities of Brazil, as noted in my interviews, often agreed reluctantly to have their young people make the journey, putting temporary sacrifices ahead of promised rewards. The unsavory profits that labor brokers accrued were accepted as a necessary cost of the process.

Although *Nikkei* working in Japanese factories in the 1980s earned much higher wages than they could have at home, they did not enhance their professional skills or education while in Japan. Yet this did not stop even university-educated youths from leaving Latin America in search of economic opportunities in Japan. As one Brazilian businessman shared, "There are ten equally trained and educated individuals, many of them *Nikkei*, ready to step into a vacancy created by those who leave South America." For those living in the stagnated South American economy of the 1990s, wages in Japan continued to appear extraordinarily high when compared with those of Brazil or Peru. Afraid to return to Brazil without anything to show for their efforts, and without any guarantee that they could make a return on their investments, many *Nikkei* remained in Japan far longer than they expected (Yamanaka, 2003). Their families in Brazil, although generally proud of their children's accomplishments, continue to hold out hope that their loved ones will return to the fold unscathed.

But few come home without scars of humiliation, physical and mental disability, and disequilibrium. The number of accidents resulting from working in dangerous, dirty, and difficult jobs, combined with precarious living conditions, have left a generation of middle-class Latin Americans with little to show for their sacrifices. As one *Nikkei* pastor in São Paolo confessed, "What really is heartbreaking is the destruction of the essential basis for family, both those who go and those who stay. So many with separations, infidelities, degrading experiences, they come to me by the thousands in despair. A lost generation; a great spiritual loss."

For many adult *Nikkei*, Brazil remains their home. Japan represents a temporary abode where quick financial gain is presumed to enhance their professional opportunities or benefit their parents. They work hard, often live in low-quality housing, and seldom have contact with their extended families that never emigrated from Japan. These distant relatives often see *Nikkei* as traitors for having left Japan during the hard times, or worse yet, fear that association with them will bring shame. This cold reception, combined with a need for comfort and survival, throws the *Nikkei* together with other immigrants from around the world and with *Burakumin* and Okinawans who have experienced similar stigmatization. For those *Nikkei* who have attempted to shed their *Burakumin* ancestry in South America, or never knew about it, the risks of possible exposure can be intense (DeVos, 1992). This ambivalence of not knowing the reason for the ostracism casts a shadow over *Nikkei* enclaves, making remembrances of Brazil appear warm and welcoming. Yet for many it is difficult to imagine returning home without having at least some success, especially in terms of advancement for their children.

In contrast to their expectations, *Nikkei* have found steadily decreasing levels of income and lengthening periods of residence in Japan, which present serious challenges for their families (Gordon, 2008a). Access to education, for which the *Nikkei* fought so desperately in South America, has been limited for their offspring living in Japan, where the government policies regarding compulsory education do not extend to newcomers (Okano, this volume; Sugino, 2008). And without a high school education, it is difficult to function within Japan, a country that prides itself on its nearly universal high school attendance level. Unable to pass exams in a language few have mastered, most *Nikkei*, in the words of one principal, "lack the basic skills and knowledge to live a decent life in Japan." With the Japanese unemployment rate, even for high school graduates, having reached an all-time high, *Nikkei* youth in Japan, with few skills and minimal education credentials, are doomed to a life of manual work, often under conditions similar to those of their parents (Yasuda, 2003).

During my numerous discussions with social workers, translators, and other cultural intermediaries, I was amazed at how candidly they discussed problems in the *Nikkei* community and how these problems have been exacerbated by the host society. The blame was seldom left solely on the shoulders of any one party.

Maybe this was because the vast majority of these people had family who had made the journey back and forth to South America, often more than once, and knew of the confusion and disillusionment that result from the perpetuation of myths that suggest returning to Japan will solve their problems. The interaction of such economic and social variables tends to be left out of discussions of immigration, regardless of the countries involved. But the case of *Nikkei* differs from other groups. *Nikkei* retain a strong perception that, as Japanese descendants of pure blood, they should have equal access to Japan's economic success (Reis, 2002). It was this quest to gain advantage via higher wages that took many *Nikkei* to Japan in search of illusive wealth, only to end up back in South America, damaged emotionally and physically from laboring in jobs shunned by mainstream Japanese.

HISTORICAL LEGACIES

The cycle of push and pull that in the 21st century has brought *Nikkei* to Japan as migrant workers is not so different from the process that led their ancestors to make dangerous voyages to the Americas a hundred years ago. Living under a hierarchical social structure reinforced by the Tokugawa regime, traditionally marginalized groups, such as *Burakumin* (Amos, 2011), Okinawans, and the rural landless classes, suffered great oppression and poverty (Endoh, 2009). At the end of the 19th century, Japan opened its doors to the world after 200 years of semi-isolation and began to prepare to arm itself as a world power. To further its ambitions, the nation began importing people from its newly acquired colonies, such as Korea, to work as laborers. Also, it allowed its citizens to emigrate, thereby removing from rural areas those Japanese who were perceived as a burden due to overpopulation and underproduction. Faced with poverty and discrimination, the illusion of a better life drew those of the lowest classes and most difficult circumstances into a dangerous and uncertain voyage to the Americas.

Arriving in Latin America in the early 1900s, the *Nikkei* faced backbreaking work and difficult living situations. An agreement between the Brazilian and Japanese governments facilitated the transfer of Japanese immigrants to Brazilian coffee plantations left vacant by the emancipation of African slaves and European immigrants who refused to do difficult agricultural work. The first boat of mostly destitute Japanese left for Brazil in 1908, though the major transnational shift did not occur until the 1930s, when Japan reached the peak of its military power. The complex reasoning behind the selection of who would leave is carefully developed in the work of Endoh (2009), who examines labor unrest, *Burakumin* protest, and government efforts to diffuse both by inducing emigration to Brazil and other South American nations. One crucial indication of *Burakumin* participation in emigration during the 1930s is described in the work of the *Yûwa* Association (later affiliated with *Dôwa kyôiku*):

> From 1928 to 1934, the *Yûwa Jihô*, the national newspaper of the *Yûwa* Association, actively promoted Brazilian-bound migration under state sponsorship. . . . As a representative of the Overseas Emigration Association put it, South American emigration allowed "*Burakumin's* emancipation from the agony of discrimination and despisal" and the elimination of domestic troublemakers. (Endoh, 2009, p. 143)

Endoh (2009), Geiger (2011), and Ito (1996) are clear about the difficulties of quantifying the numbers of *Burakumin* among any of the immigrant waves, but the impact of their presence, both real and perceived, is crucial to understanding contemporary Japanese prejudices toward the *Nikkei*.

Ironically, because Japanese immigrants to South America could not and would not do the work they had been contracted to engage in, they became known as unreliable and of questionable worth (Masterson & Funada-Classen, 2004). This stigma lasted through the war years, creating a situation that reinforced their isolation and distrust of outsiders. Having to rely on themselves, they set up *colonias* that followed Japanese traditions and values, including the retention of social hierarchies that many had longed to escape. Throughout this history, *Burakumin* did not lose their outcaste position, and Okinawans retained their stigma as outsiders.

When opportunities arose to move out of the stifling and stultifying rural *colonias*, it was those who had suffered the greatest amount of oppression, the Okinawans and *Burakumin*, who left to find a better life in Brazil's cities (Lesser, 2003). These people became the entrepreneurs, the shopkeepers, and the ones who negotiated for a living. As a result, their image improved from being untrustworthy to being reliable in both business and trade. Prejudice and the necessity of survival, not only in Japan, but also in the *colonias*, enabled these people to recreate themselves.

Freeing themselves of their stigmatized identities, since both *Burakumin* and Okinawans were viewed by other Japanese Brazilians as tainted, these urban *Nikkei* took on identities that they themselves had been denied or had eschewed back "home" in Japan. In the postwar years, these outcaste groups came to acquire the positive characteristics often associated with Japanese (hardworking, thrifty, clean, polite, and taciturn), and "passed" as regular *Japones* in South America (Amemiya, 1998; Mori, 2003). Such ascribed status within the South American context provided these *Nikkei* with a sense of confidence and assertiveness. Many of them gradually moved into positions of relative privilege, sending their children to university and developing professional middle-class standing.

There were others, however, who suffered emotionally from the trauma of migration to South America, often carrying with them illusions of what life could have been like had they remained in Japan. Forgetting the poverty, destruction of war, and the discrimination many of them experienced while in Okinawa or Japan, parents fed their children images of Japanese society as orderly, polite, democratic, and secure. Such cognitive dissonance was necessary to justify their attempts to retain a separate, acceptable, and detached, if not elite, status within a new and foreign land.

While Japan was being transformed into a modern nation state with new codes of conduct, the Japanese communities formed by the Diaspora remained in suspended animation (Lesser, 2003). Many held onto frozen images of an ideal life in Japan, which most had never experienced. They celebrated Japanese culture and traditions, only distantly related to their lives in Japan. In Brazil, Peru, Bolivia, and Colombia, they established schools where Japanese was spoken along with the local language, either Portuguese or Spanish. In fact, prior to leaving Japan, many of the Okinawans had communicated mostly in their own language, Uchinanchu, or some distinct dialectic version of Japanese (Arakaki, 2002). With these images in mind, the children and grandchildren of these immigrants accepted the possibility of a better life in Japan, particularly when the economic crisis hit South America in the 1980s.

Upon their return to the ancestral homeland, however, *Nikkei* have found their hard-won identities as Japanese to be of little value, in part because of continuing inequities within Japanese society. Denied the Japanese identities they formed in South America, many *Nikkei* youths resist their newly ascribed subservient status in Japan and take on yet another rarified identity, a construction of Brazilian that feeds into Japanese fantasies of the exotic "Other."

Tsuda (2003) and Linger (2001) offer clear depictions of how Japanese nationals perceive newcomers of Japanese ancestry as both foreign and low-class. Many Japanese nationals view *Nikkei* as having descended from failure in Japan and remained failures throughout their time in Brazil (Tsuda, 2003). Their willingness to accept undesirable jobs in Japan only serves to reinforce these assumptions. This view, contradicted by the fact that most *Nikkei* who come to Japan are middle-class and many of them professionals, is derived from the minimal contact that Japanese nationals have with *Nikkei*. The fact that *Nikkei* end up working in factories is due to Japan's need for labor in these areas and a willingness to pay very high wages to *Nikkei* workers who agree to the terms of their temporary contracts, sometimes higher wages than those offered to Japanese nationals (Roth, 2002; Tsuda, 2003).

Yet when faced with choices of identities, the vast majority of the South American *Nikkei* in Japan that I interviewed proudly claimed to be "Brazilian." The assumption is that they would rather be a foreigner than a low-caste Japanese, an ascription some of their ancestors, ironically, may have had to bear. The ability of *Nikkei* to take on the identity of proud Brazilians is in part due to their success in Brazil after two to three generations. Even though *Nikkei* Okinawans and *Burakumin* living in South America continue to experience discrimination from other Japanese immigrants, they have been able to capitalize on the common perception in Brazil that they are, in fact, Japanese. While this pride might sustain them in their personal lives, it does not protect them from ostracism or isolation within mainland Japanese society. Nor does it provide their children with a sane and healthy context within which to create identities that are grounded in the realities of being born and raised in Japan (Gordon, 2008a).

CONCLUSION

Japan is undergoing a process of extensive reform as its society attempts to deal with decades of economic stagnation and the perception that Japanese children lack crucial abilities to participate in an evolving global community (Fujita, 2010). My research questions the effectiveness of educational reforms, embodied in the improvised practices of urban schools attempting to meet the needs of immigrant and other marginalized communities. These policies and practices are constrained by the conventions of national policymaking and by societal norms that demarcate who belongs and who does not. In addition, many educational reforms apply varying policies and levels of support to each Japanese minority group. Although these programs are based on a presumption of ethnic continuity, the complexity of cultural difference has become increasingly apparent (Okano, this volume; Frey, this volume). Educating the children of immigrants has proven a difficult challenge for both parents and teachers as they struggle to accommodate youths whose life chances depend on their performance within a highly structured educational system (Gordon, 2005). Providing access to consistently high-quality education is difficult during the best of times—and profoundly difficult during times of economic duress.

Transnational research enables us to view our worlds differently, seeing commonalities and structures based not on culture alone, but on periods of "development" and orientations to the nation-state. Assumptions and practices that hold a society together at times have created and reified the perception that some external threat or "Other" will dilute or contaminate that which is viewed as the "real" or "pure" essence of that particular entity (Befu, 2001). The presence of this insider/outsider mentality in Japan is most clearly displayed in the treatment of *Burakumin*, as well as Koreans and Okinawans (DeVos, 1992). Guiding this work is a critical interrogation of the ideology of Japanese racial and cultural homogeneity. That ideology has undermined the recognition of longstanding minority groups and continues to shape the nation's treatment of immigrant communities, including the education provided to their children.

Beginning in the late 19th century and continuing throughout the postwar period, Japanese citizens sought education, employment, and investment in many other nations. The resulting experience profoundly changed those who left Japan as well as those who have returned, whether after a few months or a few generations. The restrictions experienced by these individuals and groups, combined with evolving definitions of Japanese identity, provoked a national debate that drew attention to the education of marginalized youth. As in other contexts, the effects of marginalization experienced by newcomer families in Japan have both reinforced foreign identities and intensified pressure for assimilation. Given the pattern of migration, stratification, and resistance, the Okinawan identity in mainland Japan today is a mixture of exotic adoration in popular culture and marginalization in everyday life. For *Burakumin* it is one of fading glory, a fight fought through *Dôwa* education reforms. Those reforms fell out of favor as Japan experienced pressure to move away from policies that targeted specific ethnic groups, and instead embrace its newly arrived brethren, whether they be from China, Korea, or South America.

While this homogenized treatment of minorities within a global context might be viewed as a positive outcome, it can also mean a dilution, not only of services, but of identity that could easily leave the two most traditionally stigmatized groups, *Burakumin* and Okinawans, outside of popular discourse (Gordon, 2008b). The situation is exacerbated when *Nikkei* display prejudice against Burakumin and Okinawans as the *Nikkei* themselves try to hide their own ancestry in the hopes of gaining greater acceptability in their "homeland." The findings of this research leave me with many questions, two of which I close with now: Would the elimination of discrimination against this mythical group, the *Burakumin,* stigmatized for hundreds of years as "impure or polluted," require Japan to accept its historical legacy of inequality and class distinctions? And if so, how would this acceptance influence Japan's response to its immigrant population and its changing role in the world order?

REFERENCES

Amemiya, K. K. (1998). *Being "Japanese" in Brazil and Okinawa.* Occasional Paper No. 13. Tokyo: Japan Policy Research Institute.

Amos, T. D. (2011). *Embodying difference: The making of Burakumin in modern Japan.* Honolulu: University of Hawai'i Press.

Arakaki, R. K. (2002). Theorizing on the Okinawan Diaspora. In R. K. Nakasone (Ed.), *Okinawan Diaspora* (pp. 26–43). Honolulu: University of Hawai'i Press.

Befu, H. (2001). *Hegemony of homogeneity: An anthropological analysis of Nihonjinron.* Melbourne, Australia: Trans Pacific Press.

DeCarvalho, D. (2003a). *Nikkei* communities in Japan. In R. Goodman, C. Peach, A. Takenaka, & P. White (Eds.), *Global Japan: The experience of Japan's new immigrant and overseas communities* (pp. 195–208). London and New York: RoutledgeCurzon.

DeCarvalho, D. (2003b). *Migrants and identity in Japan and Brazil.* New York: RoutledgeCurzon.

DeVos, G. A. (1992). *Social cohesion and alienation: Minorities in the United States and Japan.* Boulder, CO: Westview Press.

Endoh, T. (2009). *Exporting Japan: Politics of emigration toward Latin America.* Urbana and Chicago: University of Illinois Press.

Fujita, H. (2010). Whither Japanese schooling? Educational reforms and their impact on ability formation and educational opportunity. In J. A. Gordon, H. Fujita, T. Kariya, & G. LeTendre (Eds.), *Challenges to Japanese education: Economics, reform, and human rights* (pp. 17–53). New York: Teachers College Press.

Geiger, A. (2011). *Subverting exclusion: Transpacific encounters with race, caste, and borders, 1885–1928.* New Haven, CT: Yale University Press.

Gordon, J. A. (2000). *The color of teaching.* London: Falmer Press.

Gordon, J. A. (2003). A shoelace left untied: Teachers confront class and ethnicity in a city of Northern England. *The Urban Review, 35*(3), 191–215.

Gordon, J. A. (2005). Inequities in Japanese urban schools, *The Urban Review, 37*(1), 49–62.

Gordon, J. A. (2006a). Assigned to the margins: Teachers for immigrant communities in Japan. *Teaching and Teacher Education: An International Journal of Research and Studies* (Australia), *22*(7), 766–776.

Gordon, J. A. (2006b). From liberation to human rights: Challenges for teachers of the *Burakumin* in Japan. *Race, Ethnicity and Education, 9*(2), 183–202.

Gordon, J. A. (2008a). Transnational migration and identity: Brazil and Japan share a work force. In J. Dosch & O. Jacob (Eds.), *Asia and Latin America: The encounter of two continents. Political, economic and social dynamics* (pp. 70–85). London: Routledge.

Gordon, J. A. (2008b). *Japan's outcaste youth: Education for liberation.* Colorado Springs, CO: Paradigm Publishers.

Gordon, J. A. (2009). Children of the *danchi*: A Japanese primary school for newcomers. *Ethnography and Education* (United Kingdom), *4*(2), 165–179.

Higuchi, N., & Tanno, K. (2003). What's driving Brazil-Japan migration? The making and re-making of the Brazilian niche in Japan. *International Journal of Japanese Sociology, 12*, 33–47.

Ikeda, H. (1999). *Buraku children and their cultural identity.* Paper given at International Conference of the Japan Society of Educational Sociology, Tokyo.

Ito, H. (pseudonym). (1996). Japan's outcastes in the United States. In G. DeVos & H. Wagatsuma (Eds.), *Japan's invisible race: Caste in culture and personality* (pp. 200–221). Berkeley and Los Angeles: University of California Press.

Lesser, J. (2003). Japanese, Brazilians, *Nikkei*: A short history of identity building and homemaking. In J. Lesser (Ed.), *Searching for home abroad: Japanese Brazilians and transnationalism* (pp. 47–66). Durham and London: Duke University Press.

Linger, D. T. (2001). *No one home: Brazilian selves remade in Japan*. Palo Alto, CA: Stanford University Press.

Masterson, D. M., & Funada-Classen, S. (2004). *The Japanese in Latin America*. Urbana and Chicago: University of Illinois Press.

Mori, K. (2003). Identity transformations among Okinawans and their descendants in Brazil. In J. Lesser (Ed.), *Searching for home abroad: Japanese Brazilians and transnationalism* (pp. 47–66). Durham and London: Duke University Press.

Nabeshima, Y. (2010). Invisible racism in Japan: Impact on academic achievement of minority children. In J. A. Gordon, H. Fujita, T. Kariya, & G. LeTendre (Eds.), *Challenges to Japanese education: Economics, reform, and human rights* (pp. 109–130). New York: Teachers College Press.

Ninomiya, M. (2002). "The dekasegi phenomenon and the education of Japanese Brazilian children in Japanese schools." In L. R. Hirabayashi, A. Kikumura-Yano, & J. Hirabayashi (Eds.), *New worlds, new lives: Globalization and people of Japanese descent in the Americas and from Latin America in Japan* (pp. 246–260). Palo Alto, CA: Stanford University Press.

Reis, M. E. F. (2002). *Brazilians in Japan: The human tie in the bilateral relationship*. São Paulo: Kaleidus-Primus. Second Revised Edition, Organized by Masato Ninomiya.

Roth, J. H. (2002). *Brokered homeland: Japanese Brazilian migrants in Japan*. Ithaca and London: Cornell University Press.

Shimizu, K. (2000). The reverse side of "Nippon": "Dekassegui" South Americans of Japanese descent and Japanese schools. *Sociology of Education Research Seminar, 66*, 21–39.

Sugino, T. (2008). *Nikkei Brazilians at a Brazilian school in Japan*. Tokyo: Keio University Press.

Takenaka, A. (2003). Paradoxes of ethnicity-based immigration: Peruvian and Japanese-Peruvian migrants in Japan. In R. Goodman, C. Peach, A. Takenaka, & P. White (Eds.), *Global Japan: The experience of Japan's new immigrant and overseas communities* (pp. 222–236). London and New York: RoutledgeCurzon.

Tsuda, T. (2003). *Strangers in the ethnic homeland*. New York: Columbia University Press.

Yamanaka, K. (2003). "I will go home, but when?": Labor migration and circular diaspora formation by Japanese Brazilians in Japan." In M. Douglass & G. S. Roberts (Eds.), *Japan and global migration: Foreign workers and the advent of a multicultural society* (pp. 123–152). Honolulu: University of Hawai'i Press.

Yasuda, Y. (2003). High school graduates who cannot find work, *Japan Echo 30*(2), 56–62.

PART IV

The Outcome of Educational Reform

Evaluating Policies Introduced to Mitigate Inequality and Expand Opportunity

CHAPTER 9

Growing Educational Inequality in Japan During the 2000s

Hyunjoon Park & Yeon-Jin Lee

In response to growing criticism of the standardized, centralized, and test-focused system, Japanese education has undergone some major changes in its structure, curricula, and overall orientation. In particular, the 2002 reforms (announced in 1998), often described as "*yutori kyôiku*" (relaxed education or low-pressure education), have produced significant changes in the schools. Major components of these reform measures include full implementation of the 5-day school week, reduced class hours especially for core academic subjects, and introduction of integrated studies courses that cut across traditional divisions of academic subjects and aim to enhance student interest and motivation for learning through hands-on experiences (Bjork, 2009; Bjork & Tsuneyoshi, 2005). The fundamental goal of *yutori kyôiku* is to shift the overall direction of Japanese education away from "traditional" curricula and instruction toward nurturing self-motivation and self-direction for study, individuality, and independent thinking (Tsuneyoshi, 2004).

Even before the scheduled implementation of the reform in 2002, however, critics from diverse ideological positions warned that *yutori kyôiku* would weaken the academic performance of Japanese students. The release of the PISA 2003 (Programme for International Student Assessment) results intensified the debates on "educational crisis" in Japan (Takayama, 2007, 2008). Declines in the international rankings and average scores on mathematics and reading among Japanese 15-year-old students from PISA 2000 to 2003 stirred widespread concern about the diminishing academic performance of Japanese students, and raised serious questions about the potential consequences of the *yutori* reform. As Takayama (2008) illustrates, compared with their overall positive reactions regarding the PISA 2000 results, major Japanese newspapers responded to PISA 2003 with sensational and provocative articles that fed into the national "panic" about the declining academic abilities of Japanese students.

Opponents of relaxed education, concerned that reduced school hours and decreased emphasis on academic achievement would undermine the academic abilities of Japanese students, often argued for a return to the traditional system that emphasized high academic standards (Tsuneyoshi, 2004). On the other hand, those who had long been critical of this traditional approach tended to reject the crisis diagnosis, instead emphasizing the issues of low motivation to study and lack of engagement in academics, and argued that these problems were caused by the high-pressure and test-oriented system (Tsuneyoshi, 2004).

In this chapter we do not aim to summarize the ideological stances or frameworks of those who criticize or defend recent educational reforms. Instead, we are interested in assessing whether or not the academic performance of Japanese students has actually changed since those reforms were adopted. The key to answering this question, we believe, is to use better data and analyses than have been used in previous studies of academic achievement in Japan.

Interestingly, scholars who speak in favor of and against the 2002 educational reform often base their arguments on patterns in student achievement data. However, as several individuals have pointed out, few high-quality sources of data that could be used to trace temporal trends in Japanese student academic performance exist. And selective and superficial uses of data, often resulting in misrepresentation of the trends, continue to dominate public discourse. Reports on the PISA 2003 results clearly illustrate this trend (Takayama, 2007, 2008).

In this sense, our study echoes earlier studies such as Kariya (2001, 2002) that attempted to ground trends in academic performance of Japanese students in strong empirical evidence. However, our study differs from those earlier studies in some major ways. First, our investigation of trends in academic performance of Japanese students improves upon previous literature by using high-quality student achievement data that are comparable over time. Specifically, we compare levels of student reading literacy across 2000 to 2006 PISA surveys.[1] Most previous studies relied on nonnational samples of students and on measures of academic performance that are not directly comparable over time, making it difficult to precisely identify trends in academic performance. PISA provides student scores on the reading literacy scale that are directly comparable over time.[2]

In addition, we examine how student attitudes toward mathematics have changed between 1999 and 2007 by using data from another international survey of student achievement, the Trends in International Mathematics and Science Study (TIMSS). A nationally representative survey of 8th-grade students that is administered every 4 years, TIMSS is a dependable source of data that can be used to examine trends in student outcomes. Studies published during the 1990s revealed a decline in academic performance of Japanese students and also in student interest, effort, and motivation for study (Kariya, 2001, 2002). Focusing on the level of student general attitudes toward mathematics, we explore whether the trend in the 1990s continued into the 2000s. Due to the lack of data on attitudes toward reading (or language education), we focus on attitudes toward mathematics.

Second, our study directly addresses trends before and after the adoption of the 2002 *yutori* education reform. It is true that there is some continuity between the 2002 educational reform and earlier reforms in regard to overall direction. Given that debates about the "educational crisis" intensified after the adoption of the *yutori* reforms and the release of the PISA results in the early 2000s, however, we choose to analyze trends in academic performance in the 2000s with reference to debates about the education crisis rather than those observed in earlier periods. We acknowledge that the time periods we examine with PISA (2000–2006) and TIMSS (1999–2007) are relatively short and perhaps it is too early to draw any definite conclusions about the impacts of the recent educational reforms. On the other hand, analyzing these data can provide some preliminary insights into the effects of reforms implemented in the early 2000s.

Finally, we examine trends in academic performance separately for students at the higher and lower ends of the academic achievement spectrum. In other words, we do not assume that educational policies will have uniform effects on students of different abilities or of different family backgrounds (Park, forthcoming). Instead, we explore how *yutori kyôiku* has produced differential outcomes for different groups of students. Research that examined changing educational outcomes in Japan during the 1990s highlighted more substantial declines in various educational outcome measures among low-performing and/or socioeconomically disadvantaged students than their counterparts of high-achieving and/or socioeconomically advantaged students (Kariya, 2001, 2002). Park (forthcoming) identifies a similar pattern in PISA and TIMSS mathematics scores.

CHANGING DISTRIBUTIONS OF READING PERFORMANCE

Table 9.1 presents basic descriptive statistics that illustrate how the reading performance of 15-year-old students has changed across three PISA surveys administered in Japan.[3] Most Japanese students who take the PISA tests are first-year high school students from academic as well as vocational high schools. PISA 2000 measured reading performance among students in OECD (Organization for Economic Co-operation and Development) countries on a scale with a mean of 500 points and a standard deviation of 100 points. Reading scores in PISA 2000, 2003, and 2006 are all comparable.

Table 9.1. Means and Percentile Scores in PISA Reading Scores,
Japan 2000–2006

	2000	**2003**	**2006**
Mean Scores	522	498	498
Percentile Scores			
10th percentile	407	355*	361*
90th percentile	625	624	623
Difference (90–10)	218	269	262
Total variance	7306	11297	10918
Within-school variance	3910	6253	5410
Between-school variance	3396	5044	5508
% of between-school variance	46	45	50

* Indicates that this value is significantly different from the 10th-percentile score in 2000.

One significant trend that emerges from these data is that mean scores substantially declined between PISA 2000 and the later versions of the survey. In 2006, the average reading score (498) was 24 points lower than the average score in 2000. Looking at the trend separately for the lower (10th percentile) and higher (90th percentile) ends of the distribution, however, reveals that the decline in reading performance was not uniform. The mean score for students in the 10th percentile declined substantially, from 407 points in 2000 to 361 points in 2006, while the score for students in the 90th percentile remained virtually constant. Although most newspapers and public discussions of PISA results focused on average scores for the entire population of test-takers, the more significant change was the growing gap between high- and low-performing students. Park (forthcoming) observes a similar pattern in PISA mathematics and science scores.

Changes over time in the distribution of test scores confirm growing differences among Japanese students. Total variance can be broken down into two different elements: within-school and between-school variance. Within-school variance indicates the differences among students within schools; between-school variance pertains to variation due to school differences. Table 9.1 shows that both between-school and within-school variance increased in Japan between 2000 and 2006. However, the increase in between-school variance was more substantial than the increase in within-school variance. The proportion of total variance due to differences between schools increased from 46% in 2000 to 50% in 2006. The finding that half of total variance in reading was due to between-school differences highlights comparably high degrees of difference in student performance among Japanese high schools (Park, forthcoming).

FAMILY BACKGROUND AND STUDENT PERFORMANCE IN READING

Next, we turn our focus to how reading scores are connected to family background factors and how those relationships have changed over time. One important advantage of PISA surveys over previous international surveys is that PISA collected a variety of information related to socioeconomic background of student families, including parental education and occupation (Buchmann, 2002). In PISA 2000, unfortunately, a large number of Japanese students did not answer questions about the education levels and occupations of their parents, which prevented us from using those traditional measures of family background. Instead, we use three alternative measures that tap into related but different aspects of family background and home environment.

The first indicator of family background we rely on is the number of books available in a student's home. It is debatable whether the number of books in the home is a reliable proxy for more traditional measures of family socioeconomic status (SES) such as parental education and occupation, or perhaps the measure reflects a separate dimension of family environment, i.e., home literacy environments. However, numerous studies have shown that the number of books in a home is closely associated with child's academic achievement and educational attainment (years of education and transitions to the next level of school) in a variety of contexts (Buchmann, 2002; Evans, Kelly, Sikora, & Treiman 2010; Park, 2008; Wößmann, 2003). We classify students into three groups: those with 0–10 books, 11–100 books, and 101 or more books.[4]

The second measure of family environment, family's possession of cultural items, pertains specifically to cultural resources available in the student's home that potentially affect academic performance. This aspect of family background has been widely studied in relation to children's educational outcomes in research on cultural capital (Bourdieu, 1984; DiMaggio, 1982). In both PISA 2000 and 2006, students were asked to indicate whether each of the following cultural items was in their home: classic literature, books of poetry, and works of art (yes or no). By adding students' answers to each question, we constructed the variable of the number of cultural items available in the home, with values of 0, 1, 2, and 3. The higher values indicate higher levels of cultural resources available in the student's home.

We also consider educational resources available in the student's home as an indicator of family background. Although availability of educational resources does not necessarily indicate the actual use of those resources, evidence suggests that educational resources available in the home are positively related to children's educational outcomes (Teachman, 1987). In both PISA 2000 and 2006, students were asked to indicate whether the following items were available in their home: dictionary, quiet place to study, desk for study, and textbooks (books to help with your schoolwork). Combining student answers to the four questions, which had two responses (yes or no), we created the variable of the number of educational resources in the home, with values that ranged from 0 to 4. However, we found that more than 70% of the sampled students in each PISA study had all four educational resources. Therefore, we combined the first four categories (0–3) to distinguish from the last category of all four items. Panel A in Table 9.2 presents the distributions (percentages) of three family background variables. (Panel B does so for other variables used in our analyses, which will be introduced below.)

Figures 9.1–9.3 illustrate how reading scores differ among students from varying family backgrounds with respect to each indicator, and also how the relationship between reading performance and family background changed between 2000 and 2006. Figure 9.1 shows higher scores among students with more books in the home in PISA 2000: Those with 101 or more books scored 544 points on average, 56 points higher than their counterparts with 10 or fewer books. Reflecting the decline in the average score in PISA 2006, each group of students (with respect to the number of books in the home) earned lower scores in 2006 than in 2000; however, the decline was more substantial among those with 10 or fewer books than those with 101 or more books. Specifically, in 2006 students with 10 or fewer books scored 439 points, 49 points lower than their counterparts in 2000. The decline (29 points) in reading performance among students with 101 or more, however, was smaller than the decline among students with 10 or fewer books. In other words, the difference in reading performance between students who had the largest and smallest numbers of books increased from 56 points in 2000 to 76 points in 2006. Interestingly, students in the middle (11–100 books) showed the smallest decline between 2000 and 2006.

A similar pattern is found for another indicator of family background, cultural resources in the home. In Figure 9.2, students who had more cultural items in their homes scored higher on the reading test in PISA 2000: Students who had none of the three cultural items scored 492 points, 53 points lower than students who had all of the three cultural items. Students showed poorer performance in 2006 than in 2000 across all groups. However, the decline was particularly evident among those who had fewer numbers of cultural items. The average score of those who had none of the three cultural items declined 25 points from 492

Table 9.2. Distributions (Percentages) of Key Variables and the Sample Size

	SURVEY/YEAR	
A. Family Background	**PISA 2000**	**PISA 2006**
Number of books in home		
0–10 books	12.5%	9.6%
11–100 books	45.2%	46.3%
101 or more books	42.4%	44.1%
Sample N	*5,064*	*5,931*
Number of cultural items		
0 items	24.7%	37.4%
1 item	26.4%	26.9%
2 items	25.3%	20.8%
3 items	23.6%	14.9%
Sample N	*4,971*	*5,881*
Number of educational resource items		
0–3 items	21.1%	27.5%
4 items	78.9%	72.5%
Sample N	*4,975*	*5,920*
B. Students' Attitudes Toward Mathematics	**TIMSS 1999**	**TIMSS 2007**
I enjoy learning mathematics		
Disagree a lot	14.5%	17.9%
Disagree a little	46.7%	42.5%
Agree a little	32.8%	30.4%
Agree a lot	6.1%	9.2%
Sample N	*4,680*	*4,265*

(continued)

Table 9.2. *(continued)*

	SURVEY/YEAR	
I like mathematics		
Disagree a lot	14.1%	23.4%
Disagree a little	37.9%	40.3%
Agree a little	39.5%	26.5%
Agree a lot	8.6%	9.9%
Sample N	*4,679*	*4,281*
Mathematics is boring		
Disagree a lot	9.4%	12.4%
Disagree a little	48.7%	46.8%
Agree a little	32.9%	27.9%
Agree a lot	9.0%	12.9%
Sample N	*4,679*	*4,267*

Figure 9.1. PISA Reading Scores and Number of Books in Home by Year

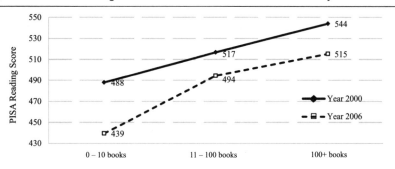

138

Figure 9.2. PISA Reading Scores and Cultural Resources in Home by Year

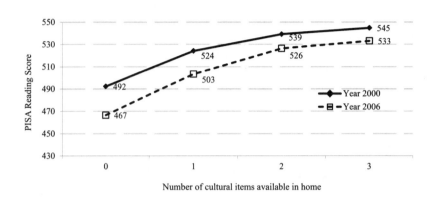

Figure 9.3. PISA Reading Scores and Educational Resources in Home by Year

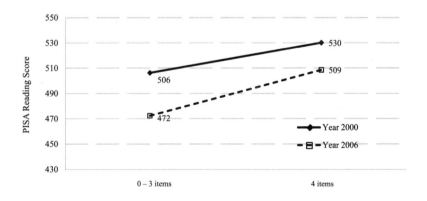

in 2000 to 467 in 2006, while the average score of those who had all three items declined only 12 points. Consequently, the performance gap between students at the higher and lower ends of cultural resources in the home became larger in 2006 (66 points) than in 2000 (53 points).

Finally, Figure 9.3 reveals a trend similar to that captured in Figures 9.1 and 9.2 with respect to educational resources in the student's home: The gap in reading performance between students who had all four educational resource items and their counterparts with three or fewer items became larger between 2000 and 2006, due to the more substantial decline among students with three or fewer items than among students with all four items.

In short, across three different aspects of family background, we observe a consistent pattern of the change between 2000 and 2006: a growing achievement gap in reading between students from advantaged families and their peers from disadvantaged families.

TRENDS IN STUDENT ATTITUDES TOWARD MATHEMATICS

Next we move to student attitudes toward mathematics. We are particularly interested in exploring whether trends in student attitudes toward mathematics are consistent with the trends in reading performance discussed in the previous section, i.e., a more significant decline among students from disadvantaged families than their counterparts from advantaged families. Ideally, we would have compared student attitudes toward reading, given our focus on reading performance in this study, but unfortunately PISA 2000 and 2006 do not use common measures of student attitudes toward reading. In fact, no comparable measure is available for mathematics or science, either. Therefore, we had to rely on a different data sources to address the trends in student attitudes toward studying: the Trends in International Mathematics and Science Study (TIMSS).

TIMSS is an international survey of student performance on mathematics and science among 4th- and 8th-grade students in a number of countries. It began in 1995 and has been repeated every 4 years since then. In this study, we analyzed changes in attitudes toward mathematics among 8th-grade students between 1999 and 2007.[5] Differences in student attitudes toward mathematics between TIMSS 1999 and 2007 should offer valuable insight into the impact of *yutori* educational reform on students' attitudes toward mathematics.

Three questions included in both TIMSS 1999 and 2007 address student attitudes toward mathematics. In TIMSS 2007, students were asked to indicate the extent to which they agree with the following statements on a four-point scale: 1) I enjoy learning mathematics, 2) I like mathematics, and 3) Mathematics is boring.

In TIMSS 1999, the same questions were asked, though different wordings and scales were used.[6] Although we recognize those differences, we believe that the questions and measurements are comparable for TIMSS 1999 and 2007. We reversed the coding so that higher values indicate more positive attitudes for the questions, "I enjoy learning mathematics" and "I like mathematics," while higher values for the question "Mathematics is boring" indicate more negative attitudes.

Because the outcome variables we use to gauge attitudes toward mathematics are ordinal, we applied an ordered logistic regression to examine how family background, which is measured by the number of books in the home, is related to the student attitudes toward mathematics (Long, 1997). Table 9.3 presents the results of ordered logistic regression for each of the three attitude measures. Note that higher values indicate more positive attitudes for "I enjoy learning mathematics" and "I like mathematics" but more negative attitudes for "Mathematics is

Table 9.3. Results of Ordered Logistic Regression for Students' Attitudes Toward Mathematics

	I Enjoy Learning Mathematics	I Like Mathematics	Mathematics Is Boring
Year (reference = 1999)			
2007	−0.362*	−0.770***	0.240^
Number of books (reference = Small [0–10 books])			
Medium (11–100 books)	0.207**	0.314***	−0.106
Large (101+ books)	0.381***	0.471***	−0.097
Number of books X Year			
Medium X Year 2007	0.300*	0.221^	−0.278*
Large X Year 2007	0.342*	0.204	−0.345*
Gender (reference = Male)			
Female	−0.432***	−0.635***	0.253***
Gender X Year			
Female X Year 2007	0.182*	0.268**	−0.032
N	8,945	8,960	8,946

*** $p < .001$ ** $p < .01$ * $p < .05$ ^ $p < .10$

boring." Therefore, the positive coefficients for the analysis of enjoying learning mathematics mean that there is a higher likelihood of having more positive attitudes toward mathematics. For example, the positive coefficient 0.381 for students with 101 or more books in the analysis of enjoying learning mathematics indicates that the odds of having more positive attitudes toward mathematics are higher for students with 101 or more books than for students with 10 or fewer books (the reference category). Students whose families have a larger number of books tend to have more positive attitudes than students whose families have a smaller number of books. Given that the year 1999 is the reference and the category of 0–10 books is the reference, the negative coefficient, -0.362, for the year 2007 means that the likelihood of having positive attitudes toward mathematics is lower for students with the smallest number of books in 2007 than their counterparts in 1999.

Given that the number of books is positively associated with the likelihood of having more positive attitudes, the positive coefficients in the interaction terms means that in 2007 larger gaps existed in the odds of having more positive attitudes between the small number and the medium number of books, and between the small number and the large number of books. For the outcome of "I enjoy learning mathematics," the interaction terms between the two categories of books and the year 2007 are statistically significant and positive, suggesting that the gaps by the number of books in the odds of having more positive attitudes toward mathematics increased between 1999 and 2007. The interaction terms are not statistically significant at the 95% level for the outcome of "I like mathematics." However, the interaction term between the medium number and the small number of books is positively significant at the 90% level, and the interaction term between the large number of and the small number of books is positive, similar to the pattern for the outcome of "I enjoy learning mathematics."

Because higher values indicate more negative attitudes for the outcome of "Mathematics is boring," the positive coefficient of the year 2007 means that the odds of having more negative attitudes toward mathematics are higher in 2007 than 1999. The results are similar to the other two measures of attitudes toward mathematics. Interestingly, the negative coefficients of medium and large numbers of books (compared to the small number of books) are not significant, suggesting that in 1999 there was no evident difference in the likelihood of agreeing to the statement "Mathematics is boring" among students with different numbers of books. However, the interaction terms between the two categories of books and the year 2007 are both significant and negative. The results indicate that in 2007 the odds of having more negative attitudes became significantly lower for students with larger numbers of books than students with the smallest number of books. Stated differently, although the gaps in the odds of having more negative attitudes toward mathematics were not substantial among students with different numbers of books in 1999, the gaps became more evident in 2007, when students with the smallest number of books showed higher odds of having more negative attitudes toward mathematics.

CONCLUSION

For both reading performance and attitudes toward mathematics of Japanese secondary school students, a clear picture of trends emerges from the analyses conducted in this study. The decline of reading performance along with the educational reform since the early 2000s mostly happened at the lower end of the distribution. Moreover, students with disadvantaged family backgrounds suffered more severely than their peers from more advantaged families. In a separate study of math performance, Park (forthcoming) observed similar trends. Not only in reading performance but also in student attitudes toward mathematics, we could find the similar trend of much more substantial decline among disadvantaged students than among advantaged students. These findings are particularly significant given that on multiple measures of academic ability and motivation, the gaps between high-achieving and/or socioeconomically advantaged students and their counterparts of low-achieving and/or socioeconomically disadvantaged students continued to become larger during the 2000s. As mentioned above, some earlier studies already showed the similar trends during the 1990s.

It goes beyond this study to answer what features of the educational reform since the early 2000s could be responsible for the trend of growing gaps in educational outcomes. Finding the similar trend in mathematics performance, Park (forthcoming) pointed out potentially negative impacts of increasingly differentiated and individualized curricula for low-achieving students. As Fujita (2010) emphasizes, the educational reform since the early 2000s has not only changed curriculum contents as focused in debates on the *yutori* reform, but importantly it has also affected structure of Japanese schools. The Ministry of Education now promotes differentiated learning, ability grouping, and school choice. These practices were rare before the educational reform. Yet their effects are rarely touched upon in discussions about declining academic achievement in Japan.

As Park (forthcoming) summarizes, several studies of curriculum tracking in other countries demonstrate that increased differentiation of learning opportunities through within-school tracking such as ability grouping or between-school tracking tends to increase educational inequality (Gamoran, 2010; Oakes, 1985). Despite the proclaimed benefits of separating students into different classes or schools according to their perceived academic abilities, research on this topic indicates that low-achieving students actually lose ground when they are grouped into classes or schools separate from high-achieving students (Gamoran, 2010; Hoffer, 1992). This research points to the need for more research that examines how increased differentiation of learning opportunities is affecting student achievement in Japan.

Changes in school structure could help to explain the recent exacerbation of gaps between high- and low-performing students—and perhaps between socioeconomically advantaged and disadvantaged students. Other important factors to consider include the reduced number of hours students spend in school each week and the expansion of elective coursework that were implemented in 2002. These changes, which reduce low-achieving students' exposure to core academic subjects, could be partially responsible for the increasing gaps in student achievement that we highlight in this chapter (Kariya, 2001, 2002; Park, forthcoming). Although we cannot draw any definite conclusions about the relative influence of any of these factors based on the findings of this study, we do think that the multiple sources of data that document steady declines in academic achievement and interest in studying among low-achieving students raise important questions about educational inequality that should concern education researchers and policymakers.

NOTES

1. Although PISA 2009 data are also publically available, we decided not to include PISA 2009 for the analysis in this study. In PISA 2009, none of private schools was selected among academic high schools and technical colleges (first 3 years). On the other hand, 95% of vocational high school students in PISA 2009 attended private schools. This pattern of sampled students by private and public schools is extremely deviant from the reality and also from PISA 2006. In PISA 2006, the majority (88%) of vocational high school students actually attended public, not private, schools, while as many as 35% of academic high school students attended private schools. The Japanese government statistics in 2010 show the similar pattern as PISA 2006 (Japan Statistical Year Book, 2012).

2. This study of changes in reading literacy performance is a companion of Park's forthcoming study of changes in mathematics using the same data source of PISA (and another source, TIMSS).

3. A brief overview of PISA (and TIMSS) surveys in regard to their target population, sampling, measures, and others variables can be found in Park (forthcoming).

4. Refer to Park (forthcoming) for the relationship of the number of books in the home with student performance in mathematics. PISA 2000 and 2006 surveys have different categories of the number of books in the home from which students select. In order to have the same categories between PISA 2000 and 2006, the operationalization used in this study seems most plausible (see Park, forthcoming).

5. Both 7th- and 8th-grade students were included for Japan in TIMSS 1995, while only 8th-grade students were sampled since then. TIMSS 2007 is the latest survey for which data are available publicly.

6. In TIMSS 1999, students were asked to indicate their levels of agreement to each item, "I enjoy learning mathematics" and "Mathematics is boring" (along with other items), under the question, "What do you think about mathematics?" Students were required to select one of the following four categories: strongly agree, agree, disagree, strongly disagree. In 2007, the categories were: agree a lot, agree a little, disagree a little, disagree a lot. A question in a separate section asked students, "How much do you like" mathematics (and science), with four choices of which to select one: like a lot, like, dislike, dislike a lot.

REFERENCES

Bjork, C. (2009). Local implementation of Japan's integrated studies reform: A preliminary analysis of efforts to decentralize the curriculum. *Comparative Education, 45*, 23–44.

Bjork, C., & Tsuneyoshi, R. (2005, April). Educational reform in Japan: Competing visions for the Future. *Phi Delta Kappan, 86*, 619–626.

Bourdieu, P. (1984). *Distinction: A social critique of the judgment of taste*. Cambridge, MA: Harvard University Press.

Buchmann, C. (2002). Measuring family background in international studies of education: Conceptual issues and methodological challenges. In A. C. Porter & A. Gamoran (Eds.), *Methodological advances in cross-national surveys of educational achievement* (pp. 150–197). Washington, DC: National Academy Press.

DiMaggio, P. (1982). Cultural capital and school success: The impact of status culture participation on the grade of U.S. high school students. *American Sociological Review, 47*, 189–201.

Evans, M. D. R., Kelly, J., Sikora, J., & Treiman, D. J. (2010). Family scholarly culture and educational success: Books and schooling in 27 countries. *Research in Social Stratification and Mobility, 28*, 171–197.

Fujita, H. (2010). Wither Japanese schooling? Educational reforms and their impact on ability formation and educational opportunity. In J.A. Gordon, H. Fujit, T. Kariya, & G. LeTendre. (2009). (Eds.), *Challenges to Japanese education: Economics, reform, and human rights* (pp. 17–53). New York: Teachers College Press.

Gamoran, A. (2010). Tracking and inequality: New directions for research and practice. In M. Apple, S. J. Ball, & L. A. Gandin (Eds.), *The Routledge international handbook of the sociology of education* (pp. 213–228). London: Routledge.

Hoffer, T. (1992). Middle school ability grouping and student achievement in science and mathematics. *Educational Evaluation and Policy Analysis, 14*, 205–227.

Japan Statistical Yearbook. (2012). Table 22-6. Students of upper secondary schools by course (regular course). Available from http://www.stat.go.jp/english/data/nenkan/1431-22.htm

Kariya, T. (2001). *Education in crisis and stratified Japan* (in Japanese). Tokyo: Yushindo.

Kariya, T. (2002). *The illusion of educational reform* (in Japanese). Tokyo: Chikuma Shobo.

Long, J. S. (1997). *Regression models for categorical and limited dependent variables.* Thousand Oaks, CA: Sage Publications.

Oakes, J. (1985). *Keeping track: How schools structure inequality,* New Haven, CT: Yale University Press.

Park, H. (Forthcoming). *Re-evaluating education in Japan and Korea.* Routledge.

Park, H. (2008). Home literacy environments and children's reading performance: A comparative study of 25 countries. *Educational Research and Evaluation, 14,* 489–505.

Takayama, K. (2007). A nation at risk crosses the pacific: Transnational borrowing of the U.S. crisis discourse in the debate on education reform in Japan. *Comparative Education Review, 51,* 423–446.

Takayama, K. (2008). The politics of international league tables: PISA in Japan's achievement crisis debate. *Comparative Education, 44,* 387–407.

Teachman, J. D. (1987). Family background, educational resources, and educational attainment. *American Sociological Review, 52,* 548–557.

Tsuneyoshi, R. (2004). The new Japanese educational reforms and the achievement "crisis" debate. *Educational Policy, 18,* 364–394.

Wößmann, L. (2003). Schooling resources, educational institutions, and student performance: The international evidence. *Oxford Bulletin of Economics and Statistics, 65,* 117–170.

CHAPTER 10

Government Spending, Socioeconomic Background, and Academic Achievement in Tokyo

Tomoaki Nomi

The decline of academic standards and the widening gaps in student performance in elementary and secondary schools in Japan have received wide attention in recent years (Asahi Shimbun Shuzai Han, 2003; Kariya, Shimizu, Shimizu, & Morota, 2002). Data from a number of international achievement tests suggest that analyses of student achievement published in the 1980s and 1990s do not apply to the current cohort of pupils. At the same time, the gap in income and wealth in what used to be a very egalitarian society has become more visible (Saito, 2001; Sato, 2000; Tachibanaki, 1998, 2004). This chapter tries to link these two trends by examining the relationship between the academic achievement of Tokyo elementary and secondary school students and their socioeconomic backgrounds. It carefully examines economic as well as structural changes in school communities, and how those changes have influenced the academic experiences provided to K–12 pupils.

Changes in the socioeconomic backgrounds of students living in those communities could influence their academic performance in various ways. For example, more affluent school districts usually have more money to spend on school. Wealthier parents can also spend more money on their children's supplementary education such as afterschool classes (*juku*) and private tutoring. Finally, more educated parents tend to be better at guiding their children to academic success. While each one of these factors might be significant, understanding their relative importance is a crucial component in formulating education policies. Remedies that fail to do this could prove counterproductive. For example, several recent reforms have focused on economic aspects of education, but overlooked the social dynamics of schooling. Initiatives that take such a narrow approach to school improvement and fail to address the underlying causes of the achievement gap could actually exacerbate the problems they were designed to address.

WHAT WE KNOW ABOUT ACADEMIC STANDARDS
AND STUDENT PERFORMANCE

The 2003 Programme for International Student Assessment (PISA) study (OECD, 2004) confirmed two trends in Japanese education that have been widely perceived in recent years: the general decline in academic standards of Japanese students and the growing bifurcation in student performance. While the performance of the highest tier of Japanese students in math and science remained at the top internationally, average performance declined and the number of students at the lowest level increased.[1]

The decline in academic standards has been debated prior to, and particularly since, the Ministry of Education announced a reduction in elementary and secondary school curriculum content in 1998. This curriculum change was introduced for at least two reasons. First, since formal instruction time at public schools was reduced with the elimination of half-day classes on Saturdays, less content could be covered. Second, the pace of instruction was slowed so that more students could keep up with the classes. Students' inability to keep up with the pace of instruction was considered a source of behavioral problems and a basic contributor to dropping out of school. The change was deemed necessary to reduce the burden on and stress level of the students.

Recent reports indicating the inability of growing numbers of university students, including graduates of the most selective schools, to solve elementary school–level math problems attribute this trend partly to the reduction in school curriculum content.[2] They argue that further reduction in curriculum content would only make the situation worse. The Ministry's 1998 decision was initially popular. Many people believed that stress stemming from excessive schoolwork and intense competition contributed to rising incidences of school violence and withdrawal syndromes. The Ministry of Education hailed a shift in emphasis from knowledge acquisition to encouraging a "zest for living." The new approach is referred to as *yutori kyôiku*, which the English version of *The White Paper on Education* (MEXT, 1999) describes as "liberal, flexible, and comfortable" education. Declining performance aside, official statistics indicate no significant improvement in student behavior since the curriculum reform. The total number of elementary and junior high school students who refuse to go to school increased from 66,817 in 1990 (0.47% of all students) to 138,722 in 2000 (1.23%). Cases of violence at school increased from 23,621 in 1996 to 34,595 in 1999 before dropping to 31,278 in 2002. The dropout rate from senior high school has remained relatively constant, fluctuating between 1.9% and 2.6% in the years 1982 to 2002 (MEXT, 2004).

The second trend confirmed by the PISA study is increasing bifurcation that is most apparent in the growing percentage of students ranked at the lowest level of achievement. For example, the percentage of students in the bottom of six levels in reading comprehension increased from 2.7% in the first survey to 7.4% in the second survey, a figure that now surpasses the OECD average (6.7%). By contrast, the percentage of students in the top level remains virtually unchanged (9.9% in 2000 and 9.7% in 2003), still above the OECD average (8.3%). While the percentage of students at the bottom level in mathematics (4.7%) is still below the OECD average (8.2%), it is higher than that in other countries with comparable mean scores, such as Finland (1.5%), Canada (2.4%), South Korea (2.5%), and the Netherlands (2.6%). At the other end of the spectrum, Japan has a higher percentage of students in the top level of mathematics (8.2%) than any other OECD member, twice the OECD average (4.0%). Science scores among the top 10% of students from Japan improved from the 2000 survey, while the scores in the bottom decile dropped. In short, while the performance of the high-achieving Japanese students in math and science remained at the top internationally, the average declined, with a notable increase in the number of students at the lowest level. What we see is a hollowing out of the middle levels with a shift of students from the middle range to the lower range.

This bifurcation was a predictable result of curriculum content reduction. Students at lower levels of academic achievement are studying and learning less because the curriculum is less demanding. In the 2003 PISA study, Japanese 10th-graders reported studying 6.5 hours per week outside of school, compared to 8.9 hours for the average of all OECD countries. This includes time spent at *juku*. Due to declining fertility rates and a concomitant reduction in the size of the pool of potential new college entrants, there is also less pressure from entrance examinations, except for students pursuing elite universities. The number of 15-year-olds today is about one-third lower than it was 15 years ago, while the number of openings for first-year college students has increased significantly with the opening of new colleges. As a result, many colleges and high schools now admit most (and some admit all) applicants without competitive exams, further undercutting student motivation to study. On the other hand, competition to get into the most selective schools is still intense enough to motivate large numbers of Japanese students with high aspirations.

Particularly ominous is the possibility that this bifurcation may not be an unintended consequence of reform. For most of the postwar period, the Ministry of

Education focused on raising average achievement. In the mid-1980s, however, Prime Minister Nakasone established a cabinet-level advisory council, the Ad Hoc Council on Education (AHCE, or *Rinkyôshin*), which called for a changing focus in Japanese education. The AHCE was established outside the jurisdiction of the Ministry of Education to provide a forum for people from various backgrounds to discuss education. Many participants in the AHCE discussions voiced concerns about the failure of the educational system to promote originality and creativity. They attributed the problem to a curriculum and teaching methods that were tailored to boost average levels. Their assumption seems to have been that rapid learners were spending too much time on topics they had already mastered, and too little time, if any, on developing creative skills, original thinking, and advanced techniques. They proposed greater variety and flexibility for the curriculum.

The AHCE issued its final report in 1987, after 3 years of intense discussion. Many of its ideas were implemented in the 1989 curriculum change and thereafter. Those ideas included allowing parents to choose public elementary and junior high schools regardless of where they lived, creating 6-year public schools that combined junior and senior high schools, creating public high schools with flexible curricula that did not set a time limit for graduation, and allowing universities greater flexibility in selecting students. If there was an unexpected result from the implementation of the AHCE changes, it was that the bifurcation was accompanied by a decline in average performance. Rather than raising the level of top performers, the new curriculum lowered the performance of the middle and bottom performers. The increasing number of low-level performers could result in the creation of large numbers of "unemployable" people among the younger generation at the very moment when demographics create a situation of growing labor shortages and corporate strategies increase the number of part-time workers. Such results undermine one of the foundations of Japan's postwar economic success: the high levels of skill and motivation of the rank-and-file labor force.

The PISA survey results stimulated wide-ranging discussion about improving standards. Proposals included increasing instruction time in math and science, restoring Saturday classes (eliminated with the 1989 curriculum change), reviving national standardized tests for all students (abolished in the 1960s), introducing ability-based groupings, and offering more school choice along with 6-year public secondary schools. Whatever the effects on mean test scores, many of these changes seem likely to accelerate bifurcation, boosting the top performers while having a marginal positive impact on lower achievers. Therefore, it is very important to ask which policy goal is really targeted.

LINKS TO ECONOMIC CHANGES

The PISA study also investigated the impact of socioeconomic background on student performance. In Japan, this correlation has been among the lowest of OECD countries, probably due to two factors that differentiate Japan from many other countries, i.e., immigrant background and the language spoken at home. Japan's relatively low level of immigration and corresponding high level of Japanese spoken at home minimize factors that might explain educational differentiation elsewhere. A third trend, single-parent families, is on the rise in Japan, but is still less prevalent than in most OECD countries.[3]

The issue of socioeconomic background has received less public attention than the recent decline in academic standards or the growing bifurcation in academic achievement. At least two reasons might explain this situation. The first reason is that differences in socioeconomic backgrounds and student performance levels were until recently among the lowest in the world (Rohlen, 1983). Therefore, while the link between socioeconomic background and student performance may have been visible, it has been marginalized. For example, Okano and Tsuchiya (1999) examine the issue of "equality and diversity" as experienced by students in vocational, evening, and correspondence courses. Their underlying supposition is that a high degree of homogeneity exists among the two-thirds of students who attend academic senior high schools.

However, assumptions about the relative equality in income levels and in academic performance have been challenged in recent years. The expanding gap in student performance has been documented in the PISA study, among other places. There is also a growing perception that both equality and social mobility in Japan have been threatened in recent years. For example, the poverty level (percentage of households with income under one-half of the national median) in Japan increased from 12% in 1985 to 16% in 2009 (Ministry of Health, Labor and Welfare, 2011). Japan's poverty rate of 15.7% in 2006 ranked the fourth highest of OECD countries, behind Mexico, Turkey, and the United States (OECD, 2008).[4] Therefore, assumptions about the disparities in both income distribution and student performance need to be reexamined.

The second reason that the issue of socioeconomic background has not received enough attention is that, until recently, most students surpassed the educational levels of their parents. In the first few decades after World War II, the rapid growth of school enrollment rates at the secondary and tertiary levels made it possible for students to achieve a higher educational level than their parents by simply graduating from high school. This was even true for students at vocational and evening schools, though they were near the bottom of the educational ladder among their cohorts (Rohlen, 1983). By the early 1990s, however, young people had stopped expecting that their children would receive more education than they did themselves (Okano & Tsuchiya, 1999).

Historically, the public elementary and middle schools in Japan have insisted on "formal equality," following a uniform national curriculum and resisting any forms of ability-based classes. Teachers, too, have generally followed an egalitarian pedagogical approach (Okano & Tsuchiya, 1999). Rohlen (1983) attributes the relatively small variation (at the time) in student achievement to pedagogical uniformity and lack of tracking in elementary and middle school education. Recently, however, this traditional model has changed, even among the public schools that are supposedly providing "egalitarian" education.

TEST SCORE TRENDS

One source of data that can enhance our understanding of the links between economic trends and academic performance is the standardized tests for public elementary and secondary school students administered by the Tokyo Metropolitan Government Board of Education. These tests were first given to secondary school students (8th-graders) in 2004 and to elementary school students (5th-grade) in 2005 in response to concerns about declining academic standards in public schools. The tests included questions designed to measure student understanding of the contents of the national curriculum. They also attempted to measure student ability to apply basic knowledge to "real-life" situations, similar to the PISA survey.

A total of 68,144 8th-graders from 651 junior high schools participated in the first test in January 2004. In January 2005, 88,531 5th-graders from 1,342 elementary schools, and 71,866 8th-graders from 651 junior high schools participated. The tests included four subjects (Japanese language, arithmetic, social studies, and science) for the 5th-graders, and five subjects (Japanese language, mathematics, social studies, science, and English language) for the 8th-graders. The average scores for 23 wards and 26 cities were published in June 2004 for the first exam, and in June 2005 for the second exam.[5]

I examined the average scores for those 49 municipalities (23 wards and 26 cities) and considered the socioeconomic characteristics of each municipality. Since there are no data for the households of students for most variables, the characteristics of residents within the municipality are used as the closest available proxy. Of course, significant limits arise from the use of municipalities as the unit of analysis, given that some municipalities are more diverse than others and none is homogeneous in terms of the socioeconomic background of residents.

For example, Edogawa-ku (ranked 36th out of 49 in average income) and Koto-ku (32nd in average income), both located on the eastern edge of Tokyo, have among the lowest average income levels of the 23 wards (*ku*). But they still have redeveloped areas with relatively better-off families. Ota-ku (13th in average income) has one of the most upscale residential neighborhoods in Tokyo, while its eastern part is occupied with small factories with modest income level. On the other hand, cities in the Tama region (western part of Tokyo) have relatively homogeneous population. Cities like Kokubunji (11th in average income) and Mitaka (12th in average income) have similar income levels as Ota-ku, but they are mostly made of middle-class neighborhoods unlike Ota-ku.

Aside from data availability, there is additional difficulty with using a smaller unit of analysis than municipalities. Nineteen of 23 wards and seven of 26 cities have some form of school choice system, either at the elementary or junior high school level, resulting in a significant number of students attending schools outside of their own designated school districts. Schools in high-income districts with more educated residents tend to attract high-achieving students from other districts. As a result, looking at the relationship between school district characteristics and student performance may end up overestimating the impact of socioeconomic background. There are also a small number of students who attend public schools outside of their municipalities. By aggregating data at the municipal level as opposed to the school district level, the potential measurement bias is significantly smaller.

HYPOTHESES AND ANALYSIS

The first part of this study is an attempt to explain the test scores of each municipality. Multiple regression method is employed in order to separate the impacts of different socioeconomic factors (income level, educational level, and government expenditure). While all of the factors might contribute to academic performance, some factors might be more important than others. Multiple regression method allows us to estimate the impact of each independent variable when other variables are held constant. (For example, how much impact does educational level have if both income level and government expenditures were constant?) Additional variables such as gender ratio, foreign student ratio, and single-parent ratio are included to control the impacts of those factors.[6]

The second part tries to examine which segment of public elementary school students advance to private or national junior high schools. The hypothesis here is that it is a function of 1) student academic achievement in elementary school, 2) household income, and 3) educational level of parents. Therefore, all three independent variables are expected to be positively associated with the dependent variable.[7]

Results of multiple regression are summarized in Table 10.1. Educational level is positively associated with the test score with a statistical significance at the 0.01 level for all four equations. Income is also positively associated with the test score with a statistical significance at the 0.10 level for the elementary school data. This suggests that parents with high socioeconomic status are successfully using both their financial and cultural resources to bolster their children's academic achievement in elementary school. However, the data also show that only cultural resources remain relevant to junior high school student academic achievement. On the other hand, individual student expenditure does not have statistical significance, although it is positively associated with test scores in two of the four equations. Thus, it seems that the expenditure levels in each of Tokyo's municipalities largely exceed the minimum threshold of adequate quality of instruction.

Gender is negatively associated with test score with a statistical significance at the 0.05 level for elementary school students. This indicates that municipalities with a higher ratio of girls have lower test scores. One possible explanation for this is that more girls attend private elementary schools. About 6% of girls attend private elementary schools, while only 3.6% of boys do. In other words, 60% of private elementary school students are girls, while only 48.4% of public elementary school students are girls. Although private elementary schools do not choose their applicants based on their academic accomplishments, it is still conceivable that their students have higher levels of academic achievement than their cohorts in public schools.

The results for the control variables are mixed. First, single-parent household has an expected sign (in this case, a negative relationship between the single-parent household and test scores), although it is not statistically significant. Second, foreign student ratio has an unexpected (positive) sign, although it is not statistically significant. This might be due to the fact that the "foreign" students include a large number of Koreans whose native language is Japanese. Finally, the impact of private school enrollment is inconclusive with positive sign for one year and negative sign for another year. The "bright flight" (Kariya, 2001, p. 105) does not seem to produce a big enough impact to cause a decline in achievement among students who are left in the public schools.

Test score and income are positively associated with private school enrollment with statistical significance at the 0.01 level. This indicates that parents who have high-achieving children and who can afford to send them to private schools are likely to do so. However, the level of education attained by parents does not seem to have a significant impact on parental decisions to send their children to private schools. This explains why household income is a more important factor in explaining student achievement at the elementary school level than at the junior high school level in this survey. Financially well-off families might be using their

Table 10.1. Multiple Regression Analysis

	8th Grade (2004)	8th Grade (2005)	8th Grade (pooled)	5th Grade (2005)	Primary-> Secondary
Dependent Variable		*Test Score*			*Private School Ratio*
Intercept	300.734*** (14.018)	323.694*** (12.848)	319.475*** (21.396)	306.914*** (16.710)	-1.454*** (-2.770)
Test Score					0.553*** (4.201)
Educational Level	1.838*** (8.477)	1.309*** (3.096)	1.407*** (8.531)	0.768*** (5.418)	-0.001 (-1.187)
Income	-6.052 (-1.622)	0.044 (0.488)	-1.412 (-0.496)	3.402* (1.725)	0.088*** (5.904)
Expenditure	9.652 (1.250)	-6.034 (-0.669)	-0.469 (-0.086)	1.620 (0.281)	
Private	-1.180 (-.0048)	22.539 (0.908)	19.856 1.216		
Gender	10.862 (0.537)	-1.987 (-0.112)	4.530 (0.376)	-34.503** (-2.082)	
Foreign Student	1.047 0.661	1.236 (0.627)	0.106 0.124	1.458 1.026	
Single-Parent	-0.332 (-0.251)	-1.807 (-1.049)	-0.809 (-0.809)	-0.038 (-0.039)	
Dummy05			-17.387*** (-7.724)		
R^2	0.8579	0.7258	0.8381	0.8087	0.8536
Adj. R^2	0.8336	0.6790	0.8235	0.7813	0.8403
F	35.357***	15.504***	57.589***	29.585***	64.149***
N	49	49	98	49	49

t-statistics in parenthesis; *** $P < 0.01$, ** $P < 0.05$, * $P < 0.1$.

resources in the form of supplementary education at the elementary school level, but they are certainly using their means to send their children to private schools at the junior high school level.

EXAMINING THE DATA

Educational level seems to have the most robust impact on test scores at both elementary and junior high school levels, even after other variables are controlled. This indicates that social class has a strong influence on student performance, independent of economic factors. Income level seems to have a significant impact only at the elementary school level.

This contrast might be due to a difference in the percentage of students who attend private schools at the two levels. Fewer than 5% of Tokyo elementary school students attend private schools. However, almost 25% of Tokyo junior high school pupils do. Families with financial resources are more than likely to send their children to private junior high schools. Therefore, economic factors are much weaker among junior high school students who attend public schools. On the other hand, economic factors have a stronger impact at the elementary school level, since most children, including those from financially better-off families, attend public schools.[8]

This point has serious policy implications. Many of the public school reforms that have been implemented as countermeasures to the perceived decline in public school education standards have only considered the impact of economic factors. Those initiatives include 6-year public secondary schools, larger school districts for public senior high schools, "enrichment" classes for advanced students, and greater school choices for public elementary and junior high school students. While those efforts may help reduce the impact of economic background, they may also increase the impact of students' social backgrounds.

The issue of school choice is a particularly sensitive one. The school district boundaries for elementary and junior high schools in Japan were enforced rather strictly until the 1990s. This has been relaxed since the turn of the century. Shinagawa-ku was one of the first municipalities in the country to introduce a school choice system at the elementary school level in 2000, and at the junior high school level in 2001. By 2005, 19 of 23 wards and 7 of 26 cities had introduced some kind of school choice option at the junior high school level, and 14 of 23 wards and 5 of 26 cities did so at the elementary school level (Minei & Nakagawa, 2005).

There are many reasons that students and their parents choose schools outside of their designated districts, including commuting convenience, neighborhood safety (and school safety), quality of facilities, and extracurricular activities. At the junior high school level, academic reputation is among the factors most frequently mentioned by parents (Minei & Nakagawa, 2005). On the one hand, this may have a positive impact on the academic performance of higher-achieving students, since they tend to be concentrated in a smaller number of schools where they enjoy greater positive peer effects. On the other hand, the exit of higher-achieving students from their designated schools might have a negative effect on the students who are left behind in their districts.

The most extreme example of the negative effects of school choice might be the 6-year schools that combine junior and senior high schools. This practice has been popular among many private schools, because it allows for a streamlining of the curriculum. It also has been effective in preparing students for university entrance examinations. The growing number of entrants into the most competitive universities who have matriculated from 6-year schools in recent decades indicates their advantage.

Responding to these changes, many local governments have established 6-year public high schools (Tsuneyoshi, this volume). Prefectural (or metropolitan) governments usually accomplish this by creating junior high schools that are affiliated with existing senior high schools because most public senior high schools are administered by the prefectural or metropolitan government. Most elementary and junior high schools, in contrast, are administered by municipal governments.

Tokyo opened its first 6-year public high school in 2005, and 10 more schools have since been established. Students from anywhere in Tokyo are eligible to apply to these schools, and admission is determined by essays, elementary school grades, interviews, and academic aptitude assessments. Parents who send their children to these schools are most likely those who would be otherwise interested in private junior high schools, but cannot afford that option. Overall, students in these schools have higher levels of academic achievement compared to students in other public schools, although the "academic aptitude assessments" they use are slightly different from conventional entrance examinations most commonly used by private schools.

The teachers in the newly established junior high schools have been openly recruited from other public junior and senior high schools in Tokyo, and were selected based on quality of classroom instruction. While this provides excellent quality of instruction for the 6-year schools, the quality of instruction at the remaining public schools may suffer with the departure of their best teachers. Six-year public high schools were established with an objective of closing the gap between private and public secondary schools. But they may also exacerbate disparities between those who attend the 6-year public schools and those who remain at other public schools. Conventional public schools have lost or are losing some of their best teachers and their highest-achieving students to the 6-year public schools.[9]

The public use of financial resources does not seem to have a significant impact on student performance, perhaps because the central government of Japan has traditionally tried to even out expenditures across municipalities. The national government also sets maximum class size for public elementary and junior high schools (currently 40), providing subsidies to local governments to hire teachers to achieve this size. Local governments, in turn, are free to use their own resources to hire additional teachers in order to lower the class size. However, this has not been done widely so far. On average, Tokyo classrooms include 29 to 36 students at the junior high school level.

The lack of focus on additional public spending on education might be due to the fact that many of the financially well-off parents in affluent municipalities send their children to private junior high schools, and are not interested in improving the quality of public junior high schools. Most of them, however, still enroll their children in public elementary schools. Perhaps they think that instruction at the elementary school level is not nearly as important. Even when preparing children for junior high school entrance exams, parents sometimes rely more on supplementary education, such as *juku*, rather than on elementary school instruction. Therefore, even with the increased local autonomy in school funding under the current "administrative reforms," expenditure levels may not have a notably greater impact on student performance.

CONCLUSION

The results of this study indicate that among the factors that influence student performance, cultural capital may be the most important. This is rather unfortunate, since it is much harder to address the gap in cultural capital through policy tools. Is there any way to reduce this gap? One possible way is to provide learning opportunities for public school students outside of formal classroom instruction. This can be done through extracurricular activities, such as science and history clubs, and book clubs or reading programs that encourage students to read outside of the school curriculum. So far, these initiatives have been largely left to individual schools, but local governments could take more active roles in identifying successful practices and encouraging other schools to adapt them. These activities can also be more fully integrated into traditional afterschool programs at the elementary school level.

The trend of increasing socioeconomic inequality in Japan is long-term and results from the structural changes of the global economy rather than from deliberate policies of the government. Therefore, it is not likely to be reversed anytime in the near future. Education policy has to take these trends into consideration—at the national as well as the local level. If the goal is to minimize the impact of socioeconomic background on student performance, the starting point must be a correct understanding of this impact. Reducing the problem to a matter of income level could lead to misguided policies that increase the inequality rather than decrease it.

NOTES

1. A portion of this chapter was published in Nomi (2006), including a more detailed discussion of these two points.

2. The elementary and secondary school curriculum contents have been reduced three times in the last 3 decades: in 1977, 1989, and 1998. The first PISA survey tested students educated under the 1977 curriculum. Those in the second survey were educated under the 1989 curriculum. The most recent curriculum went into effect in 2002, and the first cohort of students who are studying under it did not reach the 9th grade until 2009.

3. Rohlen (1983) clearly shows the negative impact of single-parent families on student academic performance. While only 1–2% of students at three academic high schools in his study were missing one or both parents, the figure was 13–15% for students at vocational and evening schools.

4. On the issue of inequality and social stratification in Japan, see Saito (2001), Sato (2000), and Tachibanaki (1998, 2004), in addition to Kariya (1995, 2001).

5. A minor correction of the data was released in December 2005. This paper is based on the revised data that can be found at http://www.kyoiku.metro.tokyo.jp/press/pr051215s.htm. The average scores for towns and villages were not published because they either had too few schools or too few students to meet the standard set by the board of education. These minimums, of three schools and 100 students, are required for mandatory disclosure, although each municipality and school is allowed to publish its own scores on its own accord.

6. The dependent variable (test score) is the total score of four subjects combined for the 5th-graders and the total score of five subjects combined for the 8th-graders in each of the 49 municipalities. Since the bivariate correlations among the average scores for four/five subjects are very high, the combined score is treated as one variable instead of being divided into four/five separate variables.

Educational level is the percentage of residents over 15 years old who have finished 4-year universities, 2-year junior colleges, or technical colleges. (People who are still in school are excluded from the total.) Since these data are published only every 10 years, 2000 census results are used for this study. It has been documented that parents with higher educational level are generally more interested in their children's educational achievement, and they tend to know better about how to guide their children to academic success (Kariya, 2001; OECD, 2004). Although this variable is not a direct measurement of the parents' educational level, it should be a close enough proxy. This variable is expected to be positively associated with the dependent variable.

Income is the per capita income of residents in each municipality. Higher household income is supposed to give students an advantage in academic achievement through private use of household financial resources such as supplementary education such as cram schools, private tutors, or correspondence courses. Although this variable does not directly measure the household income of student population, it should be a close enough proxy. It is expected to be positively associated with the dependent variable.

Expenditure is the per student expenditure by each municipal government. In addition to the private use of financial resources mentioned above, parents who live in more affluent districts are able to use financial resources on schools through public spending. Although spending money is not a sufficient condition for high student performance, it seems to be at least a necessary condition to a certain extent. In other words, more expenditure does not guarantee better student performance. But there is a certain level of expenditure that is almost necessary to give students enough opportunities for success (OECD, 2004). This variable is expected to be positively associated with the dependent variable.

Private is the percentage of students in the 8th grade from each municipality who attend private schools. The board of education only publishes the data on the percentage of public elementary schools who enter private or national schools. Therefore, the students who attend private elementary schools have to be excluded from this estimation. Although this creates a measurement problem, it is a relatively minor one, considering the relatively small percentage of students who attend private elementary schools (fewer than 5% in 2004, as opposed to over 25% among junior high school students in the same year). The private junior high schools have been attracting students with higher academic achievements, especially in the last few decades as the public school education has become less rigorous with curriculum content reductions and entrance exam reforms (Kariya, 2001). It is expected to be negatively associated with the dependent variable, since higher percentage implies more students with high academic achievements having chosen private schools after elementary school. This variable is added only for the model that explains the performance level of junior high school students, since the students in private elementary schools are not chosen by their academic merits.

Gender is the girls-to-boys ratio in respective grade level in all the public schools of each municipality. PISA 2003 shows that boys tend to score higher in math and science, while girls tend to score higher in reading, although the difference in science is not statistically significant (OECD, 2004). Since this study combines the scores for all five subjects, there may not be any gender significant difference in scores. However, Japan is one of the few OECD countries in which women's educational attainment still lags behind men's. Therefore, it is still worth examining whether gender ratio has any impact on the average score.

Foreign student is the ratio students with foreign citizenship in the public elementary or junior high schools. The board of education only publishes the aggregate data for all the grades (1st through 6th, and 7th through 9th). However, this is not a serious measurement problem unless there is a reason to suspect that this ratio is significantly different between grades. A more serious problem might be that this does not separate Korean students whose native language is Japanese. However, the obstacles than foreign students face are not limited to the language problem, although it is an important component. PISA 2003 shows that "first-generation" students (those who were born in the country of current residence) still seem to have some disadvantage, even though it is not as serious as the case for the "nonnative" students (OECD, 2004). This is expected to be negatively associated with the dependent variable.

Single-parent is the ratio of single-parent households to all households that include children under 18 years old in each municipality. These data are published every 5 years and 2000 census data are used for this study. It is often difficult for single-parent families to create and maintain environments that are helpful for students' learning, since parents are too busy with their workplace and household responsibilities (OECD, 2004). This is supposed to be negatively associated with the dependent variable.

7. Data sources:

Test Score: Tokyo Metropolitan Government Board of Education (2004a, 2005a).
Education: Toyo Keizai Shimposha (2005, 2006).
Income: Toyo Keizai Shimposha (2005, 2006).
Expenditure: Tokyo Metropolitan Government Board of Education (2004d, 2005d).
Gender: Tokyo Metropolitan Government Board of Education (2004b, 2005b).
Foreign: Tokyo Metropolitan Government Board of Education (2004b, 2005b).
Single: Tokyo Metropolitan Government Statistics Bureau (2000).
Private: Tokyo Metropolitan Government Board of Education (2004c, 2005c).

8. Since this survey does not cover private school students, there is no way to test the performance differences between public and private schools or how economic factors influence those differences.

9. See Fujita (1997, 2005) and Tsuneyoshi (this volume) on the problems with school choice and 6-year secondary schools.

REFERENCES

Asahi Shimbun Shuzai Han. (2003). *Education at a turning point* (in Japanese). Tokyo: Asahi Shimbunsha.

Fujita, H. (1997). *Education reform* (in Japanese). Tokyo: Iwanami Shoten.

Fujita, H. (2005). *Reexamining the compulsory education* (in Japanese). Tokyo: Chikuma Shobo.

Kariya, T. (1995). *Direction of mass education society* (in Japanese). Tokyo: Chûô Kôronsha.

Kariya, T. (2001). *Stratified Japan and education crisis* (in Japanese). Tokyo: Ushindo.

Kariya, T., Shimizu, K., Shimizu, M., & Morota, Y. (2002). *The true state of decline in academic ability* (in Japanese). Tokyo: Iwanami Shoten.

Minei, M., & Nakagawa, T. (2005). *Selected schools, non-selected schools* (in Japanese). Tokyo: Hachigatsu Shokan.

MEXT, Ministry of Education, Culture, Sports, Science and Technology. (1999). *Japanese government policies in education, science, sports and culture 1999.* Tokyo: Author. Retreived from http://www.mext.go.jp/b_menu/hakusho/html/hpae199901/hpae199901_2_023.html

MEXT, Ministry of Education, Culture, Sports, Science and Technology. (2004). Press release from August 27, 2004 (in Japanese). Tokyo: Author. Retrieved from http://warp.da.ndl.go.jp/info:ndljp/pid/286184/www.mext.go.jp/b_menu/houdou/16/08/04082302.htm

Ministry of Health, Labor and Welfare. (2011). *Summary of comprehensive survey of living conditions* (in Japanese). Tokyo: Author. Retrieved from http://www.mhlw.go.jp/toukei/saikin/hw/k-tyosa/k-tyosa10/

Nomi, T. (2006). Inequality and Japanese education: Urgent choices. *Japan Focus.* Retrieved from http://www.japanfocus.org/-Tomoaki-NOMI/2016

Okano, K., & Tsuchiya, M. (1999). *Education in contemporary Japan: Inequality and diversity.* Cambridge, U.K.: Cambridge University Press.

Organization for Economic Co-operation and Development (OECD). (2004). *Learning from tomorrow's world: First results from PISA 2003.* Retrieved from http://www.pisa.oecd. org/

Organization for Economic Co-operation and Development (OECD). (2008). *Are we growing unequal?* Retrieved from http://www.oecd.org/dataoecd/48/56/41494435.pdf

Rohlen, T. P. (1983). *Japan's high schools.* Berkeley: University of California Press.

Saito, T. (2001). *Unequal opportunity* (in Japanese). Tokyo: Bungei Shunjusha.

Sato, T. (2000). *Japan: Unequal society* (in Japanese). Tokyo: Chûô Kôron-sha.

Tachibanaki, T. (1998). *Economic disparity in Japan* (in Japanese). Tokyo: Iwanami Shoten.

Tachibanaki, T. (Ed.). (2004). *Sealed inequality* (in Japanese). Tokyo: Toyo Keizai Shinposha.

Tokyo Metropolitan Government Statistics Bureau. (2000). *Census survey report by municipalities* (in Japanese). Tokyo: Author. Retrieved from http://www.toukei.metro.tokyo.jp/kokusei/2000/cc-04data.htm

Tokyo Metropolitan Government Board of Education. (2004a). *Survey to achieve improvement in student academic achievement* (in Japanese). Tokyo: Author. Retrieved from http://www.kyoiku.metro.tokyo.jp/buka/shidou/15gakuryoku/index.htm

Tokyo Metropolitan Government Board of Education. (2004b). *Report on the statistical survey on public schools (School survey)* (in Japanese). Tokyo: Author. Retrieved from http://www.kyoiku.metro.tokyo.jp/toukei/16gakkoucho/toppage.htm

Tokyo Metropolitan Government Board of Education. (2004c). *Report on the statistical survey on public schools (Student exit survey)* (in Japanese). Tokyo: Author. Retrieved from http://www.kyoiku.metro.tokyo.jp/toukei/15sotsugo/toppage.htm

Tokyo Metropolitan Government Board of Education. (2004d). *Reports on the local education expenditure* (in Japanese). Tokyo: Author. Retrieved from http://www.kyoiku.metro.tokyo.jp/toukei/17chikyohi.htm

Tokyo Metropolitan Government Board of Education. (2005a). *Survey to achieve improvement in student academic achievement* (in Japanese). Tokyo: Author. Retrieved from http://www.kyoiku.metro.tokyo.jp/press/pr051215s.htm

Tokyo Metropolitan Government Board of Education. (2005b). *Report on the statistical survey on public schools. (School survey)* (in Japanese). Tokyo: Author. Retrieved from http://www.kyoiku.me tro.tokyo.jp/toukei/17gakkoucho/toppage.htm

Tokyo Metropolitan Government Board of Education. (2005c). *Report on the statistical survey on public schools (Student exit survey)* (in Japanese). Tokyo: Author. Retrieved from http://www.kyoiku.metro.tokyo.jp/toukei/16sotsugo/toppage.htm

Tokyo Metropolitan Government Board of Education. (2005d). *Reports on the local education expenditure* (in Japanese). Tokyo: Author. Retrieved from http://www.kyoiku.metro.tokyo.jp/toukei/18chikyohi.htm

Toyo Keizai Shimposha. (2005, 2006). *General survey of regional economies* (in Japanese). Tokyo: Toyo Keizai Shimposha.

CHAPTER 11

Junior High School Entrance Examinations in Metropolitan Tokyo

The Advantages and Costs of Privilege

Ryoko Tsuneyoshi

Market-oriented reforms have introduced competition into the educational systems of many countries. Even in East Asian countries that have centralized and strongly public systems, the market metaphor is gaining popularity in education (Mochida, 2003). In discussions of market-oriented reforms, critics often note that competition widens the gap between the haves and have-nots, thereby disadvantaging those without the economic means to exercise their choice (Apple 2006; Whitty, 2002; Woods, Bagley, & Glatter, 1998, ch. 8). These critics focus their attention on families that live in communities with fewer educational opportunities and who lack social capital (MacLeod, 2009). It goes without saying that the education of the disadvantaged is a central educational issue; at the same time, it is not as often noticed that market competition influences everyone, not just the underprivileged.

Very few studies mention the potential cost of living in affluent areas with a thriving private educational sector. More capital and more choice tend to be automatically equated with privilege. Families living in these affluent communities, however, pay a price for their "privilege." This chapter describes the cost that the educationally privileged pay in a market-driven context focusing on the case of junior high exam-taking in Japan. In the following pages, I argue that the Japanese high-stakes entrance examination system for junior high, increasing private school domination, and the rise of private learning centers (*juku*) form a system in which certain urban centers experience greater market choice, but conversely suffer from its consequences (e.g., weakening of public education).

This chapter treats the Japanese junior high entrance exam-taking phenomenon as a symbolic case, illustrating the cost that even the privileged pay in a market-driven system, and provides insights into the negative impact privately driven education can have on the public purpose of education. It draws on observations of key elementary and junior high schools and *juku*, interviews with teachers, and analyses of education materials, made during the years 2008–2010 in a Tokyo ward that has a high rate of junior high exam-taking. This was supplemented by *juku* observations from Saitama City (2002–2006) in neighboring Saitama prefecture, where junior high exam-taking was newly taking hold. The first junior high exam-taking boom peaked around 1990, leveled out, and then increased again in the early 2000s, as public criticism toward the government's relaxed (*yutori*) education policies mounted and the economy showed signs of recovery (Diamond Magazine Editing Unit, 2012a; Morigami, 2009). There are now signs that the second boom has passed, with the peak around 2007–2009, depending on the prefecture and information source.

The Tokyo ward in question, which I will call B ward, is one of the most market-oriented wards, even for Tokyo. This ward harbors one of Japan's most prestigious universities and many of Japan's most famous national and private secondary schools. In other words, there is ample school choice. The case of junior high school exam-taking, however, reveals that there are few real winners in the high-stakes educational market, even in privileged districts such as this.

THE HIGH-STAKES
EXAM-TAKING SYNDROME

Junior High School Exam-taking

High-stakes testing has long been part of the educational landscape in East Asian countries, and the growing emphasis on market competition, accountability, and testing has brought this phenomenon to the educational landscape of many Western countries. High-stakes testing receives criticism for privileging tested subjects over others, encouraging teachers to "teach to the test," placing stress on students, encouraging cheating, and diminishing developmentally adjusted teaching (Berliner & Biddle, 1996; Jones, Jones, & Hargrove, 2003; Nicholas & Berliner, 2007).

East Asian countries suffer from all of these symptoms. In the Japanese case, the Western educational literature includes many references to the examination hell faced by students vying for entrance into top Japanese universities. This image is somewhat misleading, however, since the first sorting process occurs at the high school entrance level, when compulsory education ends, not at college entrance. Recently, for those living in urban privileged areas, however, entrance examinations have begun shifting to even younger children. At many private or national schools, junior high is attached to high school, creating junior/senior high schools. As a result, in affluent urban centers, the earliest and most extreme competition occurs for coveted top-ranking junior/senior high schools. Living within commuting distance of such schools is in itself a privilege. But this privilege comes with a cost, i.e., hyper-high-stakes entrance examinations.

The topic of this chapter, junior high school exam-taking, is primarily an urban phenomenon, a trend that has emerged in Tokyo and other major urban centers. Tokyo is a model case in this regard, because many of Japan's most famous private schools—kindergartens, primary, and secondary—and universities are in the area, and school choice is the norm. In a 2007 study of parents of 6th graders on junior high school choice in metropolitan Tokyo, fewer than 20% answered that they had no private school options. In rural areas with fewer than 50,000 residents, this number rises to more than 70% (Benesse Kyôiku Kenkyû Kaihatsu Sentâ, 2008b, pp. 24–25). In Tokyo today, the potential school choice options following elementary school level:

1. public junior high school,
2. exam to enter a private junior high school,
3. exam for a national school,
4. aptitude test to enter one of the public junior/senior high schools, founded since 1999.

Items two, three, and four are junior high exam-taking categories, and the percentage of students in the Tokyo metropolitan area (Tokyo and the neighboring prefectures) pursuing these options in 2010 was estimated at 15–21%.[1] Needless to say, living in a district within commuting distance from a brand private or national school, and being able to pay *juku* fees and private school tuition in itself implies a certain level of affluence. And although category one may imply direct enrollment into a neighborhood school, because most Tokyo districts presently have choice within the public sphere, there are options among public junior high schools as well (Tokyo Metropolitan Board of Education, 2012).

The New Generation of "Education Mamas"

Decades ago, the term *kyôikyu mama* (education mother) was used to describe the mentality of middle-class Japanese mothers pushing their children to excel. Yet, according to Hida (2009), who has done recent studies on the junior high exam-taking families, the education mamas of today are different from their more leisurely counterparts of the past. Their work as "partners" in their children's exam-taking has become all-consuming and externally controlled by the *juku* industry. Total physical and emotional devotion is required of these mothers.

Why did this happen? Morigami (2009) offers three reasons. First, major chain mega-*juku* have taken over the junior high exam-taking market, establishing branches nationwide and pushing out the smaller *juku*. Second, these mega-*juku* have standardized programs across the country, controlling more aspects of the child's life, including the longer hours spent studying. And because the clients are elementary school children, mothers become involved. Third, the gap between what the school provides and what the children need in order to pass the competitive junior high school entrance examinations has become so great that external adult assistance becomes almost mandatory.

Moreover, many junior high schools are requiring applicants to take tests in four subjects (reading, math, science, social studies), even more than the entrance examination for private high schools and colleges. The shift toward thinking skills and problem-solving—in itself a welcome trend—when translated into a 40- to 60-minute written exam, requires skills that are difficult to acquire on one's own or at school. At the same time, the 2002 revisions to the national curriculum standards further reduced content in order to make room for the children to grow, exacerbating the gap between the public school curriculum and entrance examination content. Around this era, junior high exam-taking rates went up every year, until they peaked and began decreasing around the 2008 Lehman stock and related financial crises.

As the more impersonal, standardized, and businesslike approach of the mega-*juku* overwhelms the small, personalized neighborhood *juku*, families must follow the intense mega-*juku* calendar, which does not adjust for individual circumstances. All of these changes lead to a lifestyle where *juku* commuting, class time, and *juku* homework consume a large part of life outside of school for the exam-taking child and mother. In these mega-*juku*, summer sessions often run through most of the vacation, with homework far more intensive than in regular schooling. Frequent tests divide the children into ability groups with mock exams (local, *juku*, and nationwide), and the child's progress is monitored and reported constantly to the parents.

Mega-*juku* such as Nichinoken, Sapix, and Yotsuya Otsuka develop their own instructional materials, based not on the school curriculum, but on what the child must learn to keep pace with the exams scheduled for the end of 6th grade. The *juku* content is so accelerated that it may be more than a year ahead of the school curriculum, requiring speed in reading, writing, and computing that baffles even educated adults.

The author observed workshops for parents offered by two of the largest mega-chain *juku* prior to the 2003-04 school year, at the beginning of the second junior high exam-taking boom. The initiation workshops were filled with mothers and often their children, along with some tense fathers taking notes sometimes with their sons. The *juku* gave many examples of past questions and emphasized that parental attitudes were critical for the pupils to pass. It was quite clear, unlike the *yobikô* (cram schools for college entrance), that *juku* for junior-high school exam-takers were trying to educate the parents as much as the pupils, albeit in a different way.

The target of these *juku* are the new generation of education mamas—and papas—urban, middle-class, and ever more reliant on the education industry than their predecessors. Junior high school exam-takers are basically taking the exam to enter a private school (or one of the few national schools or newly emerging junior/senior attached public schools). Private schools can offer entrance examinations that are far removed from what children study in elementary school and what counts above all is the score on the written entrance examination, not one's grades in school. This phenomena differs from the high school exam-taking scene in which public high schools usually ask for grades and keep exam content aligned to the junior high school curriculum. Thus, compared to high school, junior high exam-taking is extremely test score–oriented: The score on written exams is everything. Years of total devotion and sacrifice of free time on the part of the child and family focus on the day of the hyper-high-stakes test, taken by the top tier of the elementary school population. Even in Tokyo, less than 20% of the cohort pursues this option, and one can assume that they are mostly relatively affluent families with dedicated mothers. The privilege that offers them this opportunity, however, comes with a cost.

THE WORLD OF THE JUNIOR HIGH ENTRANCE EXAMINATIONS

Exam-taking Before the "Great Divide"

Although the English literature on Japanese schooling pays more attention to examination hell for students about to enter college, the first "sorting-and-selecting" occurs before college entrance. Today, over 98% of students of the relevant age group (including students enrolled in correspondence programs and night schools) go on to high school (MEXT, 2012). Despite this universality, compulsory education ends at junior high school and students must pass some kind of entrance examination to enter the post-compulsory high school stage. Thus, most children pass through the neighborhood public school at the elementary and junior high school levels, then face an exam, what I call the "Great Divide." Given this in-stitutional characteristic, it is no surprise that studies on tracking in Japan have focused on the hierarchical ranking of high schools, rather than on the sorting process within schools or the differentiation made before high school (Iida, 2007; LeTendre, Hofer, & Shimizu, 2003).

Juku offer mock tests and rank the difficulty of high schools based on the standard deviation scores of the students who pass their entrance examinations. This ranking also corresponds to the ability of the high school to send its students to prestigious universities. Information on how many students from a particular school were accepted by certain colleges is available on the school's homepage as well as in commercial guidebooks published by the education industry. For lower-ranking high schools, the information shifts to how many went on to col-lege, sought work, and entered various professions.

Today, however, there is a segment of the urban population that does not wait until the Great Divide, and pushes its children at the elementary school level (sometimes even before this stage) to take the entrance examinations for private or national junior high schools. In addition to the regular route, whereby a child attends a public elementary school followed by a public junior high school, and then takes a high school entrance examination (public, national, or private), as mentioned previously, there are now alternative routes that connect the public system at the elementary level to the junior high transition level. A student can apply to enter either a private or national junior high school, and both of these op-tions require the passing of a school-based entrance examination. Another route, available since 1999, is to enter a public junior high school that is attached to a public high school (*koritsu chûkô ikkankô*). For this option, an evaluation of appropriateness (*tekisei*), which is supposed to be more moderate than the tests for private or national junior high schools, determines entrance. As of the school year 2011-2012, there were 420 junior/senior high schools (private, public, and national); 179 of them were public (MEXT, 2011).

In rural districts, the only option may be the neighborhood public high school. In Tokyo and several other mega-cities with the most school choice, all of these options are available. A high school's relative ranking correlates with the number of graduates placed in the University of Tokyo and other top universities. In an earlier era, public high schools, led by Hibiya Metropolitan High School, dominated the top of the list of high schools that sent graduates to the University of Tokyo. Then came an era of private junior/senior high school dominance in the university entrance examination competition. This shift also signaled the begin-ning of junior high exam-taking in which public schools increasingly faced the challenge of the private sector. The next section will review how this happened.

The Rise of Private Junior/Senior High Schools

Junior high exam-taking is as yet a very urban, geographically restricted phenomenon, though it is one with a symbolic message. The urban centers are where the major actors of junior high exam-taking come together: 1) brand private schools that challenge or have overtaken public schools in their exam competitiveness; 2) educationally oriented and affluent parents who wish to place their children ahead in the education race, or who can place their children in private schools for whatever reason; 3) public junior and senior high schools that are faced with the challenge of private schools; and 4) mega-*juku* that are relentless in their advertising and provision of services.

According to Nichinoken, a mega-*juku* specialized in junior high exam-taking, 8.7% of metropolitan Tokyo elementary school children took the junior high exam in 1988, while 2 decades later, the rate has more than doubled to 20.6% (Nichinoken, 2008a). Many factors seem to have come together to push up the rate of exam-taking. First and most quoted is the decline of competitiveness of public high schools and the rise of private junior/senior high schools in the Tokyo area. The metropolitan Tokyo high school reform of 1967 (with its counterpart in other prefectures) is widely accused of bringing down the competitiveness of metropolitan high schools. This reform, an attempt to control the intense competition to pass the entrance examinations of brand schools, grouped public high schools into units (*gakkôgun*) and required students to apply to a grouped category, rather than to individual schools.

After this era, Hibiya Metropolitan High School quickly lost its top position to private junior/senior high schools and national high schools in the ranking of institutions based on the largest number of students passing the University of Tokyo entrance examination. In 1975, Tokyo metropolitan high schools totally disappeared from the top-ten list. From 1982, the private boy's Kaisei High School jumped to the top, and has maintained its top position for decades. Private high schools with affiliated junior high schools currently dominate the league table. Data from 1950 to 2009 show that students from the top 30 high schools constitute 43.7% of the total that were admitted to the University of Tokyo (Kobayashi, 2009).

Under the regime of Governor Ishihara, the Tokyo metropolitan government launched efforts to revive public metropolitan high schools that include designating former brand schools as focus schools for college entrance instruction (*shingaku shidô jûtenkô*). The first of these, Hibiya, created its own entrance examination tests rather than use the common metropolitan tests, and other such schools followed in its steps. The establishment of public junior/senior high schools also added to public school choice. In recent years, many people are noting the revival of Hibiya and the public junior/senior high schools in the numbers they send to the University of Tokyo (and other top universities). The Lehman shock of 2008 and economic stagnation are also said to have pulled down the numbers of exam-takers applying to private and national schools (Diamond Magazine Editing Unit, 2012a).

To summarize, what has influenced public versus private dominance? From the previous discussions, the following can be mentioned: 1) policy, especially zoning and rules on those eligible to attend (e.g., Tokyo's 1967 school grouping); 2) the impact of relaxed education, a trend that had been continuing from the late 1970s into the 2000s. This reform reduced curricular content, introduced a 5-day school week, and created new curriculum (e.g., class periods for integrated studies). Some things that were previously taught in schools were removed from the curriculum but remained on the entrance examinations or in the *juku* curriculum (Nichinoken, 2008b; Tsuneyoshi, 2004); 3) access: With the opening of new train lines, some schools were able to attract students from a wider geographic area; 4) increase in school choice, especially in urban areas: The establishment of public junior/senior high schools pushed families who otherwise would not have joined the entrance examination race to take part. Establishment of new private junior/senior high schools in urban centers also contributed to school choice; 5) private junior/senior high school advantage on the exam: These schools often adopt techniques such as ability grouping, summer courses, early mornings and extended days, and special courses targeted to match the entrance requirements of specific elite universities (Kobayashi, 2009; Komiyama, 2007; Nichinoken, 2008b). We can add to this list the state of the economy, i.e., the economic recession.

It is important to note at this point that the popularity of junior high exam-taking among a certain urban segment of the population is not a simple matter of more choice, but of what kind of choice. It is about the relative decline of public education as a choice for educationally ambitious families in urban districts.

Pushing Exam Hell into Younger Grades

The decline of real "choice," especially for top students, has taken place in both the public and private sectors, pushing the competition age downward. Top junior/senior private high schools can accelerate the curriculum and cover material at a higher level and at a faster pace than the public schools, which has helped improve their success in the entrance examination competition. Schools sometimes complete the high school curriculum a year early, for example, leaving 1 year free for exam preparation; other private schools adjust the curriculum, emphasizing certain exam subjects over others in order to prepare for the exam more efficiently.

In Tokyo, the private challenge to public schools is most visible, since there has emerged a range of private schools that caters to all kinds of achievement levels. To the anguish of many parents, however, many private junior/senior high schools have stopped recruiting students for entrance at the high school level. This trend is most prominent at all-female private schools in the Tokyo district. For example, the three top women's high schools at the junior high exam-taking level (Futaba, Jyoshi Gakuin, and Oin) do not recruit for high school, which necessitates junior high exam-taking for families aiming for these schools. Azabu and Musashi, leading boy's schools in the Tokyo area, also do not recruit for high school. This trend is often noted by *juku*, a a factor that creates pressure on Tokyo families to participate in junior high exam-taking (Nichinoken, 2008a).

Table 11.1 shows the standard deviation scores of selected top junior high schools for girls, a number indicating a student's chances of passing the entrance examination to a particular school. Such scores are computed by various major *juku*, based on mock tests. Table 11.1 is taken from the Yotsuya Otsuka's test, one of the three major mock tests for junior high exam-takers. The schools in bold font do not recruit at the high school entrance level, making the junior high exam the last chance to gain entrance. Boys and girls take the exam for different schools (except the co-ed ones, indicated by an asterisk in the table), so the scores are computed by gender. Table 11.1 is for girls.

Such data tend to feed parental fears of being left behind. The biggest difference between junior high exam-taking and high school exam-taking is that the former is usually about leaving the public system. Especially for higher-ranking Tokyo female students, if one waits until the high school entrance examination level, the major options would be: 1) metropolitan public high schools, 2) the few competitive national schools, and 3) the remainder of private schools that continue to recruit for high school. Many of the top-level girls' schools are no longer an option. According to a male *juku* spokesperson working in central Tokyo, the usual advice given to parents, especially of daughters, who come to his *juku* and ask whether they should place their child in the junior high exam-taking course or regular non-exam course is: "If you don't mind sending the child to a third-ranking school, the child does not have to take the junior high exam" (Interview, December 11, 2009).

In prefectures outside of the larger metropolitan Tokyo area, the private sector is not as strong, and the most sought after school is usually the leading public high school. For urban residents like those in Tokyo, however, junior high school exam-taking is not simply an act of privilege for those who can afford the *juku* and private school fees. Ambitious families in these districts have little choice but to pursue earlier entry into the exam race or risk the negative consequences. The attractive private, national, and public junior/senior school options within

Table 11.1. 2010 Standard Deviation Scores Necessary for an
80% Probability of Passing: Data for Girls for Junior High
School Entrance (Selected Schools in the Tokyo Area)

Standard Deviation Scores	Exam Date	Name of School
70	Feb. 3	Keio*
	Feb. 1	**Oin**
69	Feb. 3	Tsukuba (national)*
68	Feb. 2–4	Toshimaoka Girls (1st–3rd exams)
67	Feb. 1	Waseda Jitsugyo* **Joshi Gakuin**
	Feb. 3	Ochanomizu (national)*
	Feb. 5	**Shibuya Kyôiku Gakuen** (3rd exam)*
65	Feb. 1	**Ferris** **Futaba**
	Feb. 3	Tokyo Gakugeidai (national)*
64	Feb. 1	**Shibuya Kyôiku Gakuen** (first)*
	Feb. 2	Aoyama*
62	Feb. 2	**Shirayuri** (regular)
	Feb. 4	**Ohyu** (third exam) **Kichijyo Girls** (third exam)
61	Feb. 1	**Rikkyo Girls**
	Feb. 2	**Ohyu** (second exam) **Kichijyo Girls** (second)
	Feb. 3	**Gakushuin Girls** (regular B) **Koishikawa** (public junior-senior) * Musashi (public junior-senior high school) *
	Feb. 5	**Shoei Girls** (second)
		Scores continue down to the 30s

Note 1: Schools that do not recruit for high school are highlighted in bold.
Note 2: Co-ed schools are indicated by an asterisk (*); the remaining are
all-female schools.

Source: Based on the 2010 data of the cram school Yotsuya Otsuka *Juku*'s
mock test results (*Gofugokaku hantei* test). http://www.yotsuyaotsuka.com/
index.php.

commuting distance create the appearance of more school choice, but ultimately these families have less public school choice in the real sense, especially when gender is considered.

Tokyo B Ward: The Costs of Being Privileged

This section looks more closely at the costs that the "privileged" pay, using the example of B ward. Within the junior high exam-oriented Tokyo metropolitan area, this ward has one of the highest percentages of exam-oriented families. Some of Japan's most prestigious secondary schools are concentrated within its area.

At M school, the elementary school with the highest rates of exam-taking in the district, *juku* figures put the percentage of students taking entrance examinations at 80–90% (Theory Magazine Editing Unit, 2008). Only about 30% of the pupils of this school eventually enter the public junior high school of the district (Interview with the junior high principal, November 20, 2007, and December 4, 2008). On Parents' Day, this school has a very different feel from most public elementary schools in Japan. The parents are uniformly well dressed, and the school has a private school feel. Unlike in private schools, however, the vast majority of children are studying for the entrance examination, and in the hallways, mothers exchange information on *juku*.

The schedule for junior high exam-taking starts early in Saitama and Chiba, prefectures that border Tokyo. These schools start their exams in January while Tokyo (and Kanagawa) schools start on February 1. The same school often offers multiple exams so that pupils who failed or who were taking the test of another school can schedule the exam. Some schools have morning and afternoon exams, so that a student can take the tests at two schools on the same day. Even in Tokyo, pupils who do not plan to attend a Saitama or Chiba school use exams in these prefectures as practice. Thus, schools in Saitama and Chiba sometimes have more than 2,000 applicants. In 2012, Sakae Higashi, a high school in Saitama, topped the list by totaling 8,172 applicants.[2]

Tokyo elementary schools, like M school, in which a large portion of the class takes the junior high school exam, find that they cannot maintain classes during the exam season, since most of their students will be gone taking examinations. In contrast to junior high, some elementary school pupils will miss school for days on end to study for the examination and to avoid contact with peers from whom they might catch influenza. Nevertheless, although these pupils are absent from school, they typically continue to attend *juku*.

This choice reflects two factors: 1) The gap between the school curriculum and the exam is so wide that even top students cannot rely on schools to prepare for the test. Also, since school grades do not count in the private junior high admissions process, such truancy seems to make pragmatic sense; (2) the stakes of missing exam day are extremely high, given the years of joint sacrifice on the part of the child and mother. The possibility of becoming sick on exam day worries mothers. During the examination period, it is easy to identify anxious junior high exam-taking families in a crowd. The mother and child are wearing white surgical masks. Again, since elementary school children do not fully understand the system, it is basically the parents and *juku* that are giving them advice.

Such obsessive behavior is more often displayed in elementary school than in junior high school, where most of the students know that the score they receive on public high school entrance examinations is only one of the factors used in determining admission along with school grades. In elementary schools of B ward, teachers commented that pupils would sigh with relief when summer vacation finally ends and they are freed from intensive *juku* seminars. Such behavior indicates how removed private junior high school exam-taking is from regular public schooling, and how much it relies on parental and *juku* involvement.

R junior high school accepts the 30% of M elementary school children who chose or had to continue in the public system. The principal at R junior high noted that low self-esteem and low social skills are considered a challenge at this school. Most of these students have failed the junior high exam after many years of intense examination preparation, or could not take the exam for one reason or another, perhaps because of low *juku* scores or economic hardship. Actually, the level of the students at R junior high school, as measured by the Tokyo metropolitan tests, is high. Yet teachers worry that the students come into R school feeling like "losers" in the exam scene, having watched many of their classmates enroll in private or national junior high schools. The principal explains that the board of education recognizes that the scores of R junior high school students are lower than those at M elementary school, and puts pressure on the school to improve. He wonders how they can, however, given that the top and average scoring students "have all left" (Interview with the principal, November 29, 2008).

According to the principal, students enter R junior high saying that they will make up for their failure on the junior high school examination. Alhough their years of exam preparation were not enough to earn them entry into a competitive private junior high school, their scores still put them among the better-prepared group of metropolitan students. In fact, R school is one of the most competitive public junior high schools in the district.

The spokesman for a mega-chain *juku*, which has many branches in the area, tells a similar story. According to him, the reputation of children living in B ward is that by the time they sit for the junior high exam, they are likely to have already failed two exams—one for entrance to a brand private kindergarten and the other for admission to a private or national elementary school. Such are the costs of having so many brand schools within commuting distance. Therefore, according to the spokesman, one of his *juku*'s first responsibilities in working with these students is to boost their self-esteem so they can effectively face yet another entrance examination. Unfortunately, the spokesman adds, the mothers tend to "rub salt into the wound" by saying things like "if you don't do better, you will fail again." These comments further paralyze the children (interview with spokesman of the *juku*, December 11, 2009).

The above-quoted principal of R school, the most competitive public junior high school in B ward, noted that some parents of the public elementary school in the neighborhood who are not admitted to the school of choice place their children in lower-ranking private schools that yield lower results (based on entry into high school), rather than in his public junior high school. Since some private high schools also accept students at the high school level, he feels like telling parents that "anyone from this junior high school can get into" that particular high school (interview, November 29, 2007). For junior high school exam-taking, the rivals are limited to the top of the elementary school cohort with years of intensive *juku* commuting. For high school entrance, everyone else participates. As a result, the standard deviation scores estimating the probability of entering a particular school—and which are relative—tend to jump up for any particular child.

Teachers at R junior high school and others in similar districts I have visited often described the act of placing a child in a low-ranking private school even though there was a perfectly good public junior high school nearby as an exercise carried out simply to gratify "parental ego." From the parents' perspective, however, it is understandable not to want their children labeled as belonging to the bottom 30%, nor do they want their children (or themselves) to feel like the years spent preparing for the exam were wasted. They are the victims of the junior high school exam phenomena—the exam of the "privileged."

Enclosure of the Children by the *Juku*

When discussing junior high exam-taking, one cannot ignore the presence of the *juku*. In comparison with entrance into high school, junior high exam-taking to top schools relies even more heavily on *juku*, since the contents of the exam and the school are so far apart. Public high schools follow the national curriculum on their entrance examinations. On the other hand, private schools face few restrictions regarding exam content. *Juku*-related books warn parents that the gap between exam content and the school curriculum is so wide in junior high school exam-taking that it is impossible to earn acceptance to brand schools without *juku* assistance (Komiyama, 2007). Previously used exam questions from brand schools are sold in stores, and many can also be obtained from the Internet. These problem sets confirm for parents that the advice given by *juku* is fairly accurate.

To give an example, according to an analysis conducted by a major chain *juku* in the greater Tokyo area, the average word count for the reading tests given by junior high schools is 6,000 Japanese words, going up to a high of about twice that much for some schools. The authors excerpts for the tests are similar to those used in high school—or even college—examinations. Referring to the reading section of entrance tests, a *juku* spokesman used an invented Japanese term, *otonado*, meaning "the degree (*do*) to which a child can think like an adult (*otona*)" (statement at a recruitment session of *I juku*, March 2005). In many ways, junior high school exam content requires the child to think like an adult: The social studies questions ask about international politics that even high school students may find perplexing.

It is clear that developmentally appropriate teaching is not the norm at *juku* that prepare children for junior high school entrance examinations. In fact, the complete opposite is the norm: The child shouldn't think like a child. According to a lecturer at a major Tokyo chain *juku* that is best known for its competence in dealing with the new public junior/senior high school essay exams, the *juku* had students recall and write down what they wrote on their actual exam and analyzed the factors that led to success. In the *juku*'s view, the most important characteristic of children who passed top public junior/senior high examinations was the ability to "write like adults" (interview with *juku* lecturer, October 15, 2010). It goes without saying that this finding is reflected in what the *juku* is teaching.

It is no wonder that the *juku* schedule becomes ever more consuming of the lives of the mother and child. Knowing that there is so much to cover, *juku* operators, looking for business opportunities, respond with additional programming. For example, Table 11.2 outlines the summer programs offered by one of the largest mega-*juku* for junior high exam-taking in Japan. For 5th- and 6th-graders, summer sessions take up most of their vacation, with long days that might include eating lunch or dinner at the *juku*.

Yotsuya Otsuka, Nichinoken, Sapix, and Waseda Academy are some examples of large chain *juku* that help students with junior high exam-taking. Each has its own characteristics, and prepares its students for exams given by specific junior high schools. Some of these *juku* also have classes to prepare students for high school examinations. In addition, all of the major *juku* use entrance tests of their own to select students and place them in appropriate ability-grouped classes at the *juku*. Mock exams are available at national *juku* chains, the three major ones created by Shutoken Moshi Senta, Yotsuya Otsuka, and Nichoken. In addition to these, there are *juku*-level tests. As a result, children are tested constantly, and the results are shared with parents.

Thus, *juku* provide ultimate tracking alongside the untracked Japanese elementary educational system. They sort their students into classes of different levels, even though public elementary schools avoid this practice. The major *juku*

Table 11.2. Example of Schedule and Price for Summer Sessions at Nichinoken
    Juku: 2012 (at one of the Tokyo branches)

	GRADE			
	3rd	**4th**	**5th**	**6th**
Class days	6	6	18	24
Test days	1	1	3	4
Hours	8:40 –11:10	8:40 –13:55	14:25 –19:30	7:20 –13:55
Fees	¥20,422 approx. $240	¥38,535 approx. $450	¥117,705 approx. $1,400	¥170,730 approx. $2,000

Note: Examples are for the regular classes, so the advanced classes would be more demanding.
Source: From the homepage of Nichinoken (*juku*), http://www.nichinoken.co.jp.

test their pupils regularly, and the scores on these tests determine whether they move up or down. In locations where junior high school exam-taking is the norm, *juku* have large numbers of students, and many levels of classes. As a result, in competitive *juku*, small mistakes on tests can lead to placement in a lower class.

The irony of all this comes from the function of the entrance examinations—to select certain students for success and to fail the others. The junior high exam-taking market, as noted previously, is dominated by mega-chain *juku* that are standardized, systematic, and efficient. Ironically, as *juku* become more efficient, exam content must become more difficult in order to differentiate among students. In other words, the exams exist to select students, not to assess mastery of the school curriculum.

It is not difficult to see that junior high exam-taking is a major time- and money-consuming enterprise that requires years of preparation by the children and their parents, mostly mothers. Estimates of how much families aiming at top junior high schools pay for *juku* fees alone exceed 1,000,000 yen (approximately $12,000) per year,[3] more than the figures for high school or college entrance *juku* (*yobikô*), which is quite an investment for a single child.

CONCLUSION

There is something ironic about the present situation of junior high exam-taking in Japan's urban centers. On the one hand, the media are trumpeting the arrival of universal acceptance to higher education. In April 2012, according to the National Association of Private Schools, 45.8% of the junior colleges and 4-year colleges could not fill their openings (Nihon Shiritsugakkô Shinko/Kyosai Jigyodan 2012). Yet in certain urban pockets of wealth, exam competition dominates the lives of many young children, who rely more and more on systematic *juku* assistance.

At first glance, this is a structure of privilege. The junior high exam-taking communities are those of the middle-class metropolitan urbanites. Sending a child to *juku* for years, and then paying private junior high school fees, requires a certain level of affluence. Studies suggest that households with 5th- and 6th-graders about to take the junior high school exam spend three times more on educational expenses than families that do not pursue this option (Benesse Kyôiku Kenkyû Kaihatsu Sentâ, 2008a). These are families in privileged regions that can afford *juku* fees in the preparation period and, later, private junior/senior high school tuition.

As noted at the beginning of this chapter, the usual discussion about this "exam for the privileged" focuses on the winners and the widening gap between the haves and the have-nots. Undoubtedly, such privatization of elite education, both in its end (private schools) and process (*juku* usage), raises questions of equity. At the same time, this system takes its toll even on the residents of "privileged" locations, where an underlying mechanism leads parents to push their children toward junior high exam-taking. In high-exam-taking schools, such as M elementary school, most pupils pursue the junior high school exam option. When the high- and middle-ranking pupils are all studying for the exam, it is natural for other families to consider signing up for the junior high exam. But the system also creates "losers" out of otherwise highly competent children who feel they are left behind to enroll in the public system, having failed the exam that made it possible for their peers to attend private junior high schools.

For "privileged" children at this stage, striving for the top is an all-consuming enterprise. According to a 2007 survey of 6th-graders and their parents, one could illustrate the average life of the junior high exam-taking child as something like the following: The child studies about 3 hours on weekdays (with about a third studying for more than 4 hours daily). A majority (57.6%) says they almost never play with friends or with video games (64.5%); more than 80% attend (or have attended) a *juku*. About half of the children in exam-oriented *juku* attend three or more times a week, for 3 hours and 14 minutes on average (30% exceeding 4 hours or more). The typical time these students return home is 8:35 P.M., with 10% coming home after 10:00 P.M. The families whose first choice is a private junior high school spend an average of 60,457 yen (approximately $700) per month on education fees, compared to 13,924 yen (approximately $170) for those who do not. When asked which would be more useful in the future, school study or *juku* study, over 70% answered "*juku*" (Benesse Kyôiku Kenkyû Kaihatsu Sentâ, 2008b).

Here, we see an exam-taking preparation period that extends for years, consumes both the child's and the mother's life, and is *juku*-driven. This is the contemporary version of the "education mama," directly intervening in the child's educational process, but regulated by the mega-*juku* that dominate the Japanese junior high exam-taking scene today. This chapter underscores what one might call the "commercialization of exam-promoting parenting." Such analysis points to the costs of the market-oriented context in some of Japan's most affluent districts. Though there may be more private school choice, the weakening of the public schools combined with the monopolization of exam preparation by mega-*juku* increase the pressure to enter the exam competition at an early age. This is the cost of "privilege" in a context in which high-stakes testing, private industry (*juku*), and market-oriented education dominate.

NOTES

1. Shutoken Moshi Senta estimates 15.3%, Yotsuya Otsuka Shingaku Kyoshitsu estimates 17.8%, and Nichinoken estimates 20.2%, for the year 2010. Taken from the homepage of the Gakken, Shutoken Chugakujuken Net. Retrieved from http://www.chu-j.net/.

2. Zenshigaku Shinbun, online newspaper, March 13, 2006, "06 Shutoken shigaku chûgakujyukenshi kyôiku no tokushoku, shôraisei ni kôhyôka, jyukenseizô no keiko." Retrieved from http://www.zenshigakunp.jp/news_01.php?y=2006&m=3&d=13&newsid =1721&archive=true. Zakzak, online news, "Chûgaku nyûshi de shingashazô toppu wa Saitama no Sakae Higashi." Retrieved from http://www.zakzak.co.jp/society/domestic/ news/20120601/dms1206010744012-n1.htm.

3. Yahoo!Research and Shukan Toyo Keizai, "Chûgakujyukensha sokuho ripôto," Retrieved from, http://prtimes.jp/data/corp/624/cb126ac880ad67ebcc5cec0b5007ab96. pdf. See also Diamond Magazine Editing Unit (2012b).

REFERENCES

Apple, M. W. (2006). *Educating the "right" way: Markets, standards, god, and inequality* (2nd ed.). New York: Routledge.
Benesse Kyôiku Kenkyû Kaihatsu Sentâ. (2008a). *The third child-rearing life fundamental survey, release, parents in the larger Tokyo area* (in Japanese). Tokyo: Author.
Benesse Kyôiku Kenkyû Kaihatsu Sentâ. (2008b). *A report on junior high school choice* (in Japanese). (Vol. 48). Tokyo: Author.
Berliner, D. C., & Biddle, B. J. (1996). *The manufactured crisis: Myths, fraud, and the attack on America's public schools*. New York: Basic Books.

Diamond Magazine Editing Unit. (2012a). The private junior high exam-taking bubble has burst, affiliated schools to private colleges and middle to lower ranking schools have lost applicants in large numbers (in Japanese). *Weekly Diamond (online)*. Retrieved from http://diamond.jp/articles/-/16382

Diamond Magazine Editing Unit. (2012b). The strongest *juku* & *yobikô* (in Japanese). *Weekly Diamond, 25*, 28–79.

Hida, D. (2009). The state of the home environment surrounding junior high school exam-taking (in Japanese). In Morikami Kyôiku Kenkyûjo (Ed.), *The choice of age 10: Educational discussion on junior high school exam-taking* (pp. 17–34). Tokyo: Daiamondosha.

Iida, K. (2007). Challenging the inequality gap in secondary school: Concerning the high school gap (in Japanese). *Kyôiku Shakaigaku Kenkyû, 80*, 41–58.

Jones, M. G., Jones, B. D., & Hargrove T. Y. (2003). *The unintended consequences of high-stakes testing*. Lanham, MD: Rowman & Littlefield.

Kobayashi, T. (2009). *The rise and fall of high schools sending students into Todai: Analyzing 60 years of ranking* (in Japanese). Tokyo: Kobunsha.

Komiyama, H. (2007). *Junior high school exam-taking and the quest for living* (in Japanese). Tokyo: Nihon Hyoronsha.

LeTendre, G. K., Hofer, B. K., & Shimizu, H. (2003). What is tracking? Cultural expectations in the United States, Germany, and Japan. *American Educational Research Journal, 40*(1), 43–89.

MacLeod, J. (2009). *Ain't no makin' it: Aspirations and attainment in a low-income neighborhood*. Boulder, CO: Westview Press.

MEXT, Ministry of Education, Culture, Sports, Science, and Technology. (2011). *The progress of high school education reform* (in Japanese). Tokyo: Author. Retrieved from http://www.mext.go.jp/b_menu/houdou/23/11/__icsFiles/afieldfile/2011/11/02/1312873_01.pdf

MEXT, Ministry of Education, Culture, Sports, Science, and Technology. (2012). *The cross-national comparison of education indicators for 2012* (in Japanese). Tokyo: Author.

Mochida, K. (2003). Contemporary issues on academic achievement in Japan (in Japanese). *Hikaku Kyôikugaku Kenkyû, 29*, 3–15.

Morigami, N. (2009). How much did junior high school exam taking change in the last 20 years? (in Japanese). In Morikami Kyôiku Kenkyûjo (Ed.), *The choice of age 10: Educational discussion on junior high school exam-taking* (pp. 8–15). Tokyo: Daiamondosha.

Nichinoken. (2008a). Chûgakujuken no ABC (in Japanese). *Kid's Radar* (p. 2). Tokyo: Author.

Nichinoken. (Shingaku Jôhôshitsu). (2008b). *Public junior/senior high schools* (in Japanese). Tokyo: Chikuma Shobo.

Nicholas, S. L., & Berliner, D. C. (2007). *Collateral damage: How high-stakes testing corrupts America's schools*. Cambridge, MA: Harvard Education Press.

Nihon Shiritsugakkô Shinko/Kyôsai Jigyodan. (Shigaku Keiei Sodan Center) (2012). *2012 private colleges/junior colleges etc. state of candidates* (in Japanese). Tokyo: Author. Retrieved from http://www.shigaku.go.jp/files/shigandoukou24.pdf

Theory Magazine Editing Unit. (2008). Where is the elementary school whose pupils pass the entrance examination into the top private junior high schools? (in Japanese). *Theory 2*, 136–143.

Tokyo Metropolitan Board of Education. (2012, April). *Tokyo public school numbers, the state of school choice system, and the establishment of community schools* (in Japanese). Tokyo: Author. Retrieved from http://www.metro. tokyo.jp/INET/OSHIRASE/2012/03/20m38300.htm

Tsuneyoshi, R. (2004). The new Japanese educational reforms and the achievement "crisis" debate. *Educational Policy 18*(2), 364–394.

Whitty, G. (2002). *Making sense of education policy: Studies in the sociology and politics of education*. London: Paul Chapman Publishing.

Woods, P. A., Bagley, C., & Glatter, R. (1998). *School choice and competition: Markets in the public interest?* London & New York: Routledge.

Change upon Change
Whither Japan, Whither Japanese Education?

Victor Kobayashi

The phrase, "You never step into the same river twice," sets a theme for this concluding chapter: Heraclitus wasn't just talking about rivers, but about the many phenomena, which, like rivers, are in constant flux. Changes continually take place, including in education. And, as the participants involved in any human phenomenon themselves change, so, too, do the signs and the signified.

One of the keys to understanding education in contemporary Japan is that new reform measures established by the central government require several years for any effects, including unanticipated ones, to become visible: Time is required for entering cohorts of students to move through a particular new school program. During this time, subsequent policies are enacted, adding to the complexity. In the meantime, Japanese media report what is happening in specific areas, perhaps looking only at newly implemented policies, and their interpretations influence politicians who may press for even more change. All of this takes place before the original policy can fully demonstrate its effect.

It may take several years for schools to accept and adjust to new policies, and the players—the principal, teachers, and students themselves—must alter their behaviors and attitudes, which vary from individual to individual, by geographic area, and by other characteristics. In the end, not all of the changes may be desirable. Furthermore, individual members of the educational bureaucracy themselves may have mixed feelings about the worthiness of the effort and may delay implementation, even as the political leaders and much of the public laud the new policies. Indeed, it is difficult to recalibrate settings when the targets also change.

The move toward the reform that included *yutori* (relaxed education that would make schooling less stressful for children) came about in part as a response to media reports of increased violence among children and other symptoms of dysfunction. It was also a response to the perceptions of a rigid and authoritarian secondary school and top-down, highly centralized national system of compulsory schools. The *yutori* reforms, to provide teachers more flexibility as they confronted new challenges, seems also to be playing out in school guidance.

Bjork and Fukuzawa's chapter on school guidance in middle schools describes the changes in the interaction between teachers and students over the last 30 years. In the manner of a documentary film that fuses archival video clips of specific events (with flashbacks and flash-forwards), they describe the guidance system where teachers work to nurture children by improvising and experimenting with their practices in response to a society that has become more complex and difficult for young people as they move into adulthood. Even with the acknowledged gaps in their research, the authors' depiction is convincing: Most Japanese teachers remain empathetic and nurturing, albeit troubled, as they continue their previous approaches, focusing on the whole child at a time when the newer generation of middle school children themselves have become less accepting of the authority of elders and teachers. Despite such societal changes, the "river" remains: There is continuity in the ethos among teachers that shows a deep concern for the moral and spiritual development of youth.

Tsuneyoshi's chapter illustrates the effect of Japan's embracing of the neoliberal ideas of privatization and market choice in education, especially in the large metropolitan areas of Tokyo. After primary school completion, students and their parents now face various alternatives besides the local public middle school, many of them requiring examinations and other forms of entrance requirements. The complexity of this process has resulted in an increase in attendance at for-profit *juku* that meet the needs of many parents as their children move through the educational system.

Juku may be viewed as thwarting the emphasis of *yutori* education on developing well-rounded persons, but from the point of view of many parents they provide children with greater opportunity to enter better schools. Like them or not, they are an important feature of Japanese education. As Tsuneyoshi indicates, *juku* have evolved to meet the changing needs of their clientele outside of the formal school system. *Juku* have a long history in Japan, dating back centuries and they have taken on many forms to adapt to changing circumstances. The current manifestation seems to be adding a support function for anxious parents as the "education mothers" of an earlier era have become "helicopter parents" hovering around, yet still uncertain about what is best for the education of their children.

When I first visited one large *juku* in Tokyo in the 1970s, I found the building well equipped with up-to-date facilities and materials. The personnel seemed proud of their work as they assisted young people in finding the appropriate colleges to aim for, given their ability level, while also helping them prepare for the examination. This particular corporate *juku* also employed able lecturers, some of whom taught at prestigious universities.

Many Japanese words shift in meaning in everyday conversation and are part of the rapid pace of change in Japan. Before the modern era, the term *juku* signified various kinds of private schools with a focus on a master teacher who attracted students and taught various subjects and skills. Some of the students were disciple-apprentices, who would continue the *juku*, providing succession and perpetuation of the area of expertise to new generations (Mehl, 2003). A variant of this type of *juku* continues to thrive to this day in subjects such as traditional music, martial arts, calligraphy, and dance. The schools coexist outside of the formal Western-style (and now global-type) educational system, allowing both youths and adults opportunities to enjoy leisure pursuits that round out their education and provide opportunities for aesthetic pursuits. Many Japanese view tradition-based cultural pursuits (*kyôyô*) as an important part of education based in the Confucian tradition of self-cultivation and refinement. Once reserved for the literati, they are now part of the everyday lives of many Japanese, both children and adults. As a term, however, *juku* in this context is considered old-fashioned and is seldom used today to refer to schools that teach Western arts such as violin, harp, piano, ballet, jazz, and vocal music.

Christopher Frey's chapter shows how Japanese public schools had long been open to children of Ainu descent, but the goal was assimilation, without any concern for Ainu culture. In 2007, the United Nations General Assembly adopted the Declaration on the Rights of Indigenous Peoples, with Japan as one of the signatories. The following year, the Japanese Diet passed a resolution that recognized the Ainu as "Indigenous Japanese," calling for an end to discrimination.

The government's recognition of Ainu as Indigenous, due in part to the increased global networking of international Indigenous groups, was an important step in the breakdown of Japan's self-image as a racially homogeneous nation. The official recognition of Ainu as Indigenous to Japan is significant in that it requires a change in mindset by many Japanese: It has problematized the term and idea of *zainichi* (literally "longtime resident of Japan"), which had been used to refer to longtime minority groups residing in Japan. These changes illustrate the way global forces have altered internal discourses in Japan. Even Emperor Akihito helped destroy the myth of "pure Japanese" at a news conference in December 2001 when he referred to the blood ties between Japan's imperial family and the ancient Paekche people of Korea, a kinship that had been noted by Korean scholars for a long time (Makino, 2010).

Okano's chapter on ethnic schools in Japan points out that despite the increased tolerance and inclusiveness of diverse minority groups in mainstream schools (about 300 full-time schools offer schooling in a language other than Japanese), the credentials of students graduating from such schools are not recognized in the mainstream employment market. Nevertheless, the government, including at the local levels, has made some progress toward greater inclusiveness, encouraged by the work of recently formed associations, itself a sign of the progress of civil society. Okano provides an example of one prefecture's generosity in funding ethnic schools that formed the Hyogo Prefecture Association of Schools for Foreigners in the aftermath of the major earthquake disaster in January 1995. These organizations have also evolved and now support all-Japan forums of ethnic schools among other activities.

The chapter by Gordon discusses the complex plight of a relatively new group marginalized in Japanese society, the Latin Americans (mostly Brazilians) of Japanese descent, who come to Japan as workers. She also shows that some of the Latin American *Nikkei* are also of Okinawan and *Burakumin* background. Again, global forces complicate the picture of the marginalization of minority groups in Japan.

Whither Japanese education? Japan's ranking has slipped to third place behind the United States and China in the contest for the largest economy of the world. Japan will perhaps move lower as larger countries—India and Brazil, for example—move up in the rankings. Japan's bubble economy collapsed in the 1990s, followed by "stagnation" and then a slow recovery. The catastrophic Tohoku earthquake and tsunami, and the subsequent meltdown of the Fukuoka No. 1 nuclear reactor, set the economy back, but Japan is again on the road to recovery, even if the future of nuclear energy makes the situation problematic, as it does for all nations dependent on imported fossil fuels.

A strong relationship between modern educational systems and economic development has been taken for granted, and Japan's high scores on international achievement tests in literacy, mathematics, and science have been held as proof of the quality of its educational system. In the early 21st century, however, Japan's rankings in these tests of critical fields have fallen, leading many Japanese and foreign observers to see this change as part of Japan's overall decline.

The research of Christopher H. Tienken (2008) indicates that the relationship between international achievement in mathematics and science and a country's future economic growth was stronger among those nations with weak economies. Among nations with already developed economies, the correlation was "nonsignificant." This suggests to me that, as a mature "modern" nation, Japan may now be in a dilemma that all nations face; i.e., given the global ecological crises that include climate change and nuclear considerations, the competition for economic power seems futile even as it escalates. As the late Kenneth Boulding, the maverick economist, once said, "Anybody who believes exponential growth can go on forever in a finite world is either a madman or an economist."[1]

Japan's population is aging and declining. Although low birthrates add to the worries about the future of schools in Japan, Irish journalist Eamonn Fingleton (2012) reminds us that Japan's dependency on food imports may make a lowering of its population necessary if the country is to become more self-sustaining in a world that is already overpopulated.

Furthermore, I sometimes think that Japan's current pathway portends the postmodern future, especially with policies focusing on economic growth weighed against the growing awareness of environmental crises. The earthquake-tsunami-nuclear disaster centered in Fukushima was a setback, but Japan seems to have the knack for regaining hope. The opportunity to change the course of its development as a civilization, including the place of thermonuclear-generated electricity, may become the rallying cry that finally supplants the focus on economic growth that began with the desire for rapid recovery after World War II.

Ganbare ("Hang in there"), a common term heard in the schools and street corners of every Japanese city and town, is used in many contexts that might otherwise elicit a deep sense of resignation, perhaps depression. But a tragic disaster is also an opportunity for a nation to reconsider its priorities, including in education, and there are many examples that illustrate Japan's resiliency in situations that otherwise might result in despair. The understanding of the limits of schools as never-ending investments in the wealth of a nation situated on a fragile planet—an island in the solar system—could lead to a greater appreciation of the value of education in conserving and advancing the best of world traditions.

NOTE

1. This quote by Boulding has been noted by many writers, often in slightly different language. It probably is based on notes taken during one of Boulding's widely given lectures on systems theories and economics.

REFERENCES

Fingleton, E. (2012, January 8). The myth of Japan's failure. *New York Times Sunday Review*, p. 1.

Makino, Y. (2010). "Emperor mentioned blood ties with Korea in 1990." *Asahi Shimbun*.

Mehl, M. (2003). *Private academies of Chinese learning in Meiji Japan: The decline and transformation of Kangaku Juku*. Copenhagen: Nordic Institute of Asian Studies Press.

Tienken, C. H. (2008). Rankings of international achievement test performance and economic strength: Correlation or conjecture? *International Journal of Education Policy and Leadership*. Retrieved from http://journals.sfu.ca/ijepl/index.php/ijepl/article/view/110/44

About the Contributors

Motoko Akiba is associate professor in the Department of Educational Leadership and Policy Studies at Florida State University. She is an associate editor of *Educational Researcher*, an author of *Improving Teacher Quality: The U.S. Teaching Force in Global Context* (2009) and the editor of *Teacher Reforms around the World: Implementations and Outcomes* (2013).

Christopher Bjork is associate professor and chair of the Education Department at Vassar College. He is the author of the book *Indonesian Education: Teachers, Schools, and Central Bureaucracy* (2005), and the editor of the volumes *Educational Decentralization: Asian Experiences and Conceptual Contributions* (2006) and *Taking Teaching Seriously* (2007).

Gary DeCoker is professor of Japanese studies at Earlham College and professor of education emeritus at Ohio Wesleyan University. He is the editor of *National Standards and School Reform in Japan and the United States* (2002) and numerous articles and book chapters on contemporary Japanese education and education in the Japanese traditional arts.

Christopher J. Frey is assistant professor of historical and comparative foundations of education at Bowling Green State University. He has published in *Comparative Education Review*, *The Journal of Curriculum Studies*, and *The Journal of American Indian Education*.

Rebecca Erwin Fukuzawa is professor of anthropology and English at Hosei University, Tokyo, Japan. She is the author of *Intense Years: How Japanese Adolescents Balance School, Family and Friends* (2001) She is currently working on two research projects. One focuses on the school-to-work transition of Japanese university students. The other examines changes in middle school guidance based on a restudy of the Tokyo schools.

June A. Gordon is professor of education at the University of California, Santa Cruz. Her books include *Challenges to Japanese Education: Economics, Human Rights, and Reform*, coedited with Fujita, Kariya, and LeTendre (2010), *Japan's*

Outcaste Youth: Education for Liberation (2008), *Beyond the Classroom Walls: Ethnographic Inquiry as Pedagogy* (2002), and *The Color of Teaching* (2000).

Akiko Hayashi is a postdoctoral fellow in education at the University of Georgia. Her publications include "The Japanese Preschool's Pedagogy of Feeling: Cultural Strategies for Supporting Young Children's Emotional Development," "The Japanese Preschool's Pedagogy of Peripheral Participation," and "Reframing a Visual Ethnography of a Japanese Preschool Classroom."

Diane M. Hoffman is associate professor of educational anthropology and international comparative education at the University of Virginia, Curry School of Education, and is widely published in such journals as *Ethos, Anthropology of Education Quarterly, American Educational Research Journal, Review of Educational Research, International Review of Education, Discourse*, and *Childhood*.

Victor Kobayashi is professor emeritus, University of Hawaii, in education and Japanese studies, and has widely published in books and journals on various topics that include Japanese education, underlying philosophies of education, and aesthetics in education. *John Dewey in Japanese Educational Thought* received the outstanding dissertation award from the John Dewey Society at the University of Michigan in 1964.

Yeon-Jin Lee is a PhD student of sociology at the University of Pennsylvania. Lee received her MS in social policy from Columbia University. Her research interests include educational inequality focused on cross-national comparison and health disparity in different racial groups by using quantitative methodology.

Tomoaki Nomi is associate professor of political science at Southeast Missouri State University. His research interests include central-local government relations, demography, migration, education policy, and gender relations. His publications have appeared in *Policy Studies Journal* and *Japan Focus*.

Kaori H. Okano is professor in the Asian studies program at La Trobe University. Her major publications include *Minorities and Education in Multicultural Japan: An Interactive Perspective* (edited with R. Tsuneyoshi and S. Boocock, 2011), *Young Women in Japan: Transitions to Adulthood* (2009), *Language and Schools in Asia* (editor, 2006), *Pendidikan moden Jepun Ketaksamaan dan kepelbagaian* (with M. Tsuchiya, 2004), *Education in Contemporary Japan* (with M. Tsuchiya, 1999), and *School to Work Transition in Japan* (1993).

Hyunjoon Park is Korea Foundation associate professor of sociology and education at the University of Pennsylvania. Park is interested in educational stratification in cross-national comparative perspective, focusing on Korea and Japan. With Emily Hannum and Yuko Butler, he has edited a book, *Globalization, Changing Demographics, and Educational Challenges in East Asia* (2010).

James J. Shields is the author of numerous books chapters, articles, and book reviews, including *Japanese Schooling: Patterns of Socialization, Equality and Political Control* (1993), *Foundations of Education, Dissenting Views* (1974), *Problems and Prospects in International Education* (1968), and *Education in Community Development* (1967). He is professor emeritus and founder and past director of the Japan Initiative at the City College, City University of New York.

Kazuhiko Shimizu is vice president of academic affairs and professor at the University of Tsukuba, Japan. He is an author of numerous books and articles on higher education reforms, university evaluation systems, and educational articulation including *Japan-US Comparison of University Credit Systems* (1998) and *Understanding University Reforms* (1999).

Joseph Tobin is the Elizabeth Garrard Hall professor of early childhood education at the University of Georgia. Among his publications are *Good Guys Don't Wear Hats: Children's Talk about the Media*, *Pikachu's Global Adventure*, and *Preschool in Three Cultures Revisited*. His newest project is a study of deaf kindergartens in Japan.

Ryoko Tsuneyoshi is professor of comparative education at the Graduate School of Education, University of Tokyo, Japan. Her books include *Minorities and Education in Multicultural Japan: An Interactive Approach* (edited with K. Okano and S. Boocock, 2011) and *The Japanese Model of Schooling: Comparisons with the United States* (2001).

Index

f, *n*, or *t* following a page number refers to a figure, note, or table, respectively.